WARS, DICTATORS
GRAMOPHONE 1

TO MY WIFE NORAH
for her encouragement
and advice throughout the
writing of this book.

Wars, Dictators and the Gramophone
1898-1945

by

Eric Charles Blake

William Sessions Limited
York, England

ISBN 1 85072 292 0

Printed in 11 on 12 point Plantin Typeface
by Sessions of York
The Ebor Press
York, England

Contents

Foreword

THIS BOOK was originally going to be a general, thematic account of the gramophone's development viewed against the changing political, economic and social conditions of its times, beginning with the interlinked subjects of wars and dictatorships. This particular starting place was chosen because the gramophone's response to war provided the opportunity for a historical sweep back, if not to the beginnings of the talking machine, at least to 1898 when Thomas Edison's innovatory cylinder, which had held the field for twenty or so years, was beginning to be challenged commercially by Emile Berliner's recently introduced flat disc. As work progressed, the twin topics of wars and dictatorships seemed (at least to the author) to beg for more extended treatment than would have been possible as part of a work with wider horizons. The book's scope was accordingly revised and what is now presented to the reader is the outcome of that change. The most fitting cut-off date was felt to be 1945 when the Second World War came to its apocalyptic end with the nuclear destruction of Hiroshima and Nagasaki. By then, coincidentally, the life of the 78 r.p.m. disc, the basic point of gramophonic reference throughout the nearly fifty years of this survey, was also drawing to a close. Historically, an appropriate moment had been reached at which to round off this study.

The brave new world it was hoped would follow the defeats of Italy, Germany and Japan did not materialise and the gramophone went on to play its part in further hard-fought wars in Korea, Vietnam, the Falklands and the Gulf, though in a less diverse way than previously. Although the latter half of the twentieth century saw the gramophone advance from the shellac 78 to the long-playing record, audio tape and compact disc (taking in the switch from monaural to stereophonic sound as it went) the parallel growth of other mass communication channels left it a much reduced field in which to operate whenever wars and dictators were the focus of international attention.

It must be emphasised that even within its relatively short time span this book is not meant to be a systematic history of the gramophone; readers seeking that type of approach should consult such standard accounts as Roland Gelatt's *The Fabulous Phonograph, 1877-1977* (2nd rev. ed. London, Cassel, 1977) and Curt Riess's *Knaurs Weltgeschichte der Schallplatte* (Zürich, Droemer Knaur, 1966) which, despite its world coverage, regrettably appears never to have been translated into English. Peter Martland's *Since Records Began: EMI: the First 100 Years* (London, Batsford, 1997) is the prime source of information on the record industry's pre-eminent company and its international network. It is admirably supplemented by Anthony Pollard's *Gramophone: the First 75 Years* (Sudbury, Gramophone Publications Ltd., 1998) which covers events from 1923 to 1998 as seen through the eyes of the leading British critical review. Those wishing to trace the technical history of the industry will find Oliver Read and Walter L. Welch's *From Tinfoil to Stereo: Evolution of the Phonograph* (2nd ed. Indianapolis, Sams, Bobbs-Merrill, 1976) an authoritative guide. For quick general reference purposes *The Guinness Book of Recorded Sound* (London, Guinness Books, 1984) is excellent.

The present book deals specifically with the many and varied roles the gramophone undertook between 1898 and 1945 - entertainer, propagandist, recruiting officer, news provider, charity worker, archivist and so forth. It does not confine itself exclusively to the flat disc but, when relevant, refers both to the cylinder and audio tape; it also goes beyond the commercial world of the gramophone industry to look at the recording activities of such bodies as broadcasting services and the use made by them of recorded material.

The relationships of record companies to each other were as complex in the industry's early days as they are a century later. Where necessary, some mention is made of the marriages, divorces and changes of name but this has been kept to a minimum and readers requiring more detailed information should consult the Company Profiles in *The Guinness Book of Recorded Sound*, the Corporate Genealogy Chart of Early Companies and Types of Records Produced in Read and Welch's work and the diagram (Figure 1) showing the evolution of Les Principaux Labels in Mario d'Angelo's *La Renaissance du Disque* (Paris, La Documentation Française, 1989).

An apology is due for not supplying catalogue numbers for the many commercial recordings I have cited, but shortage of time compelled me to omit these discographical references in order to concentrate on completing the main text. Whenever possible, though, I have identified the issuing company and sometimes the label series concerned; readers seeking further information may care to consult the various record catalogues and artist and label discographies listed in the Bibliography at the end of this book. For classical enthusiasts pursuing the composer approach the three volumes of Clough and Cuming's *The World's Encyclopaedia of Recorded Music* (WERM) still reign supreme for their coverage of the whole span of electrically recorded 78s.

Finally, a word on terminology. "Gramophone" is used in the English sense of disc-playing equipment but also as a convenient shorthand for sound-reproducing processes generally; the context should immediately make clear which usage is intended. "Phonograph" is used only in relation to cylinder-playing machines except for those instances when its American usage as a generic term may be encountered in quotations from American sources.

Huttons Ambo   E.C.B.
October, 2002

Acknowledgments

WHEN WRITING this book I needed to consult a wide range of reading matter that was neither in my own collection nor available locally; for the supply of practically all my requirements I was heavily indebted to the services of the British Library and the North Yorkshire County Library system, especially the latter's Malton branch and its most helpful and understanding staff. For the extended loan of the two following items I wish to thank Munich University Library for Curt Riess's *Knaurs Weltgeschichte der Schallplatte* and Glasgow University Library for Stengel and Gerigk's Nazi *Lexikon der Juden in der Musik*. Much research was done in the welcoming atmosphere of York University Library and I must express my gratitude for being allowed access to its collections.

Librarians and archivists near and far provided much valuable information and I must thank in particular Edwin M. Mathias of the Motion Picture, Broadcasting and Recorded Sound Division of the Library of Congress for his bibliography of the United States Armed Forces Radio and Television Service; John Pinfold, then at the London School of Economics Library, for subject listings of United States government publications on the American gramophone industry; Monique Refouil of the Bibliothèque Nationale's Département de la Phonothèque National et de l'Audiovisuel for details of works on the development of the French record industry; Marlene Wehrle, Head of the Printed Collection, Music Division of the National Library of Canada for biographical material relating to Stanley Maxted; Ursula Phillips of the School of Slavonic and East European Studies, University of London for help with matters relating to the early post-Revolution days of the Russian record industry; and Graham Camfield of the London School of Economics Library who as well as locating and sending me a copy of the decree of 20th August, 1919 which brought the Russian record industry under state control also put me in touch with the Central State Archives of Sound Recordings, Moscow whose Vice-Director, Vladimir A. Koliada, sent me a most instructive account of Russian spoken word recordings made between 1919 and 1921.

The British Library's National Sound Archive was a valuable source of information; Elizabeth Wells compiled a list of publications on the French record industry; Mavis Hammond-Brake produced figures relating to record output at HMV's Barcelona branch at the time of the Spanish Civil War and dealt with my inquiries about recordings with political connections; and Judith Barnes both looked into my questions about Lenin's recordings and kindly sent a taped copy of Ben Tillett's First World War Regal disc *A Message from the Trenches* for my use at the British Library's Document Supply Centre, Boston Spa, West Yorkshire.

Equally helpful were Ruth Edge and the staff of EMI Archives whenever I sought their assistance. Suzanne Lewis provided me with detailed information on the classic Gaisberg/Hunting descriptive *Departure of a Troopship* and kindly gave me a copy of Jerrold Northrop Moore's book *A Voice to Remember*. Particular thanks also go to Greg Burge for answering my inquiries about Piero Coppola and Jean Bérard of French HMV and for sending me copies of correspondence from 1939 relating to anti-British Arabic propaganda recordings.

Amongst the record companies, I wish to thank Decca International's Maureen Fortey for material on the Decca Dulcephone portable, so prized during the First World War and Olympia Compact Discs Ltd for a copy of the liner notes to their transfers of Lenin's recorded speeches. Alfred Kaine of Deutsche Grammophon Gesellschaft, Hamburg was a much appreciated source of information on Pietro Mascagni's 1927 Polydor recordings with the Berlin State Opera Orchestra. Three compilations issued by Pearl Records, *The Aviators* (PAST CD 9760), *The Rise of Fascism* (OPAL CD 9849) and the two LPs comprising *The Great War* (GEMM 303/4) were invaluable in re-creating the atmosphere of the times as was EMI's twin-cassette collection *The Day War Broke Out* (TC EM 134) with regard to the Second World War. In particular I am indebted to Symposium's *About a Hundred Years* (Symposium 1222) which enabled me to hear for the first time the pioneering electrical recording made at Westminster Abbey on 11th

November, 1920 during the burial service for the Unknown Warrior.

For the section covering the First World War I must record my grateful thanks to Mrs D. Grahame, Secretary of the Victoria Cross and George Cross Association, Amanda McCaffery of the Commonwealth War Graves Commission and Lt. Col. L.M.B. Wilson, M.B.E., Secretary of the Queen's Royal Surrey Regimental Association for their assistance in tracing biographical details of Edward Dwyer, V.C. of the East Surrey Regiment. I am also indebted to R. Whittaker, Assistant County Archivist of Hereford and Worcester Council for information on Captain T. Lawrence Fry of the Royal Flying Corps.

I convey my deep gratitude to Alison Sharp of the Economic History Department, London School of Economics for the work she did on my behalf at the Public Record Office sifting through large quantities of Foreign Office correspondence dealing with HMV's Barcelona branch during the Spanish Civil War and with anti-Italian Arabic propaganda recordings.

For their help in identifying the composer and true title of [Col. Roosevelt's] *Rough Riders* march I owe debts of gratitude to J.A. Meikle, Music Librarian, Royal Military School of Music, Kneller Hall, Twickenham and, in the USA, Dr Norman E. Smith of the Program Note Press, Lake Charles, Louisiana and sergeant First Class Joseph E. Mariany, Music Librarian, United States Military Academy Band, West Point who kindly sent me a copy of the solo cornet part.

Whilst at the Wiener Library, London A.J. Wells thoughtfully alerted me to the reconstruction by Dr Albrecht Dümling of the *Entartete Musik* (Degenerate Music) exhibition staged by the Nazis in Düsseldorf in 1938. In response to my inquiries Dr Dümling enabled me to cite compositions which could be heard on the push-button gramophones by the original visitors.

Of the many recently published discographies I consulted, the British label listings by Michael Smith, Frank Andrews, Ronald Taylor and others in conjunction with John Hunt's artist discographies filled in many gaps in my knowledge as did Alan Grace's and Doreen Taylor's books on British Forces broadcasting.

I had not expected to find much relevant material stemming from India's defence operations against invasion by Japanese Burma-based forces. It was therefore an unexpected pleasure when Dennis Wood of Lastingham Grange, North Yorkshire not only introduced me to the war memoirs of Major David Atkins but also kindly lent me his own copy of the book.

I am extremely grateful to Peter Burgis of Port Macquarie, New South Wales for hard to come by information on Australian patriotic discs issued during the First and Second World Wars and for his article on Australian political spoken word recordings. David Mason, who wrote the liner notes for Pearl's *The Aviators* and *The Rise of Fascism*, generously provided me with printed and audio documentation of the recorded legacy of Sir Oswald Mosley; furthermore, he kindly transferred to tape my deteriorating 78 r.p.m. acetate of William Joyce's last broadcast and gave me a much appreciated copy of the Harlequin LP *German Propaganda Swing 1940-1943* by Charlie and his Orchestra (Vol. 2. HQ 2059).

Finally I come to the valued contributions made to this book by two close friends of long standing. The late Geoffrey Miller wrote for me a fascinating, detailed account of the beginnings, activities and eventual closure of the gramophone club he was instrumental in setting up on the RAF's Second World War base at Sullom Voe in the Shetland Islands. Patrick Wallace and I met at Bruges around the time of VE Day. During the writing of this book Patrick was a never-failing source of information, suggestions and ideas; whenever I had a tricky problem whether to do with BBC or Forces broadcasting, commercial or non-commercial recordings, equipment, people or places his personal knowledge and archival materials, both printed and recorded, were time and again put at my disposal. For all his assistance I offer my deep gratitude and most sincere thanks.

List of Illustrations

The author has approached all known copyright holders to request formal permission to reproduce the illustrations appearing in this book. In those cases where no reply was forthcoming this has been taken to mean that there are no objections.

Between pages 82-83

The Edison company was quick to send patriotic cylinder recordings to its British dealers on the outbreak of World War I.

Columbia's distribution department dispatching cases of World War I patriotic recordings to British dealers.

A gramophone is well to the fore at a World War I recruiting rally in London's Trafalgar Square.

Columbia's advance publicity for Maggie Teyte's recording of the best known British recruiting song of World War I.

HMV's releases for September 1914 included this list of Patriotic Records.

Women machine workers turning out munitions at the Gramophone Company's Hayes plant during World War I.

A two-page spread in HMV's May 1915 list of new releases confirms the popularity of the wartime revues.

Lenin addresses the acoustic recording horn, March 1919.

Berlin street beggar, 1923.

Under Republican control HMV's Barcelona branch advertises a Spanish Civil War patriotic recording.

The Gramophone in Wartime, 1898-1920

IN 1898, THE year in which the phonograph attained its majority, the United States and Spain went to war over Cuba. Since the
early sixteenth century Cuba had been a Spanish possession and
the nationalist uprising of 1895 was by no means the first attempt
to throw off an alien and often oppressive government. The rebel
cause had been taken up eagerly in America, particularly by the so-
called yellow press. The New York newspapers of William
Randolph Hearst and Joseph Pulitzer competed with each other in
printing and embroidering upon reports (already highly coloured)
brought to America by Cuban refugees alleging Spanish atrocities.
The story is told that an artist covering the revolution for the Hearst
press, but who had little success in finding sufficiently lurid subjects to illustrate, was nevertheless instructed to furnish the pictures and his employer would furnish the war. Hostilities began
soon enough, not through any contriving on the part of Hearst but
as a result of the sinking of the American warship *Maine* with great
loss of life in Havana harbour on 15th February, 1898. The court
of inquiry held by the U.S. Navy attributed the cause to a marine
mine, a finding which gave additional credibility to the voice of the
pro-rebel sympathisers in American public and political opinion.

As it turned out, it was the Spanish who, on 24th April, were
the first to declare war; the United States followed suit the next
day. Nellie Melba, the internationally famous Australian soprano,
was in San Francisco at this critical time and was struck by the
depth of feeling shown by the people of the city. The streets
resounded with the noise of demonstrations for the population of
San Francisco included many who were of Spanish descent. The
opera in which Melba was due to sing was Rossini's *The Barber of
Seville*, an unfortunate choice in the circumstances and one which
it was now too late to change. That it was an Italian opera based

1

on a French play mattered little to an audience ready to take sides over anything with Spanish connotations. During the first act Melba was uneasily aware of the restiveness in the house, an atmosphere to which she was totally unaccustomed. The second act, however, enabled her to produce a reconciliation between audience and opera. When the singing lesson scene was reached Melba, accompanying herself on the piano, sang not one of her customary short party pieces but *The Star Spangled Banner*, which was received with tremendous enthusiasm, the audience joining fervently in their national anthem.

Impressively displaying her naval and military muscle America opened campaigns on two fronts. Under the command of Commodore George Dewey a naval squadron was sent from Hong Kong to the Philippine Islands, at that time, like Cuba, a Spanish territory; the Spanish fleet was neutralised without the loss of a single American life and the capital, Manila, was captured. Cuba, on the other hand, was in America's back yard, separated by a bare 100 miles of ocean from the Florida island of Key West. The course of events in Cuba also ran in favour of the United States and after their Navy defeated the Spaniards in the harbour at Santiago de Cuba the next objective was Santiago city. One of the foremost units involved in this land operation was the 1st Volunteer Cavalry, popularly known as the Rough Riders. This tough fighting force had been recruited by Theodore Roosevelt from such members of the community as cowboys, miners and policemen. Roosevelt later described the regiment as having been "raised, armed, equipped, drilled, mounted, dismounted, kept two weeks aboard transports and put through two victorious aggressive fights in which it lost one third of the officers, and one fifth of the men; all within sixty days from the time I received my commission." Not unnaturally, the Rough Riders appealed greatly to the American imagination, as did Roosevelt's flamboyant style of command. On 1st July, aided by balloon reconnaissance of the terrain, the Rough Riders, led by Roosevelt himself, captured the important Spanish position of San Juan Hill, an action which hastened the eventual American victory some two weeks later.

In Cuba landlines and cable telegraphs had, for the first time, been made specially available to newspaper correspondents, so ensuring for American readers a steady flow of news from the battle zones of a successful and popular war. Considering the way in which public interest had been stimulated by the press it is not surprising that the gramophone companies devised their own methods of celebrating the conflict from which America had emerged as a world power. Columbia was the most enterprising, soon offering on cylinder two recordings, one being an impression of life on board the U.S.S. *Oregon*, and the other an account of the taking of Santiago. In the pre-electric era, descriptives, as such recordings had come to be known, were necessarily studio products in which a handful of musicians and vocalists combined with studio staff, who provided background noises and sound effects, to create the broad outlines of a particular occasion. Many early descriptives were undoubtedly primitive efforts, tonal counterparts of the cheap souvenir trade, but they were enjoyed by the gramophone's clientele which, in those days, was largely unsophisticated and easily entertained. The companies' studios were cramped and uncomfortable and because of the limitations of the acoustic recording horn the participants had to be placed close to it and consequently close to each other. In these conditions anybody within the range of string players' bows and trombonists' slides were particularly vulnerable. An element of real danger was not uncommon and an accident that happened to Peter Dawson has become a piece of gramophone folklore. When he was still a relatively unknown singer Dawson frequented the London recording studios, offering his services whenever a suitable opportunity arose. On one occasion he took part in a descriptive called *The Wreck of a Troopship* and many years later in his autobiography he recalled:

"The assistant recorder was so busy with a huge hammer smashing at a thunder sheet he succeeded in wrenching the sheet from its moorings in the ceiling, and with a tearing crash the whole contraption, including the heavy hook, fell on me. Fortunately the iron bolt missed my head ... and after a few minutes wait, during which the 'thunder' was reassembled, we continued to founder on the troopship."

Columbia went on in 1899 to issue a cylinder of Emil Cassi playing the calls he had made the previous year as Chief Trumpeter of the Rough Riders at the battle for San Juan Hill. In this instance, though, Columbia had been forestalled because in November, 1898 Cassi had already done a similar recording on disc for the Berliner

3

company. Perhaps in some way Cassi's trumpet calls typified for Americans their country's prowess in war, for in 1902 Columbia again recorded them, this time on disc. As late as September or October, 1903 Columbia must still have felt assured of a market for post-war memorabilia when it issued a descriptive of the 71st Regiment leaving for Cuba.

Other companies were also quick to exploit the openings provided by the war with Spain, though none of them attempted to compete with Columbia's relatively lavish output. For Edison a group confidently calling itself the Peerless Band made a descriptive cylinder to mark Admiral Dewey's triumphal return to New York, whilst on a Zonophone disc the well known Victor Herbert's Band helped to relive the Battle of Manila. Victor's contribution was a record on which the male voice Haydn Quartet sang of the Battle of Santiago. The singers included Harry Macdonough, one of the highly popular tenors of the day who was constantly active in the North American recording studios either as a soloist or as a member of vocal ensembles. On this occasion he and his colleagues achieved a remarkable feat of compression. Sunday morning service aboard the battleship *Oregon* is interrupted by the sighting of the Spanish fleet; the sailors take up action stations and the order is given to fire the 13 inch gun. Success in battle is followed by feelings of compassion for the vanquished Spaniards and the cry goes up "Don't cheer boys, the poor devils are dying." The three minutes or so of this record are brought to a close, predictably enough, with *The Star Spangled Banner*. The return of peace did not signal an immediate end to America's involvement. In the Philippines the U.S. Army became the military government until 1901; this reversal of roles supplied the idea for another descriptive, the Haydn Quartet's disc entitled *Round the Camp Fire*, a mixture of humour and sentimentality reflecting the life of the occupying army. Now it is peace time the nobility of spirit displayed in the Battle of Santiago disc gives way to far less elevated sentiments as, for instance, when the homesick Private Schmelzer is unsympathetically serenaded by his comrades with the song *In Dear Old Illinois*.

It was only to be expected that sooner or later a regiment as colourful as the Rough Riders would be commemorated in music, though paradoxically it was not an American composer who performed this service. The Canadian Louis-Philippe Laurendeau was

4

a prolific writer and arranger of military band music on the staff of Carl Fischer's music publishing house in New York. The combination of Laurendeau's ready talent and the prospect of quick sales for the publisher resulted in the "marche caractéristique" *Col. Roosevelt's Rough Riders* appearing in 1898. This lively piece which incorporated the sound of shots and horses' hooves is almost certainly the *Rough Riders March* recorded by the band of the Grenadier Guards of Canada, the seven-inch single-sided disc being amongst the earliest Canadian issues of the Berliner Company when it began manufacturing in Montreal in 1900. However, despite its initial success and the benefit of the early recording the work did not secure a lasting place for itself in the military band repertoire.

Judged by present day standards there was, with the exception of the Cassi recordings, little of permanent historical value in the gramophone's response to the Spanish-American War. One consequence, though, was that the earlier type of descriptives which had been content to illustrate such familiar matters as life down on the farm were now made to seem somewhat humdrum and uninteresting. The industry had shown its ability to react imaginatively to events of national importance and in the process the gramophone had given the first faint hints of a style of war reporting which, years later, was to be developed and refined in turn by the cinema, radio and television.

★   ★   ★

The originality with which the Americans had translated important episodes in the war with Spain into purely audio terms for popular consumption was less in evidence when the London studios were faced with the challenge of the Boer War of 1899-1902. As far as the gramophone was concerned this was to be another one-sided affair, for the Boer states, like Cuba and the Philippines, had no domestic recording industry with which to produce their own patriotic material. For the watchful Gramophone Company, intent on expanding internationally, the war in southern Africa had brought into sharp focus an area with considerable commercial possibilities and in the latter part of 1903 a branch was opened in Cape Town.

In formulating their responses to the war the recording companies in Britain had a difficult problem on their hands. Although by the turn of the century the phonograph had achieved a certain

5

degree of acceptance the majority of people with any aspirations to culture viewed the talking machine as a primitive and ephemeral toy, fit merely for the nursery and below stairs. Competition between the companies was extremely fierce and the limited market offered little encouragement for departures, whether on cylinder or the new flat disc, from the true and tried material (popular songs, cornet solos, military marches, etc.) which experience told them would find ready sales.

The events leading up to the war were diverse and complex but at the heart of the matter were the two independent republics, the Orange Free State and the Transvaal, set up by the Boers nearly half a century previously. Largely enclosed by British territories, they were desirable potential additions to a country still eager to extend its holdings in southern Africa. Moreover, since the world's major currencies were then valued in terms of gold, the Transvaal's enormous resources of that precious metal constituted a further tantalising objective. In the end it was British pressure for the long-denied granting of political rights to the foreign (mainly British) population of the Transvaal which resulted in the declaration of war by the Boers in October, 1899.

The campaign began disastrously for the British with a series of defeats and with their forces at Ladysmith, Kimberley and Mafeking coming under prolonged siege. The Boers grew increasingly expert in the tactics of guerrilla warfare and earned a fearsome reputation for their marksmanship which was far superior to that of their opponents. The London newspaper *The Morning Post* had as its war correspondent the youthful Winston Churchill, whose vivid dispatches left readers at home in no doubt about the difficulties being faced by the British Army. Outnumbered on land and isolated from any outside help by the Royal Navy's blockade the Boers were eventually forced to yield, but not before they had experienced the devastation of Kitchener's scorched earth policy and the wholesale internment of their men, women and children.

In Britain support for the government's conduct of the war was by no means wholehearted. There was such strong sympathy for the Boers within the Liberal Party that, early in his political career, Lloyd George had the temerity to go to Birmingham a week before Christmas, 1901 with the open intention of making a pro-Boer speech in that staunchly anti-Boer city. The meeting was to be held at the Town Hall around which so large a crowd gathered that it looked as if the force of 350 policemen drafted in to maintain order might be faced with a serious breach of the peace. Before the speeches began an organist played *The Men of Harlech* which the large contingent of militant infiltrators in the audience countered with a spirited vocal rendering of *Tommy Atkins*. Lloyd George had scarcely started to speak before there was a rush towards the platform, whilst at the same time a fusillade of stones came crashing through the windows. At the request of the Chief Constable Lloyd George abandoned his speech as it was clear that his person, perhaps even his life, were in danger. Some time later, wearing a constable's uniform, he was smuggled away from the Town Hall to safety in the midst of a protective group of policemen.

Writers of various political persuasions defended or condemned the war in a flood of pamphlets and books. Not too reluctantly Conan Doyle put Sherlock Holmes to one side in order to join the army's medical staff in southern Africa and in 1900 brought out a substantial work entitled *The Great Boer War*. Much more widely read was his pamphlet *The War in South Africa, its Cause and Conduct* which appeared two years later. This was such a skilful justification of the government's policy that it was translated into various European languages including (no doubt with Lloyd George's Liberal fellow-countrymen in mind) Welsh and distributed free of charge. Another author whose name was shortly to become a household word was active in Africa, first in the Medical Staff Corps and then as a press correspondent. This was the versatile Edgar Wallace from whose fluent pen came stories and verse inspired by the war as well as a book of *Unofficial Dispatches* published in 1901.

The dominance of the printed word, however, was about to be challenged by a new medium of mass communication, the cinema. Some of the pioneers of the moving picture industry realised the pulling power of news items shown as a regular part of their programmes and Charles Urban's Warwick Trading Company sent one of its leading cameramen to Africa to film the war on the spot. Joseph Rosenthal's silent war reports were shipped back to Britain to be screened in theatres, fairgrounds and other places of public entertainment where people could watch the Army in camp, in training and on the move. The filming equipment of those days was so heavy and cumbersome that it was quite unsuited for taking

7

into action; this drawback did not deter Rosenthal who, on at least one occasion, arranged with the military authorities for an encounter with the Boers to be re-enacted for his camera some time after the actual event. Rosenthal's faking was a precedent discreetly followed in officially made films in both the first and second world wars. Other organisations lacking Urban's financial resources contented themselves with using small casts to depict stirring, mostly imaginary, deeds with easily accessible English countryside locations doing duty for the veldt of southern Africa.

During the war two European recordings of a Transvaal folk song appeared, one made for Zonophone, probably in Berlin in 1901 or 1902, by the soprano Betsy Schot, the other in Amsterdam in 1901 for the Berliner Company by a baritone named Thomas Denys. Whether these recordings held any political significance at the time they were actually made it is now difficult to say, but they could well have been an oblique indication of the pro-Boer sympathy that prevailed in their countries of origin and throughout Europe generally.

The London companies were necessarily cautious when public opinion was sharply divided over the justness of the war, when newspaper correspondents' dispatches provided many column inches of factual reporting and when moving pictures gave audiences the illusion of being present at happenings thousands of miles away. For the gramophone a partisan stance after the style of the press would have been commercially disastrous since, in the struggle for sales, no company could risk alienating future customers for the sake of making political or moral points. In Britain the great moments of the war tended to be ones of relief, in both the emotional and military senses of that word; the tremendous celebrations that marked the raising of the siege of Mafeking made Mafeking Night a phrase which for years was synonymous with public jubilation. Little more than a month after the outbreak of war the popular singer Ion Colquhoun, known as the "Iron-Voiced Baritone", recorded *We're not going to stand it* and *Take the Lion's Muzzle off*, but the gramophone companies soon toned down the blatant John Bullishness of such titles in favour of a more generalised (and therefore widely acceptable) type of patriotism based mainly on the gallantry of the British soldier.

The trend was characterised early on by the entry in Berliner's 1900 catalogue for Godfrey's Band playing *With the British Colours*, whilst other companies issued such favourites as *The Soldiers of the Queen*, *Tommy Atkins* and *Goodbye Dolly Gray* in a wide choice of vocal and instrumental forms. Ironically, the last mentioned tune, which has a very English-sounding ring to it, was actually an American song composed for the Spanish-American War, but too late to be of use in that short conflict. When the Boer War broke out its enterprising composers lost no time in introducing it to Britain where it has remained familiar ever since.

The record catalogues of the period reveal lists of artists whose names are now virtually forgotten except by the most knowledgeable students of Victorian and Edwardian popular entertainment. The Gramophone Company, later to become HMV, had a plentiful supply of material directly related to the war with which to tempt record buyers. The Municipal Military Band and the tenor H. Scott Russell both gave their versions of the somewhat premature *Marching to Pretoria* and the Darnley Brothers contributed *The Song of Mafeking*. Two other songs, *C.I.V.s* and *Welcome C.I.V.*, had been inspired by the City Imperial Volunteers, a force that had immediately won the public's (especially the Londoners') admiration. The Municipal Military Band further explored the possibilities of war-related titles with *Patrol of the Boers* and *The Transvaal Patrol*, while Mr. C. Foster, who recorded prolifically for the Gramophone Company, added *The Boers have got my Daddy* to his long list of sentimental and comic songs. On the Zonophone label Ion Colquhoun augmented his output of topical airs with recordings of *Tommy Atkins*, *The Young British Soldier*, *Marching on Pretoria* and Leslie Stuart's *The Soldiers of the Queen*, a song which pre-dated the Boer War and contained robust patriotic sentiments. Zonophone later noted proudly that Colquhoun had sung *The Soldiers of the Queen* more than 500 times in his appearances at London's Alhambra Theatre during the war; with equal pride they commended his records for being "very loud, clear and sympathetic."

It was with music of this kind that the Edison Bell Consolidated Phonograph Company advertised itself with considerable panache on the evening in mid-November, 1899 when Sir Charles Wyndham opened his new theatre in Charing Cross Road. The crowds flocking to the charity premiere gave a go-ahead Edison Bell director a promotional opportunity not to be missed. He positioned a phonograph in the window of the Company's first floor office directly opposite the theatre and, to the delight of theatregoers and casual passers-by alike, played a programme of patriotic tunes from Edison cylinders. So great was the enthusiasm that the police had to be called in to control the throng. Despite official requests to desist, the director stood his ground and went on playing his cylinders, thereby landing himself in court where he paid, no doubt willingly, the small fine that was imposed. The recital quite possibly stimulated the first-nighters at Wyndham's to give even more generously than might have been expected, for *The Times* reported that, through the channels of the War Relief Fund, the Aldershot branch of the Soldiers' Wives and Families Association benefited by the then considerable sum of £4,000. The value of the excellent publicity gained at minimal expense by Edison Bell could not, of course, be calculated in such simple monetary terms, but bringing the high quality of its phonographs and cylinders so tellingly to the notice of a large and receptive audience must, at the very least, have resulted in a useful boost to sales and a greatly increased public awareness of the products.

The Gramophone Company earned the distinction of making the most notable recording to be inspired by the Boer War. Fred Gaisberg, who with his brother Will had come over from the United States in 1898 as Emile Berliner's British recording manager, gave much thought to subjects that might be turned into a descriptive reflecting some aspect of Britain's part in the war. This was no easy matter as the uphill struggle in Africa offered little encouragement for recording artificial heroics in the studio. Also in London was Gaisberg's friend and fellow-American Russell Hunting, another pioneer of the industry, who was thoroughly versed in its creative, technical and business sides. Gaisberg had taken part, usually as piano accompanist, in many of the records made by Berliner, but Hunting had grown famous in his own right in North America and Britain for the highly popular recordings he had made in the comic character of Michael Casey. Though Hunting was working for the British Zonophone Company the two men discussed and rejected various topics for the descriptive, amongst them Gaisberg's idea (not the most promising of scenarios) concerning raw recruits facing a Gatling gun.

Eventually they concentrated on the emotional mood of the British public and transferred that feeling with conspicuous success to *The Departure of a Troopship*, a recording that became a classic of its genre. Issued in both seven- and ten-inch formats the descriptive was made by the Gramophone Concert Band and, in Gaisberg's own words, portrayed

"crowds at the quayside, bands playing the troops up the gang plank, bugles sounding 'All ashore', farewell cries of 'Don't forget to write', troops singing 'Home, sweet home', which gradually receded in the distance, and the far-away mournful toot of the steamer whistle."

A report in *The Times* in February, 1900 confirms how well Gaisberg and Hunting caught the spirit of such occasions. The special correspondent who watched the embarkation of troops at London's Albert Docks noted the "inexhaustible cheerfulness, the pervading and abiding serenity displayed alike by those going and those left behind." Jingoism was not in evidence and the writer was impressed by "the quiet determination - equally removed from fear and boasting - the self-reliance, self-control, and absolute devotion that animate all classes in all parts of the country."

Written nearly forty years after the end of the Boer War, Gaisberg's autobiography gives the impression that the *Troopship* was conceived and issued in the course of the war, but in actual fact it was not until April and May, 1905 that the seven- and ten-inch discs respectively went on sale. Not to be outdone, British Zonophone, also in May, 1905, produced its own variation on the troopship theme, giving it the same title as that used by the Gramophone Company. Zonophone's recording was a thoroughly professional piece of work; even today, despite the inevitable heavy surface noise, the listener is aware of the engineer and the London Regimental Band bringing off a masterly fading of the National Anthem at the end as the ship departs.

Of all the works inspired by the Boer War the most famous in its day was undoubtedly *The Absent-Minded Beggar*. The recently established *Daily Mail* newspaper achieved a notable double in persuading Rudyard Kipling to write and Sir Arthur Sullivan to set to music what was in effect an appeal for money to support the wives and families of the soldiers (the absent-minded beggars of the title) fighting in southern Africa. The *Daily Mail* published Kipling's

11

verses on 31st October, 1899 and Sullivan's setting received its first performance (and encore) at the Alhambra Theatre on the evening of 13th November, conducted by the composer. A few hours later Sullivan noted in his diary: "Packed house - wild enthusiasm. All sang chorus!" The piece was recited or sung, publicly and privately, up and down the country and was played on barrel organs in the street everywhere; all proceeds from the sales of words and music went to charitable funds which acquired the remarkable sum of a quarter of a million pounds.

The Absent-Minded Beggar was so deeply rooted in the Boer War that not even the combined talents of Kipling and Sullivan plus a recording by the stentorian Colquhoun were sufficient to ensure it any lasting fame once the time of need had passed. Colquhoun's recording for the Gramophone Company, however, secured for itself a special place in the history of the industry, though for purely technical rather than artistic reasons. Kipling's four lengthy stanzas far exceeded the time available on a ten-inch single-sided disc, for double-sided discs were not produced as a standard format until the Berlin-based Odeon company brought them out in 1904. So it was that *The Absent-Minded Beggar* became the first piece to be spread over two sides (in this case two discs) in order to be presented in its entirety.

Even with its welter of leather-lunged singers and their strong-armed piano accompanists, to say nothing of solo banjoists, flautists and cornetists without number, the gramophone at this early point in its life could offer only the most limited competition to the live entertainment provided by the theatres and music halls throughout Britain. The gramophone's war descriptives had much in common with the dramatic scenes which formed part of the regular fare at the vaudeville theatres. The popularity of these items is clear from posters of the London Coliseum which in 1904 was running four houses daily; patrons had the choice of two alternating programmes, one of which included memories of a past war, whilst the other staged an episode from a war currently in progress. Though the South African conflict was long over the Coliseum's clientele obviously still relished seeing Miss Madge Lessing playing the part of Bugler Taps of the C.I.V.s at a camp outside Johannesburg on the night before the battle. This "stirring military song scene" was entitled *A Little Boy Called Taps* and in addition to Miss Lessing it called upon a military fife and drum band and a detachment of the British Army Reserves. The second military item stemmed from the hostilities in the Far East between Russia and Japan and took the form of a "grand musical spectacle" depicting the Japanese land and sea attacks on Port Arthur. The music for this highly topical production was by the aptly named composer Walter Slaughter.

★　　★　　★

The Russo-Japanese War of 1904-05 was the outcome of a dispute over territorial rights and spheres of influence in Korea and Manchuria, the flash-point occurring when Russia's failure to carry out an agreed withdrawal of troops from Manchuria was met with a retaliatory attack by Japan on the Russian-held Port Arthur (now part of Luta). With the Trans-Siberian Railway not yet fully operational the Russians could counter-attack only from the sea and accordingly the Baltic Fleet set out in October, 1904 on a seven months voyage to the other side of the world. Admiral Rozhdestvensky's force had barely entered the North Sea when serious deficiencies in its command became apparent. At night the Russian ships encountered the Hull fishing fleet and, under the impression that the trawlers were enemy vessels, bombarded them for twenty minutes. Amongst the casualties were two fishermen who had been decapitated by the shell-fire, a macabre tragedy that was given much prominence in the British press. Feelings against the Russians understandably ran high and their ambassador, Count Benckendorff, was booed and jeered at by crowds in the street as he drove about his duties in London. To the disabled fishermen and the families of the men who had been killed King Edward VII and Queen Alexandra tendered both their sympathy and immediate financial aid of more than £300. Elsewhere throughout the world the news of the Russians' naval incompetence was greeted with contempt and near disbelief. While Rozhdestvensky's ships sailed on, the Tsar made what diplomatic amends he could for his Admiral from whom he had received no news. The Russian commander's confused state of mind continued to obscure his judgment for it was reported that he ordered his torpedo boats to redouble their watchfulness as the enemy was believed to be in the English Channel. The North Sea incident was the ominous prelude to the total defeat to be suffered in May, 1905 when, in the

13

battle of Tsushima Straits, the Japanese annihilated the Russian fleet.

The reasons for the modest scale of the record companies' response to the war are plain to see. In Japan the industry was still in its infancy, the foundations of a basic domestic catalogue having been laid as recently as February, 1903 when Fred Gaisberg undertook an intensive series of recording sessions for the Gramophone Company in Tokyo. The position in Russia was quite different as the gramophone was already well established there, amongst those classes able to afford it, both as an instrument of entertainment and as a cultural medium. The repertoire, whilst containing light material and gipsy and other folk music, was dominated by opera and song with recordings of internationally famous singers and of the many fine artists working in Russia's own opera houses being in enormous demand. Considering the taste and enthusiasm of the Russian gramophone devotees it is not surprising that the concept of the red label, premium-price celebrity discs issued by the Gramophone Company and Victor should have originated in that country. When this market profile is viewed against Russia's lack of military success in the war it is clear that recordings of a propagandist nature would have been dubious commercial ventures.

Taking their cue from world opinion the British and American companies supported Japan but, as their two countries were not involved, were prudently sparing in their war-related output. It was generally felt that the Japanese had right on their side, though whether they had the power and capability to overcome the Russians might be a rather different matter. American Columbia, drawing on its previous experience with war descriptives, made its contribution with the Columbia Band re-enacting the capture of the Russian forts at Port Arthur. The widespread interest in the events in the Far East was reflected in the British music hall programmes of the time. The two hostile powers elevated their long-drawn-out confrontation to an official state of war in February, 1904 but for a month before this the Australian baritone Hamilton Hill had been delighting London audiences with a new song unambiguously entitled *Good Luck, Japan*. The British government's policy was one of strict neutrality, but such diplomatic niceties did not extend to the world of popular entertainment and Hill was soon in the studio to record his hit for Zonophone. On the return of

14

peace Hill was again in demand, on this occasion to record *Little Brown Man of Japan* in praise of the victors.

The similarity of the London Coliseum's spectacle and American Columbia's descriptive illustrates the close links developing between the stage and the gramophone as the new century progressed. This was not merely a case of war descriptives following in the well worn paths of theatrical patriotic scenas; the relationship evolved rather from the realisation that whatever was popular in performance across the footlights also stood a very good chance of success on cylinder or disc. The short duration of the war meant there was a limited choice of subjects for the would-be makers of descriptive recordings. Nicole, one of the expanding number of firms operating in London, saw its chance and took the battle of Mukden (now Shen-yang), fought during February and March, 1905 as the basis of a recording. The artists concerned were the Nicole Orchestra which, like so many other bands impressively named after the parent company, was almost certainly a pick-up group hired for the session. Some members of this orchestra probably also played in the sets of quadrilles and lancers which Nicole produced for use at dances where live music was not available;[1] for such musicians *The Battle of Mukden* would have been a novel contrast to their usually more prosaic work in the studio.

The humiliation of the defeat at the Straits of Tsushima scarred the Russian national consciousness deeply, but for the Japanese the consequences of the war were even more far-reaching. Vastly encouraged by their victory they steadily followed an imperialist policy that eventually, in the Second World War, brought the whole of the Far East under their ruthless domination and led to the nuclear obliteration of Hiroshima and Nagasaki in 1945.

★   ★   ★

In 1914 the greater part of Europe was contained in one or other of two major power blocs. On the one side was Germany in alliance with the Austro-Hungarian empire, a grouping which had territorial ambitions in Europe (especially the Balkans) and the Middle East; on the other side were Russia, her ally France and Great Britain, all keeping close watch on the constant unrest resulting from Germany's calculated political pressures and sabre-rattling. Austria at this time coveted the neighbouring kingdom of Serbia and Russia had made clear her opposition to any takeover of her Slavonic near-neighbour. On 28th June, 1914 in Sarajevo, the capital of Bosnia, (then part of the Austro-Hungarian empire), a young revolutionary named Gavrilo Princip assassinated the Austrian Archduke Franz Ferdinand and his wife. Princip was a known supporter of the Slav nationalist cause in the Balkans, and Austria, convinced of Serbia's complicity in the murders, demanded a full investigation. When the Serbs failed to respond to this and other veiled threats Austria declared war on 28th July. This action triggered other declarations and by 4th August, when Britain entered the conflict, Germany was already at war with Russia and France. As a British encyclopaedia of the 1920s succinctly put it: "Armageddon had begun."

Today the predominant images of 1914-1918 are still those of barbed wire and mud, even though the frontiers of warfare had been extended into the air and beneath the sea. The British Isles themselves were no longer safe from an enemy whose powerful naval guns could bombard the east coast from a safe distance, as the people of Yarmouth, Scarborough and Hartlepool were to find out before the end of 1914. From January, 1915 onwards Zeppelins began bombing London and the eastern counties and in November the following year German aeroplanes made the first of what was to be a long series of raids on the capital. Women from all classes took up the task of caring for the wounded in hospitals at home and abroad. Many of the great town and country houses were turned into convalescent homes for the men lucky enough to be returned to Blighty. Armaments were needed on a scale never before known and women now took on what had once been regarded as exclusively male work in the munitions factories. On the railways, trams and buses, in light industry, on the farms, in forestry, wherever, in fact, they could feasibly replace men who had gone into the fighting services, women became a familiar part of the work force. It was not in Britain alone that such far-reaching changes were experienced; all the major European countries involved in the fighting emerged from the war, whether as winners or losers, with the realisation that in one way or another the old order had passed away and would not return.

During the period that separated the end of the Boer War and the outbreak of the Great War of 1914-1918 the gramophone's reputation improved rapidly. It had become widely recognised as a respectable popular entertainer and an important medium through which the artistry of the finest musicians of the day, especially the singers, could be brought to a steadily widening public and at the same time preserved for posterity. The turning point in the gramophone's fortunes can be dated to the session in Milan in March, 1902 when Fred Gaisberg recorded ten arias sung by the tenor Enrico Caruso, until then little known outside his native Italy. The records sold prodigiously which was lucky for Gaisberg who was so impressed by the qualities of Caruso's voice that, without authorisation, he had far exceeded the Gramophone Company's upper limit when negotiating the session fee of £100 with the singer. The success of these recordings persuaded many famous operatic stars who had previously doubted the gramophone's ability to reproduce their voices satisfactorily to follow in Caruso's footsteps; within a few years the catalogues were embellished with treasures from such internationally renowned names as Nellie Melba, Adelina Patti, Mattia Battistini, Geraldine Farrar and Giovanni Zenatello.

The well-known saying that the gramophone made Caruso and Caruso made the gramophone, whilst perfectly true, perhaps does not do full justice to the part played by the pioneers of the industry. Ensuing generations of music lovers have cause to be grateful that the most influential of those who guided the gramophone into the twentieth century were not just hucksters intent on maximising profits without regard to standards. Louis Sterling, who set up his own record company in London, Alfred Clark, who ran the Gramophone Company's Paris studios and the Gaisberg brothers were all shrewd businessmen whose commercial acumen went hand in hand with sound artistic judgment as well as a wholehearted belief in the cultural value of the gramophone.

When the war that would end all wars and that would be over by Christmas erupted in August, 1914 the industry was to be involved more deeply than in any earlier conflict for, with its ample resources, the gramophone was now a significant source of popular entertainment. Military band recordings still tended to dominate the output but the recorded repertoire had expanded enormously and the catalogue of His Master's Voice records on offer during the war contained a good deal of classical music in a variety of forms. The music hall songs and the dance tunes of the day had been joined by favourite overtures, suites and ballet music

and even a complete symphony (the Beethoven 5th) in performances by well-known conductors and orchestras. There were
ballads and excerpts from opera in profusion, leading instrumentalists were featured and chamber music had begun to put in an
appearance, though not in the shape of complete works. The isolated movements that make up this latter category range over some
unexpected territory and shed an interesting light on the prevailing musical taste. Haydn and Mozart were absent, but anybody
fond of Schumann had the choice of the Scherzo from the Piano
Quintet and snippets of the String Quartet in A major, op. 41, No.
3, a work even nowadays not frequently recorded. The standard
repertoire was further represented by the Andante Cantabile from
Tchaikovsky's D major String Quartet, the Scherzo from
Mendelssohn's D minor Piano Trio, Op. 49, the Adagio from a
Beethoven piano trio and the Variations from Schubert's *Death and
the Maiden* quartet. The presence of the third and fourth movements of Ravel's String Quartet seems remarkably adventurous for
the time and the Scherzo from the Piano Quartet in B flat, Op. 41
by Saint-Saëns is a memorial to a piece that has now virtually vanished from disc and the concert hall.

The companies' first response to the war was to bring out quantities of patriotic music, usually marketed as special supplements
such as that issued by English Columbia in October, 1914. A dozen
ten-inch discs included the national anthems of Britain, France,
Belgium and Russia; the Anglo-French alliance was celebrated by
the march *The Entente Cordiale* and the *Namur March* paid honour
to war-torn Belgium. Stanford's famous song *Drake's Drum* was
given by the baritone Thorpe Bates whilst the bass baritone Robert
Howe, accompanied by the Band of the Scots Guards, sang
Onward, Christian Soldiers, aptly backed by the sailors' hymn *Eternal
Father, Strong to Save*. Despite the rapidly shrinking demand for
cylinder recordings the Edison company was not to be outdone by
its disc-producing rivals and brought out a group of patriotic numbers for its small but faithful British clientele. However, the cylin-
der business was so far in decline that suitable recordings for the
October list had to be sent from the Edison headquarters in
West Orange, New Jersey. The performers, of course, were
American and included the Edison Military Band, the New York
Military Band and the National Guard Fife and Drum Corps, but
to restore the balance exclusively British artists were featured in

the company's November and December issues. Another Edison patriotic supplement came out in June, 1915, but economic necessity again dictated an all-American batch of recordings. The efforts of the ailing company to satisfy the demand created by the upsurge of British patriotism were totally inadequate to the occasion and, as the war progressed, the sales generally of Edison and other makes of cylinders withered away in the market where the supremacy of the 78 r.p.m. disc was now beyond all doubt.

The patriotic supplements were useful enough contributions to a nation at war but the gramophone was soon playing a more positive role. Up until 1916 when Britain introduced compulsory military service enlistment was on a voluntary basis. The main stimulus came from the recruiting drives and rallies at which the blandishments of regular servicemen, commissioned and non-commisioned, were interspersed whenever possible with appropriate music. If a military or local brass band was not available it was a simple matter with the help of a gramophone to play the sort of stirring tunes calculated to encourage the potential volunteers to sign on.

A potent exhortation, and one that could be used on many different occasions, was the purpose-made recruiting song. The importance that governments attached to this particular form of inducement is clearly seen in the letter the Canadian Minister of Trade and Commerce, Sir George E. Foster, sent in October, 1914 to Columbia's Toronto office concerning the most famous one of all to be composed during the Great War. He wrote:

"I learn that you would consider a request to have a record made of Paul Ruben's [sic] Recruiting Song 'Your King and Your [sic] Country Want You.'

I would be very glad if you could find it possible to do this and would consider it a notable contribution to the Patriotic cause in Canada."

Columbia had no difficulty in obliging for a recording had already been made in London by the soprano Maggie Teyte. This song, sponsored by the *Daily Mail* newspaper, was a far cry from the repertoire with which she was then associated, since not only was she a fine Mozartian but, at Debussy's wish, had sung the role of the heroine in his opera *Pelléas et Mélisande*. When asked to record Paul Rubens's *Your King and Country Want You* and its backing,

The Homes They Leave Behind by Paul's brother Walter, Maggie
Teyte's acceptance may have been influenced as much by personal
as by patriotic considerations. Paul, whose musical comedy scores
delighted British theatre-goers, and Walter were members of the
wealthy, well-connected Rubens family that had recognised the
remarkable talent of Maggie Teyte when she was a mere fifteen
years old. Through their generous patronage Teyte had received
the best possible tuition to set her on the road to stardom. By 1914
she had become famous in Europe and America and this recording of songs by the two brothers enabled her to show her gratitude
in a most befitting way; it was also in the nature of a farewell to the
Rubenses for Teyte was about to return to her operatic career in
the United States. She remained there until the war was over but,
with her home country much in her thoughts, she included two
numbers by the rising composer Ivor Novello amongst the songs
she recorded in Columbia's New York studios in the summer of
1916. They were the long-since forgotten *Laddie in Khaki* and the
evergreen *Keep the Home Fires Burning*. The latter had immediately
endeared itself to the hearts of British soldiers and civilians and is
still remembered as one of the most evocative songs to be inspired
by the war. Whether American Columbia decided that Novello's
music would have less appeal on their side of the Atlantic is uncertain, but both recordings remained unissued.

HMV featured the contralto Edna Thornton in their version of
Your King and Country Want You and although her name has not
endured as Maggie Teyte's has done her motherly voice even now
sounds extraordinarily sincere and persuasive; her rendering of the
well-known words "We don't want to lose you, but we feel you
ought to go" must have spurred many a young man's entry into the
forces. Another newspaper, *The Daily Telegraph*, also had its own
recruiting song, *Courage*, recorded by HMV, the singer this time
being Ruby Helder who was interestingly described as a "lady
tenor".

Amongst the many public buildings that became centres for
recruiting drives was the Mansion House in the City of London
and here the gramophone again came to be used as an integral part
of the recruitment process. The Lord Mayor for the session 1915-
16 was Sir Charles Wakefield (later Lord Wakefield of Hythe), the
founder of the Castrol lubricating oil concern who in January, 1916

offered the Mansion House as a special recruiting centre for a week. So great was the response that a further seven days were needed to deal with the flood of volunteers and Sir Charles promised there would now be "additional accommodation, more clerks, better facilities for medical examination, and no waiting." As printed in *The Times* of 10th January, Sir Charles's original appeal was couched in emotive terms. The "imperishable glory" of those who fought and died at Ypres, Neuve Chapelle and Loos was referred to, but to ensure victory "We must fill the gaps. We must keep the ranks full... Come and do your duty. You will be received as worthy sons of our ancient city. Your comrades in the trenches call you. Hear and obey their call." It was sentiments such as these that HMV recorded at the Mansion House on 25th January, 1916 on the occasion of a recruiting speech delivered by the Lord Mayor. Thus there became available an appeal that could subsequently be played for recruitment purposes wherever there was a gramophone to hand. A short postscript to these events appeared in *The Times* two months later. "Eight members of the Lord Mayor's household at the Mansion House have joined the colours. One was killed at Loos. The remaining three of military age have attested, and are preparing for being called up by drilling by gramophone."

During 1915 it was the shortage of shells rather than manpower that posed the British Army's most serious difficulty and in early May the costly and inconclusive battle of Festubert in northern France brought the problem to crisis point. *The Times* was in no doubt that "the want of an unlimited supply of high explosives was a fatal bar to our success"; other national newspapers took up the theme and Lord Kitchener, the Secretary for War, was severely criticised.

The unpalatable fact was that the shell-producing factories were delivering only a small percentage of their contracts on time; something had to be done immediately to remedy the situation and a Ministry of Munitions was set up, headed by Lloyd George. In July Parliament passed the Munitions of War Act which had amongst its objectives the prevention of strikes and trade union restrictive practices and the referral of all disputes to arbitration. Technical schools provided training courses for men and women entering the munitions industry and by the end of 1915 there were thirty three national shell factories in operation. When Lloyd George on the

21

death of Kitchener became War Secretary in July, 1916 matters had improved to such an extent that what in 1914-15 constituted a year's output of field howitzer ammunition could now be manufactured in a fortnight; as a result, an artillery battery that had been rationed to a mere eight rounds a day was now in a position to fire fifty times that number of shells.

English Columbia had launched its mid-price Regal discs in 1914 and it was on this label with a recording by Ben Tillett that, in June, 1915, the gramophone added its voice to the insistent call for more munitions. Securing Tillett as their speaker showed considerable shrewdness on Regal's part for not only was he totally convinced of the need to defeat Germany but he was widely known and respected as a leader of organised labour.

When only a boy of eight Tillett left home to join a circus and went on to serve in the Royal Navy and as a merchant seaman. Returning to shore life he became a London docker and led the strikes of 1889 and 1911 in the cause of better working conditions, whilst in the wider political arena he was amongst the founders of the Independent Labour Party and the present Labour Party. He worked tirelessly on behalf of the war effort. At home he spoke regularly at patriotic meetings in halls and theatres, sharing platforms with celebrities of the time. He travelled extensively on visits to the soldiers at the Western Front, encouraging them in their struggle against the Germans and reporting their needs to the appropriate authorities. A constant subject of his public speeches was the ammunition shortage and this is emphasised time and again in his recording, *A Message from the Trenches*.

"He belonged to the evangelistic days of trade-unionism, when men spoke with natural oratory." The accuracy of the *Dictionary of National Biography's* description of Tillett's style is amply borne out by Regal's recording. Studio conditions clearly had no inhibiting effect and the listener is conscious from the start of Tillett's sincerity and deep personal concern. Even the occasional verbal slip does nothing to diminish the urgency of his appeal. He addresses himself to "My dear fellow-countrymen and women" and refers to the "glorious old Motherland". He speaks of the scenes of death and destruction he has witnessed and of the atrocities committed by the enemy against French and Belgian women. Above all, he pleads fervently for more shells and support of every kind for the

22

fighting men and their families, asking for this backing "in the name of liberty, in the name of freedom" since "the fight is for all of us".

A Message from the Trenches prompts an intriguing question: did the government have a hand in the planning of this recording? The appearance of the disc coincided with the government's initial moves to restructure the munitions industry, which strongly suggests there was official involvement at some stage. The engineers had captured a splendid example of vibrant patriotism which could be used to advantage in places where a gramophone and receptive listeners were to be found in conjunction. Although outwardly the *Message* was addressed to a general audience its prime target was unmistakably the work force in the munitions industry and we can safely conclude that both Regal and the government saw the potential of the heartfelt appeal by Tillett, the workers' champion, as a means of sparking off the desperately needed increase in productivity.

There has never been such an assured sale for recordings of national anthems as there was during the 1914-1918 war. We may now find it difficult to imagine *God Save the King* being played on the gramophone in domestic surroundings, but played it certainly was in many homes at that time and those gathered around would, equally certainly, have stood as a mark of respect. Whenever it was proper to affirm the national spirit at public meetings (and no less than 899 were organised by the National War Aims Committee between 25th September and 10th October, 1917, the time of Passchendaele) any lack of live musical resources could be remedied by playing the anthem on a gramophone record. Versions by orchestras, military bands or singers catered for all needs.

Deutsche Grammophon, the German arm of the Gramophone Company, produced an ingenious disc of their house orchestra playing *Deutschland über alles*. To complement the anthem the label was graced by the German eagle and the imperious features of Kaiser Wilhelm II, so that when displayed in shops and stores even the unplayed record became yet another patriotic stimulus. Furthermore, a note on the label informed every purchaser of this truly multi-purpose disc that it was sold in aid of the German armed forces and their dependents.

In this way gramophone companies channelled welcome funds to the war charities. For each copy sold of Maggie Teyte's *Your King*

23

and Country Want You Columbia paid a royalty to the Prince of Wales's Fund and Canadian Columbia gave 15 cents to their country's Patriotic Fund. While their menfolk were on active service or furthering the war effort in other ways at home the women of the aristocracy worked tirelessly for charitable causes. One of the most well-known was Lady Maud Warrender, the wife of Admiral Sir George Warrender. Her much-admired contralto voice had been professionally trained and during the war she gave many recitals in churches, cathedrals, concert halls and hospitals as well as in elegant society music rooms. Typically, her generosity extended to her HMV recording of two popular ballads, her royalties from which she donated to naval charities. The most serious music to appear as a charity issue was on the four single sides of excerpts from Elgar's *The Dream of Gerontius* recorded in 1916 with Dame Clara Butt and Maurice D'Oisley as the soloists with an orchestra and chorus conducted by Sir Henry Wood; the beneficiary from the special royalty on these discs was the British Red Cross. The studio session was not without incident for, as Wood recalled in his autobiography, Dame Clara

> "came in with her entire family and some of her friends. Arthur Brooks, the recording manager, came forward and told her that nothing could be done unless he could have complete silence; she forthwith packed her relatives and friends off home. She was always inclined to be a law unto herself ..."

Austria used the gramophone to publicise a charitable cause and a notable recording coup was achieved in the process. No less a personage than the Emperor Franz Josef was persuaded to speak and in Vienna on 14th December, 1915, amid the rococo splendours of the Schönbrunn palace, the Lindström company recorded his appeal to his loyal subjects on behalf of the Austro-Hungarian Military Widows and Orphans Fund.

The war brought great changes to HMV's recently built studios and factory on the western outskirts of London. The enormous demand had made it uneconomic to continue recording at the City Road premises from where the masters had to be sent over to Germany to the Gramophone Company's Hanover plant for pressing. The search for a suitable site had led finally to Hayes in Middlesex where, in 1907, Melba laid the cornerstone of the building in which all HMV's recording and manufacturing processes were to be concentrated. Within three weeks of the outbreak of war HMV patriotically offered its City Road building as additional space for the City of London Regiment (Royal Fusiliers) whose headquarters were just opposite. At Hayes much of the factory was rapidly converted to the production of munitions and long lines of heavy industrial machinery operated by women began turning out materials needed at the fighting fronts. The war workers sometimes enjoyed a unique compensation for the monotony of their daily routines as many of HMV's most popular artists visiting Hayes to make new recordings would entertain during the canteen breaks with impromptu concerts of the latest hits.

The war very quickly affected the German companies, particularly Lindström, which over the years had absorbed such important labels as Fonotipia, Odeon and Parlophon. On 4th August, 1914 Lindström's French branch was attacked and burnt to the ground by a crowd of outraged Parisians. The company's activities in Warsaw likewise came to an abrupt end when their premises were taken over by the Russians and in 1916, by order of the British government, their London branch was closed down. When the British naval blockade began to bite, the vital shellac on which all record manufacturers depended could no longer be imported directly into Germany and record buyers were soon in the position of having to trade in old discs for recycling when they wished to purchase new ones. However, even this measure could not make up for the short-fall in supply and German record production fell dramatically. In 1908 Deutsche Grammophon had turned out four and a half million discs; in the earlier years of the war the company was still producing about a million annually but by the end of 1917 the output had dropped to a meagre 400,000. Like HMV at Hayes, major German companies were drawn into armaments production, though Deutsche Grammophon was not immediately included in this industrial turnabout because of its legal status as part of an international corporation. The call-up of trained workers to the armed forces, the inevitable shortage of raw materials and secret doubts over Germany's ability to win the war led to much heart-searching as to how best to secure the future prosperity of hitherto flourishing concerns.

Lindström's solution was to look for an alternative commercial base outside Europe and they chose the neutral United States.

25

Accordingly, in 1914, Otto Heinemann, a senior member of the company, was sent to America. Wartime conditions made his journey a long and circuitous one for his ship was stopped and searched by a British naval vessel and Heinemann, as a German subject, was taken off and interned in England. In due course he arrived back in Germany having been exchanged for a British national interned in that country. Lindström was not to be deterred by this long delay and Heinemann set off again for America in 1915. This time the trans-Atlantic crossing was completed without incident and, despite the anti-German feeling then becoming increasingly apparent in the States, he started the Okeh company which in a few years built up a reputation for its recordings of jazz and the popular music of the day.

Lindström was not alone in the action it took. The French Pathé company in 1914 also had deep misgivings over the possible long-term effects of the war on its business. Again, a base in America seemed the solution to the dilemma and a recording studio and pressing plant were rapidly set up in the Brooklyn area of New York.

Whatever the difficulties of production the gramophone companies contributed considerably to the war effort of their respective countries. Listened to by the fireside records of descriptive sketches and military music could help those at home to while away a spare hour pleasantly enough whilst at the same time inducing the impression of sharing in some small way the life and hardships of the men in uniform. In an impressive display of their market leadership HMV brought out a set of nineteen ten-inch discs of the regimental marches of the British Army and another two discs of bugle calls, the latter starting appropriately with *The Charge*. With recordings of divine worship in camp, on a battlefield and on a battleship HMV paid due regard to the comfort and strength to be drawn from the Christian faith in time of war. Calling on the services of the Coldstream Guards Band and the singers Peter Dawson and Ernest Pike the same company also devoted both sides of a twelve-inch disc to a sound picture of *Church Parade*.

The numerous British descriptives of 1914-1918 were aimed first and foremost at boosting the morale of the home front and were of varying quality. HMV's *Departure of a Troopship* still had great staying power and competed on equal terms with its many newly recorded rivals. Columbia's main effort came in September,

26

1917 and took the form of six sketches that followed the fortunes of a group of soldiers at different times during the war; the subjects were *Leaving for the Front, In the Trenches, The Night Attack, The Big Push, For Valour* and *Back Home in Blighty*. At the time these records were issued there had been three years of bloody fighting and there was a great weariness of heart amongst those serving on the Western Front. With bleak detachment Edmund Blunden in his book *Undertones of War* savoured those years almost as if they were unpalatable vintages at a wine-tasting. Looking back from the standpoint of 1917 he recalled: "Our minds receded with actual joy to the 1916 war"; in contrast, "1917 was distasteful" - a consummate understatement - and "1918 did not look promising at its birth." On 31st July, 1917 the Third Battle of Ypres began and when, weeks later in this inconclusive struggle, Blunden and his men marched off "to be merged again in the slow amputation of Passchendaele, there was no singing." In its more than three months course Third Ypres was to cost the British between 300,000 and 400,000, the French 50,000 and the Germans some 250,000 men killed, wounded or captured.

Columbia's sketches, however, spared listeners the full horrors of life and death in the trenches. The scripts were designed to emphasise the spirit of comradeship in the ranks, to show that Tommy kept his pecker up even in the most difficult situations and could be relied upon when the need arose to perform acts of almost casual heroism. To late twentieth century ears these discs sound stilted and artificial but at the time they were made they undoubtedly struck a responsive chord amongst civilian record buyers. Columbia felt their ambitious project was important enough to warrant engaging an expert adviser, Major A. E. Rees of the 2nd London Regiment, The Royal Fusiliers. As well as ensuring there were no military solecisms Rees took part personally in the sketches; it is probably he who plays the various officers from General downwards whose main role is to speak words of encouragement and praise to the men under their command.

On The Winner label in 1917 the Edison Bell Company issued a descriptive that, despite the decidedly hammy performances, is still of more than passing interest. *The Birkenhead Spirit* in which a troopship is torpedoed is a typical action-packed vignette of the perils of the war at sea, but its backing, *An Air Raid*, broke new

27

ground by portraying the war on the home front. An Englishman employed overseas has returned home for a holiday in a quiet country town. The weather is fine, the band is playing in the park and all seems perfectly normal until a German Zeppelin is sighted. It is driven off by anti-aircraft guns and fighter planes but not before dropping a bomb or two, fortunately without doing any serious damage. The visitor deplores such barbarity and, as the patriotic core of the sketch, decides to offer his services to the government. He is an experienced aero engineer and hopes that with his help it may be possible to develop faster fighter planes that will give any German raiders an even hotter reception in the future. Edison Bell had come up with a sentiment that all British civilians in places vulnerable to Zeppelin attack could share wholeheartedly. The company could justly compliment itself on the innovative subject of this descriptive which, with its optimistic attitude towards air defence problems, was morale-enhancing into the bargain.

Occasionally the artificiality of the Great War descriptives gave way to the real world on records that were genuine historical documents. It was nothing new for the talking machine to be the creator of archival material. In the very early days of the phonograph Colonel George Gouraud, Thomas Edison's representative in London, made private recordings of the British and other royal families as well as such eminent men and women as Gladstone, Browning, Tennyson and Florence Nightingale. However, with the growth of the gramophone as a carrier of essentially light-weight entertainment it was music that dominated the releases at the expense of the spoken word, although great stage personalities like Sarah Bernhardt and Sir Henry Beerbohm Tree had their niches in the commercial catalogues.

When in November, 1915 Regal decided to make a documentary recording they turned not to a member of the establishment but to Sergeant Edward Dwyer, V.C. of the lst Battalion, the East Surrey Regiment, a regular soldier who had signed on in 1911 at the age of sixteen. The citation for Dwyer's Victoria Cross reads:

"For most conspicuous bravery and devotion to duty at 'Hill Sixty' on 20th April, 1915. When his trench was heavily attacked by German grenade throwers he climbed on to the parapet and although subjected to a hail of bombs at close quarters, succeeded in dispersing the enemy by the effective use of his hand grenades. Private Dwyer displayed great gallantry earlier in this day, in leaving his trench under heavy shell fire to bandage his wounded comrades."

Such was the intensity of the fighting that two other members of Dwyer's regiment were awarded the Victoria Cross for their bravery on the same day.

Regal's disc was entitled *With Our Boys at the Front* and on it Dwyer did not mince his words. He went over to France with the British Expeditionary Force at the outbreak of the war and was immediately caught up in the battle of Mons and the ensuing retreat, an episode he bluntly describes as "a nightmare". He gives an unvarnished description of what it was like to do a forced march of 40 miles between Saturday morning and mid-day Sunday and then, after a rest of only four hours, go into action. Dwyer tells how singing helped to ease the hardship of such gruelling marches and in his cracked, not very musical voice gives a few snatches of those sustaining songs. What we hear are the authentic, home-made efforts of the fighting soldier: *We're here because we're here* to the borrowed music of *Old Lang Syne* and the equally cynical *You'd be far better off in a Home*. At the time of its issue the disc offered a bracing contrast to the anodyne fare of most descriptives: indeed, it may have been too strong for the current taste since the rarity of surviving copies implies that it did not have a large sale. Today its forthright matter-of-factness provides a vivid glimpse of the infantryman's war as experienced at first hand. With the passing of the years we can now appreciate Dwyer's disc not only as a moving personal account but also as an outstanding example of preserved oral history. On his last home leave in London Dwyer, who knows with what feeling of premonition, entrusted his Victoria Cross to the keeping of the priest at the Church of the Sacred Heart, Holloway. He returned to France and, only a few months after his marriage to a hospital nurse, was killed in action on 3rd September, 1916. Although Regal described Dwyer at the time of the recording as Sergeant this would seem to have been a temporary appointment as the inscription on the headstone of his grave in France shows that when he died his rank was that of Corporal.

By 1917 signs of near-desperation were apparent in Germany's spoken word documentary recordings. In October of that year Field Marshal von Hindenburg recorded for Autophon the speech of congratulation he had originally made to the German 8th Army at the end of August, 1914 in celebration of their crushing defeat of the Russians on the Eastern Front at Tannenberg. The implication, presumably, was that Germany was still capable of a similar decisive stroke on the Western Front. Autophon again dipped into the store of patriotic rhetoric in January, 1918 when (no doubt by imperial command) they recorded the Kaiser in a speech also dating back to August, 1914 in which he had confidently looked forward to a speedy German victory. Except for the most blinkered nationalists relatively few of his subjects hearing the Kaiser's message at this stage of the war were likely to have shared its optimism.

The war's most distinctive historical document came from HMV who, with only the acoustic technology then available, made a recording that was far ahead of its time. It was clear by the autumn of 1918 that the war was at last nearing its end and the company felt in duty bound to preserve for posterity some of the true sounds of the battlefield. Fred Gaisberg's brother Will was sent over to France with his equipment and on 9th October he and a colleague recorded the Royal Garrison Artillery firing a barrage of gas shells as a prelude to the British troops' advance upon Lille. Gas had first been used by Germany against the Russians in January, 1915 and three months later they added it to their armoury on the Western Front. As a weapon it was unpredictable, its effectiveness depending entirely on consistent weather conditions and when the British tried it for the first time at the battle of Loos in September, 1915 it drifted back over the Allied lines. This type of warfare was feelingly described by Graham Greenwell, a company officer in the Oxford and Buckinghamshire Light Infantry in a letter written in September, 1916:

"We let off some gas last night ... it was our reply to a little dose of 2000 gas shells which the Germans sent over the day before, causing our fellows to wear their stinking helmets for seven hours on end."

The December, 1918 issue of HMV's house magazine, *The Voice*, printed Will Gaisberg's account of how in

"a wretched kitchen we unpacked our recording machines and made our preparations before getting directly behind a battery of great 4.5 inch guns and 6 inch howitzers ... Here the machine could well catch the finer sounds of the 'singing', the 'whine',

30

and the 'scream' of the shells, as well as the terrific reports when they left the guns."

With good reason he was proud that from this expedition "we brought with us a true representation of the bombardment, which will have a unique place in the history of the Great War." Tragically, Will Gaisberg's health was affected by the gas-laden air at the front and when the English winter brought with it a violent influenza epidemic his weakened bodily defences stood no chance and he died before the year was out. The twelve-inch disc came on sale in December and HMV's advertising matter spoke of it as "An historical record which should be in every home"; most appropriately, all profits were donated to the King's Fund for the Disabled. Later it was transferred to HMV's *No. 2 Catalogue* of "records of unique and historic interest" and was still available at the outbreak of the Second World War.

The recording contains a short epilogue; after the bombardment there is a pause before a commanding voice urges listeners to invest in War Bonds. Issued in October, 1917 these 5% Bonds raised over £1 billion within a year of their appearance. The public at large was the target of the spoken appeal on the gas shells recording but as a corporate measure the Gramophone Company had already actively promoted investment in government stock when in February, 1917 it granted short-term loans to its employees specifically for the purchase of War Loan.

The civilian populations had their own particular burdens to bear whether they stayed in their own country or not. Travel abroad was limited and dangerous on account of the unrestricted submarine warfare waged by Germany. The British liner *Lusitania* was torpedoed and sunk off Ireland on 7th May, 1915 with a loss of nearly 1,200 lives, many of them Americans whose homeland at that time was still a neutral state. The resulting anti-German riots that broke out in England added further complications to life on the home front and HMV, understandably not wishing to aggravate the situation, decided to withhold a descriptive they had recorded on the *Lusitania* sinking. Three months later, again off Ireland, the White Star Line's ship *Arabic* was sunk. Amongst the rescued passengers was the actor Kenneth Douglas who was in his pyjamas when the torpedo struck; stopping only to grab a couple of top-coats he managed to get into one of the last lifeboats to leave the ship. *The Times* reported Douglas's tribute to the bravery of the women passengers, one of whom, the professional singer Stella Carol, sang *It's a Long Way to Tipperary* to cheer up the survivors. This time HMV did not hesitate and brought out a recording of Douglas (who, strangely for an actor, remained anonymous) describing his experiences to the playwright Sir Arthur Wing Pinero.

Fuel and food were soon in short supply but more often than not the British way with such matters was to treat them as light-heartedly as possible. A typical response in song came from that boisterous comedienne Florrie Forde who, in the music halls and on her 1917 Zonophone recording, urged her listeners *Never Mind the Food Controller*. The same year a disc issued by the Coliseum company presented further wry comment on the food shortages from Arthur Osmond (a pseudonym of Arthur Gilbert) in two humorous songs, one on the topic of *Sugar* and the other on the self-denial required by *My Meatless Day*.

The popular songs of the late 19th and early 20th centuries could encompass staunch patriotism on the one hand and a jokey cynicism towards the nation's affairs on the other with equal certainty of their being publicly acceptable. During 1914-1918, however, patriotism was the order of the day and the music halls were more circumspect with their offerings. In the world of commercial entertainment acidic songs like *Oh, it's a Lovely War* (recorded for Columbia by Ella Shields in 1918) were in the minority but artists felt free to focus much more closely on domestic life, lampooning such things as the coupon system that accompanied food rationing in 1918. On Edison Bell Winner Ernie Mayne took a satirical swipe at the coal shortage in a song the chorus of which ran: And when we die/ We'll hear them cry:/ "Where's your ticket for coal?". It was in this type of song that the music hall in the Great War continued its tradition of thumbing its nose at the establishment.

But shortages were minor matters compared with the sorrows inflicted by the daily newspapers' column upon column of casualty lists, those ephemeral forerunners of the rolls of honour and memorials that were later to go up in schools, cathedrals and parish churches, in public parks and on village greens throughout the British Isles and Empire.

Although an efficient propaganda machine worked in shadowy ways to bolster the British image abroad and keep spirits buoyant at home, private and public mourning had their recognised places in civilian life. Rudyard Kipling voiced the grief of countless bereaved mothers in his sombre poem *My Boy Jack*. A woman seeks news of her dead son and the only crumb of comfort for her loss is that, in the time of need, her boy "did not shame his kind". The verses, published in 1916, came from the heart for Kipling's only son had been killed at the battle of Loos in the previous year. Edward German, the composer of the much-loved light opera *Merrie England*, set the poem to music and when they came to record the piece in 1917 both HMV and Columbia engaged artists of the highest standing. Indeed, HMV had the composer himself conducting for the contralto Louise Kirkby Lunn, a Covent Garden and Metropolitan Opera House singer. Columbia's recording starred Clara Butt and Sir Thomas Beecham who had given the first public performance at a Royal Philharmonic Society concert on 26th February, 1917. It was a potentially explosive pairing (Beecham once said of Dame Clara "On a clear day she may quite easily be heard in France") but the concert and recording session seem to have passed off without trouble. *The Times* was not enthusiastic about the new work, merely noting that the soloist "did much for Mr. German's song, which is neatly finished and only just misses finding exactly the right swing." A Royal Philharmonic Society concert was, perhaps, not the most suitable occasion for introducing a new patriotic song, especially as German's short work had to compete for attention in a typical Beecham programme that comprised Ethel Smythe's Overture to *The Wreckers*, two Handel arias, two Russian songs, Ravel's *Pavane pour une Infante Défunte*, Balakirev's *Tamara*, Franck's *Le Chasseur Maudit* and Mozart's *Linz* symphony. The critic of *The Times* was moved sadly to report that although the symphony "was most effective ... it did lengthen the concert somewhat beyond the dinner hour." Notwithstanding the fame of the artists who launched and recorded it, *Have You Any News of my Boy Jack?* soon slipped out of the repertoire, just as *The Absent-Minded Beggar* had done when the Boer War was over.

A gramophone, whether bought, borrowed or "liberated", became one of the most desirable pieces of non-military equipment for those in the services and contemporary photographs show the men of both sides relaxing to the music of portables or table-top models. Edmund Blunden remembered in the relative peace of Poperinghe, a rest area behind the lines, a shop where "some beautiful young persons condescendingly sold gramophones ..." For the benefit of officers dining at the British Hostel in the same town the management's instrument "was chiefly employed on a minuet by Boccherini and something 'Hawaiian' - not bad accompaniments (for the uncritical young) to Madame's chickens and wine." Curt Riess, the German historian of the record industry, relates that Britain's Navy was particularly well served by the generosity of an anonymous benefactor who footed the bill for a gramophone for every ship in the Fleet. The number required exceeded the immediately available stock of any British-made gramophone and the Navy was supplied with machines exported to England shortly before the war by the Lindström company; ironically, these bore the label "Made in Germany".

The first truly portable gramophone to be made in Britain was the Decca Dulcephone, a product of the musical instruments firm Barnett Samuel and Sons Ltd., which later became the Decca Gramophone Company. The design of the basic model was simple and compact. A case 11½ inches square by 10½ inches high contained the clockwork motor and turntable in the lower part, whilst the hinged lid housed the sound box and tone arm. With its carrying handle it looked not unlike a small travelling case and sold at the reasonable price of two guineas (£2.10). It came on the market only a week or two before the outbreak of war and its popularity amongst the forces ensured for its makers an honoured place in the history of the gramophone.

The fragility and (in bulk) the sheer weight of 78 r.p.m. shellac discs severely limited the size of the collections which men constantly on the move could carry with them. This in its turn resulted in much repetition when the gramophone was in use, a state of affairs that could quickly irritate those whose musical tastes lay in other directions. For Major Christopher Stone who, after the war, helped Compton Mackenzie to set up and edit that most influential of critical reviews *The Gramophone*, a few well-chosen records and the means to play them were the luxuries best able to make life on the Western Front slightly more bearable. On the other hand, one of Graham Greenwell's letters told how "a wheezy gramophone with bronchial catarrh is banging out the well-known strains of the

Tango and The Maxixe and life is on the same plane." But despite its limitations, the entertainment provided by the gramophone was appreciated by all ranks and classes from commoner to prince of the realm. The then Prince of Wales (later briefly to reign as King Edward VIII) once confided to Maggie Teyte that throughout the war he had always carried with him one of her records, *The Land of Might-Have-Been*. Tactfully the singer accepted the royal compliment, although she had not recorded this song which, in fact, postdated the war and was one of three written by Ivor Novello for the 1924 musical comedy *Our Nell*.

Perhaps the most moving tribute to the restorative powers of the gramophone comes in a letter written in October, 1917 to Sir Edward Elgar by Captain T. Lawrence Fry of the Royal Flying Corps who was engaged in the hazardous work of aerial observation from captive balloons. Elgar was deeply distressed by the war and, moreover, constantly doubted whether the musical public had any real appreciation for his works; coming from somebody quite unknown to him, Fry's letter could hardly have failed to reassure Elgar on the latter score. "We possess a fairly good gramophone in our mess", wrote Fry,

"and I have bought your record *Starlight Express* 'Hearts must be star-shiny dressed'. It is being played for the twelfth time over. The Gramophone was Anathema to me before this war because it was abused so much. But all is changed now, and it is the only means of bringing back to us the days that are gone, and helping one through the Ivory gate that leads us to fairy land or Heaven, whatever one likes to call it. And it is a curious thing, even those who only go for Rag-time Revues, all care for your music. Our lives are spent in drunken orgies and parachute descents to escape shelling or Bosch aeroplanes. In fact, the whole thing is unreal, and music is all that we have to help us carry on."[2]

Elgar's association with HMV began in January, 1914 when his visit to the City Road studio signalled the beginning of a special relationship between a composer/conductor and a recording company that was to be unequalled until Benjamin Britten and Decca joined forces in the 1950s. The idea had originated with Elgar's friend the conductor Landon Ronald who was also musical adviser to HMV. Ronald had no difficulty in persuading Alfred Clark,

HMV's managing director, that the name of Britain's leading composer on their roster of artists would add still further to the company's prestige. The outcome of this first session was *Carissima*, a brand new piece of light music; from this modest start Elgar went on to record most of his major orchestral output over the next twenty years.

At Hayes in the following June Elgar recorded a mixed bag of five of his most popular works, but the next session, his first in wartime, was devoted to a much more substantial composition, *Carillon*, for speaker and orchestra. The words were by the refugee Belgian poet Emile Cammaerts whose anguished cry against the German invasion of his native country moved Elgar to set the English translation of the verses to music. The first public performance took place on 7th December, 1914 with Elgar conducting the London Symphony Orchestra and with the poet's wife as speaker. Fred Gaisberg was there and was so impressed that he suggested Elgar should be asked to record the work for HMV. Serious patriotic music of this kind ran the risk of drowning in the flood of facile pieces aimed at the mass market. Elgar and the orchestra, however, went on to make a successful tour of the provinces with *Carillon* and the ensuing recording, taken at Hayes at the end of January, 1915 with the actor Henry Ainley in the speaking part, was issued while the work was still fresh in the memory of many people. This beneficial tie-up between recording and public performance was again turned to account by HMV when they brought out *The Starlight Express* excerpts and *The Fringes of the Fleet*.

Carillon occupies an ambiguous position in that grey area where patriotism and propaganda meet and intermingle. For both poet and composer it was essentially a spontaneous response to the heartbreaking events of the war and it certainly was not regarded as a piece of propaganda at the time of the first performance; indeed, the music critic of the *Daily News* thought it one of Elgar's "loftiest utterances". The provincial tour made *Carillon* relatively well known and thus it moved quite some way towards gaining the mass audience that is the target of propaganda. The tone of HMV's advertising leaves little doubt that the company's view of the recording extended well beyond its purely musical aspects. "We have ... achieved an artistic triumph", they declared, "that will serve to carry the noble voice of outraged Belgium to every corner of the

36

globe." Although *Carillon* was very much a product of its own time and, as such, departed from the regular repertoire with the end of the war it can, even today, be a moving experience given a sympathetic conductor and a speaker with the necessary conviction and vocal resonance.

The following year saw Elgar returning to Hayes for two more sessions. At the first of these in February, 1916 he was joined by the soprano Agnes Nicholls and the baritone Charles Mott in a generous four-disc selection of his music for *The Starlight Express* which had been adapted for the stage from the novel *A Prisoner in Fairyland* by Algernon Blackwood, a writer now chiefly remembered for his chilling tales of the supernatural. It was at one and the same time a children's Christmas fairy story and, on the adult level, an allegory of man's journey on the road towards spiritual regeneration. It is not surprising, perhaps, that such a hybrid work ran for only a month from its opening at the end of December, 1915, but despite the lack of critical enthusiasm for the play itself Elgar's music became very popular. Indeed, Captain Fry's letter to the composer testifies that at least one disc from the set was so enchanting that it could even, just for a little time, blot out the horrors of the Western Front. Significantly, the song that Fry and his fellow officers played so often, *Hearts Must Be Soft-Shiny Dressed*, is not a boisterous piece but moves from a tender wistfulness to an expression of hope and joy for mankind in the form of the familiar carol *The First Noel*.

The December session was given over to Elgar's most serious recording so far, the Violin Concerto (albeit a very truncated version) with Marie Hall as the soloist. This was intended by HMV as a counter to the performance by Albert Sammons and Sir Henry Wood on the rival Columbia label. In normal weather conditions Elgar and his wife enjoyed being driven to the studios along the wooded route between Hampstead and Hayes, but on this occasion the journey had to be made in thick fog. The road was up in many places and on the outward trip they were run into by a cart. The return was no better as they nearly collided head-on with a Red Cross car; after the day's concentrated work in the studio and the misadventures along the way Elgar was exhausted by the time they arrived home at Severn House.

37

Undeterred by these events he was back again at Hayes in February, 1917 directing a varied group of items - one of the *Bavarian Dances*, two movements from *The Wand of Youth*, an abridgment of *Cockaigne* and extracts from *The Dream of Gerontius*. At a further session in the following July HMV capitalised promptly on the popularity of Elgar's latest war-related work by taking a complete recording of *The Fringes of the Fleet*. This began its career as a sequence of four songs with words by Kipling, who had somewhat grudgingly given permission for his verses to be used in this way, but Elgar soon added a fifth song, *Inside the Bar*, the words of which were by Sir Gilbert Parker. The première of the four Kipling songs took place at the Coliseum, London, on 11th June, 1917 with Elgar himself conducting and his wife noted in her diary that the audience included "many admirals". *The Fringes of the Fleet* was given twice daily at the Coliseum until the end of July after which Elgar took it on a tour around the provincial music halls. In wartime this was a gruelling undertaking and, at a place like Chatham, decidedly dangerous for not all the scheduled performances could go ahead there because of German bombing raids on the naval dockyards.

As the title suggests, *The Fringes of the Fleet* concerns not the great battleships of the Royal Navy but the small craft that played a vital role nearer home. The success of Elgar's settings was due in large part to the contrasting nature of the songs which covered a wide range of tastes. *The Lowestoft Boat* which opens the sequence is in the "Yo-ho, my hearties" mould of jolly nautical ballads beloved by so many amateur singers of those days. The boat in question is one of the lightly armed vessels that patrolled the coastal waters of Britain, often manned by decidedly un-Naval crews. For the stage performances the four baritone soloists appeared in authentic seamen's costume and something of the theatre atmosphere crept into the recording studio when, in the last verse, the line "Her cook was chef in the Lost Dogs' Home" was greeted with a chorus of barks and howls, presumably encouraged by Elgar.

The remaining Kipling songs are rather more serious. The theme of *Fate's Discourtesy* is that the small craft, no less than their mighty sister ships, uphold the tradition of devotion to duty whatever the odds against may be. *Submarines* is not merely serious, it is positively sombre. The eight bleak lines of verse and Elgar's imaginative music vividly convey the sinister nature of this new type of warfare. There was, indeed, a harsh topicality to the song for in 1917 the U-boat offensive was at its height. The German shipyards were building more and more vessels to augment the 120 or so submarines in service at the beginning of the year and in April, little more than a month before *The Fringes of the Fleet* was first performed, they sank 875,000 tons of shipping, the bulk of it British. Although the poem does not say so specifically, Kipling's submarines, of course, were British ones. However, against the ominous background of the constantly mounting losses of allied shipping and sailors' lives it would not be surprising if some theatre-goers and record buyers interpreted the dark words differently. Elgar's setting subtly mirrors the stealth of the questing submarine; even the sandpaper blocks that simulate the rustle of the water against the vessel's hull can be heard with unexpected clarity in the pre-electric recording. The impressionism of *Submarines* gives way in *The Sweepers* to a graphic account of a day in the working life of a group of minesweepers from the first light sighting of mines to the final clearing of the channel at dusk. The ballad style is again evident at the end of each verse when there is a roll call of the names of the five sweepers. *Inside the Bar* is in the sea shanty idiom and brings the sequence to a tranquil close with the four soloists, now unaccompanied, singing of things dear to all sailors' hearts - homecoming, creature comforts ashore and their womenfolk.

Paradoxically, the stage success of *The Fringes of the Fleet* renewed Kipling's doubts as to the wisdom of allowing his work to be used for this sort of public entertainment and, despite the pleas of many influential people, he eventually withdrew his permission. *The Fringes* returned to the Coliseum for a final week in November, 1917 after which it was only to be heard on the gramophone. By this time Charles Mott, who had headed the four baritones in the initial run at the Coliseum and on the HMV recording, was serving in the Artists' Rifles; sadly, he died of wounds in May the following year.

Before the outbreak of the war there were already signs that the companies were overcoming their reluctance to record anything spanning more than two 78 r.p.m. sides. HMV's releases for August, 1914 included two discs rounding off their landmark issue recorded the previous year by the Gramophone Company's German branch of "the complete colossal Fifth Symphony" of Beethoven played by the Berlin Philharmonic Orchestra under the great Artur Nikisch. Such willingness to exceed the old basic format did not immediately result in large numbers of long works being recorded in their entirety, but there was a gradual broadening of the musical horizon for the record buyers. The recordings of Elgar's wartime compositions had sold well and justified HMV's decisions to issue them complete or, as in the case of *The Starlight Express*, to offer all the most important sections. The move away from the bleeding chunks policy of the industry's early years gathered momentum during the war until in July, 1918 HMV proudly announced "an epoch-making event, ranking amongst the greatest achievements of recording yet seen or heard in the Gramophone world" - Gilbert and Sullivan's *The Mikado*, complete on eleven double-sided records.

In the case of *Polonia*, the last of Elgar's war pieces to be recorded by the composer, HMV again resorted to cutting in order to fit the work on a double-sided twelve-inch disc. This symphonic prelude in the form of a fantasia on Polish national themes was written specially for a London concert given in July, 1915 in aid of Polish refugees, but four years elapsed before it made its appearance on record. The reason for this unusually long delay remains obscure. It is possible HMV thought that with *Carillon* firmly established in the catalogue *Polonia's* viability was questionable. Commercially it could be argued that one example of serious music relating to the war in a country other than Britain was as much as the market would bear; after all, HMV had not followed up *Carillon* with Elgar's other two Cammaerts-inspired works, *Une Voix dans le Désert* and *Le Drapeau Belge*. Nevertheless, by 1918 HMV had begun to show interest in *Polonia* and Lady Elgar noted in her diary that a recording session took place at Hayes in May that year. The results were presumably unsatisfactory for no disc appeared. Far-reaching political changes were soon to come about in Europe, however, and in November, 1918 Poland was proclaimed an independent republic. This important constitutional development lent a new topicality to *Polonia* and an abridged version was recorded and issued in 1919.

It is no exaggeration to say that the theatre became a lifeline for British, French and Germans alike during the years 1914-1918.

40

With music hall at one extreme and opera at the other, and with the middle ground occupied by revue, musical comedy, operetta and the straight play, a wide choice of short-term escape routes from the oppressive cares of the war was available to civilians and men of the armed forces on their leaves. Talented performers transported willing audiences across the footlights to lands of make-believe where romance, humour and a certain amount of unashamed sentimentality were the most appreciated ingredients of the entertainment.

From the very beginning, German censorship saw to it that large numbers of songs celebrating the Fatherland's military power went the rounds of theatres, dance halls and cafés. The record companies dutifully followed this lead as well as keeping a steady supply of military marches flowing from their presses. By 1916, however, with still no end to the war in sight, the German appetite for such music began to abate and in their leisure hours people looked instead for something more escapist. The central European countries were the home of operetta and it was to the romantic works of composers such as Franz Lehár, Leo Fall and Emmerich Kálmán that theatre-goers turned in search of relaxation. The German gramophone industry responded accordingly and Fritzi Massary and other famous singers of the day were recorded in excerpts from such melodious scores as Fall's *The Rose of Stamboul* and Kálmán's *Gipsy Princess*.

Despite a degree of nationalistic clamour on both sides, neither the Germans nor the British particularly wished to carry the war very deeply into the cultural life of the enemy. Sir Henry Wood relates that in August, 1914 "the lesser Press was demanding that all German music should be deleted from our published programmes". Wood and the Queen's Hall directors felt it prudent to replace the first Wagner night of the 1914 Promenade Concerts with a selection of Russian, French and British music but "The usual Wagner programme was reinstated on August 24, not to be disturbed again during the four years of the War." Later on when Wood recorded an abridged version of Richard Strauss's *Till Eulenspiegel* for Columbia the company opted for discretion and omitted Strauss's name from the label to minimise the risk of being criticised for lack of patriotism in issuing a work by a living German composer. Despite the loudly expressed antagonism of German

41

nationalists the plays of Shakespeare continued to be staged in Berlin and elsewhere, as also were those of George Bernard Shaw and Oscar Wilde. Evidence of the enduring appeal of Gilbert and Sullivan in Germany is to be found in the 1916 Lindström recording of the comedian Max Pallenberg in two numbers from *The Mikado*.

The theatre in France, too, was subject to strict censorship but stage militarism, serious or otherwise, did not appeal greatly to French taste. At the outset of the war the German army advanced to within fifteen miles of Paris before being held and pushed back; for older Frenchmen this near-disaster would inevitably have revived memories of the Franco-Prussian War of 1870-71 in which their besieged capital was forced to capitulate to the Germans. Although in 1914-1918 the enemy was never again to be so close to Paris the city remained uneasily conscious of its vulnerability and, perhaps as much as anything, it was this feeling of uncertainty which set the Parisians on an increasingly hectic quest for light entertainment. This seemingly unquenchable need was fostered rather than discouraged by air raids and the fuel and power shortages with which the theatres had to contend. By 1916 the Paris theatres were having to close one night per week and on the nights they were open lighting was severely reduced. The following year performances took place only three times a week and the buildings were unheated into the bargain; a similar closure pattern continued throughout 1918.

London's theatres were less troubled by such shortages but German air raids were as much a hazard as they were in Paris. A few months before the outbreak of the Second World War Sir Thomas Beecham, in reminiscent mood, wrote in the *Daily Telegraph*:

"Even during the really grim days of 1914-1918 London was never without an opera at some time or other of the year. I recall with special gratification certain performances at Drury Lane which I conducted myself to the sound of German bombs exploding within a few feet of the theatre, to say nothing of our own anti-aircraft guns - when neither performers nor public paid the slightest heed to such distractions, but behaved in every respect as in normal times."

The patrons of Sir Thomas's sparkling London seasons and opera lovers generally were able to indulge their musical tastes with the help of records to a remarkable extent considering war-time conditions. It was a truly golden age of vocal artistry and month by month HMV supplied the devotees with new issues by the world's most outstanding singers. The pre-eminence of the Gramophone Company in this particular field was now obvious; none could compare with their roster of artists and in the period 1914-1918 recordings by such international celebrities as Boninsegna, Caruso, Chaliapin, Emmy Destinn, Geraldine Farrar, Galli-Curci, Alma Gluck, Marcel Journet, McCormack, Martinelli, Melba, Titta Ruffo and Tetrazzini were to be had in the British shops.

Live opera, however, attracted only a fraction of the audiences that flocked to the latest musical comedies and revues. Straight plays continued to draw the crowds and British theatre managements reasoned that if the war was going to be over by Christmas then they must do their bit and look sharp about it. Consequently, in addition to the more usual fare a succession of plays with patriotic subjects and such stirring titles as *To Arms* held the stage briefly and then sank into obscurity. Over and over again, though, the memoirs of the time confirm that musical comedy and revue were the shows in which civilians and forces alike took the greatest pleasure. The dividing line between them was sometimes difficult to distinguish but, generally speaking, musical comedy had a thread of plot whereas revue used a particular theme or topical idea as a peg on which to hang a series of sketches, songs and dances.

Its informal structure made the revue an obvious candidate for the full patriotic treatment. One of the earliest to be staged in the war years was *Business as Usual* in which the flag-waving was almost non-stop. It opened in mid-November, 1914 at the London Hippodrome with a cast of well-known entertainers including the singer Violet Loraine, comedian Harry Tate and what some advertisements rather ambiguously described as "a mammoth beauty chorus". Various Edison Bell discs had been marketed in Britain since 1908 in an effort to make up for the decline in the cylinder trade and their Winner label (introduced in 1912) was quick off the mark with a recording of one of the show's still faintly familiar numbers, *Are We Downhearted? No!* amongst the December, 1914

43

issues. Five further items from this revue were added to their catalogue in February and March the following year. These records were certainly timely and it is a fair assumption that, as the artists concerned were not of the very front rank, Edison Bell concentrated on the show's most popular numbers. However, the set of five 10-inch discs issued by Columbia in January, 1915 was infinitely more desirable since the songs were performed by Ambrose Thorne, Henry Leoni, Unity Moore and Violet Loraine, all members of the original stage cast.

Columbia's issue, which included all the items put out by Winner, is a valuable reminder of how at this early stage of the war the musical theatre set out to cheer up its audiences and keep the patriotic adrenalin flowing. A brave, oppressed ally is saluted in *Three Cheers for Little Belgium*, whilst the finger of scorn is pointed at the enemy in *The Goose Step* and the punning *When We've Wound up the Watch on the Rhine*. The fighting forces, of course,were singled out for special attention with such numbers as *The Arms of the Army for Me* and *The Red, White and Blue*. The Irish element, sometimes soulful, sometimes comical, was seldom absent for very long from the popular songs of the time so it is not surprising to find Columbia including *Mary from Tipperary* in their selection. Two of the show's more sentimental numbers, *We've been Married just one Year* and *When the Angelus is Ringing* were chosen to provide the set with a suitable touch of contrast.

When it became apparent there would be no early end to the war the intense doses of patriotic fervour typified by *Business as Usual* soon lost their appeal. By June, 1918 when *Soldier Boy* was staged at London's Apollo theatre the emphasis had unmistakably switched to the soldier's long-desired return to home and family. Notwithstanding the talents of Sigmund Romberg and Edgar Wallace (who each had a hand in the creation of the show) and Columbia's original cast recordings, *Soldier Boy* was not one of the more memorable musicals of the war years. British audiences of 1916 craved a respite of an hour or two from what, outside the theatre, was inescapable and later revues obliged with entertainment as frivolous and frothy as could be desired. The titles alone proclaimed the changed nature of these shows. *Zig-Zag, Bubbly, Razzle-Dazzle, Hanky-Panky, Houp-La, Pell-Mell, High Jinks* and many more sparkled on the stage for a while before giving place to

44

their successors, but happy memories could be rekindled time and time again thanks to the recordings of Columbia, HMV and the lesser companies.

Musical comedy had been in the doldrums since well before 1914 but it was rescued and revitalised by the flamboyant actor-manager Oscar Asche whose *Chu Chin Chow* opened at His Majesty's Theatre at the end of August, 1916. The book was written by Asche himself who took as his starting point the tale of *Ali Baba and the Forty Thieves*, thus giving himself plenty of scope for a lavish and exotic production; indeed, by the standards of those days the girls' costumes were decidedly daring. The war played no part in the story and people flocked to it in their thousands until, after a record run, it eventually closed in the summer of 1921. Frederic Norton's tuneful score (*The Cobbler's Song* and *The Robbers' March* are still remembered) was yet another gift to the record companies who hastened to bring out selections and individual numbers to satisfy the show's devoted public.

Another 1916 production with equally magnetic powers of attraction was *The Bing Boys are Here*, sometimes referred to as a musical comedy, sometimes as a revue. Foremost in the cast were the comedian George Robey and the ever-popular Violet Loraine. Robey's comic sketches were masterpieces of hilarious *double entendre* in which he would chide his audiences for taking his meaning amiss and it came as a surprise to many when he joined Violet Loraine in what was to become one of the best-loved popular songs of the war - *If You Were the Only Girl in the World*. Columbia again made original cast recordings and listening to these two artists in that evergreen number one understands immediately why the show was such a smash hit. F. P. Crozier, a Brigadier in the Royal Irish Rifles, summed up the affection it inspired. Referring to 1917 he wrote:

"I spend two weeks on leave, during which period I see *The Bing Boys* five times, and come to the conclusion that George Robey and Violet Loraine are together one of our greatest war assets. And from them, strengthened by them, I hasten to join the other ... Boys on a bigger stage, in the area of Cambrai."

Although the gramophone was a cherished source of relaxation, comfort and encouragement it was sometimes used for quite different purposes, even to the extent of directly addressing the enemy on the battlefield itself.

The Gramophone Company sent Fred Gaisberg to Italy in 1916 and in the following year he was in Milan recording war songs and working tirelessly to set up a pressing plant destined to supply the Italian market with his firm's recordings. Shortages of raw materials and machinery made this a demanding task which taxed even Gaisberg's resourcefulness to the full, but by summer 1918 the new factory was in production. It was during this period that he assisted in a propaganda exercise devised by Lord Northcliffe, the proprietor of *The Times*. Gaisberg later described in his memoirs how he contributed to the operation which was

"... on the Italian front at the Isonzo, where the Slavs, Jugoslavs, Croats and Serbs, Hungarians and Czechs were manning the mountain trenches on the Austrian side, sometimes a few hundred feet from the Italian lines. I was sent to Vicenza, whence I would make excursions in army lorries, under military escort, to various prison camps. Deserters of those nationalities would record their folk-songs, dances and spoken words, urging their listeners to desert without fear as friends would receive and care for them. These records were played back at points in the trenches opposite the places where those nationals were known to be posted and ... resulted in a fine harvest of deserters."

His mission completed, Gaisberg returned to Milan but, mindful of the food shortage, took back with him "a mixed booty of bully beef and white bread and butter, exchanged for gramophone records with a section of English gunners."

The opening of the Milan factory heralded a welcome extension of their business at a time when the Gramophone Company was experiencing serious setbacks elsewhere in Europe. Their Deutsche Grammophon plant at Hanover had been confiscated by the German government, a state of affairs that was to remain in unresolved dispute for years after the end of the war. Hanover had been the Company's door to the markets of central and eastern Europe and in addition to inheriting this network the Germans also came into possession of the valuable stock of masters, the transfer of which to Hayes was still in progress at the outbreak of war. Strenuous efforts were made through neutral go-betweens to secure the return of the remaining masters to the Gramophone Company but Germany would not enter into any agreement unless supplied with copper in exchange. Understandably, the British refused to allow the shipment of this strategic metal and the project fell through. The fate of the masters was undoubtedly high on his agenda when Gaisberg, travelling on his American passport, spent a week in Berlin in March, 1915 holding discussions with his contacts in the record industry; tantalisingly, nothing is known of the substance of these meetings.

The loss of Hanover made it all the more vital for the Gramophone Company to safeguard its Russian subsidiary. Over the period 1912-14 Russian record buyers with their deep devotion to operatic music accounted for a turnover of £679,720, second only to the British market's £873,810 for the same years. Gaisberg made three difficult trips (in winter, 1914 and summer and autumn 1915) to undertake recording sessions and to protect the Company's future interests as far as was possible in the increasingly chaotic conditions that prevailed. Since 1913 discs for the Russian market had been pressed at a modern factory in Riga, but as soon as that city was threatened by the German army the machinery, masters and stock were transferred to St. Petersburg and then to Aprelevka, a little to the south-west of Moscow, where the plant continued to operate until it was taken over by the Bolsheviks at the end of 1917.

Gaisberg left a vivid description of his experiences which grew more and more like episodes from a John Buchan adventure story. On the long journeys necessitated by his recording schedules rail transport was slow, uncertain and desperately uncomfortable; throughout the country acute food shortages brought with them the threat of famine. Russia's political and economic turmoil failed to deter Gaisberg from the tasks the Gramophone Company had entrusted to him, though towards the end the cumulative pressure of events made even this optimistic man feel that all his labours would ultimately turn out to have been in vain.

In 1911 on a previous trip to Moscow Gaisberg had made two recordings which enjoyed great success. On one, the Iuchov Choir led by a sonorous bass soloist gave a moving performance of the Lord's Prayer which was fittingly complemented by a disc of Moscow church bells. As the weather had been far too cold for location work the latter was not actually made in a church but in Gaisberg's hotel where a peal was specially rigged up for him by a local foundry. During the war years the Lord's Prayer recording brought much comfort to those who drew strength from their Christian faith whilst the bells (a pervasive feature of Russian religious life) were particularly appreciated by Muscovite and other servicemen stationed far from their homes. The gramophone, of course, continued to cater in the main for less spiritual tastes and Gaisberg later recalled that "there was a great increase in the demand for records from both soldiers and civilians" with the greatest hits being *Hai-da, Troika* and *Black Eyes*.

When the search for a factory building in or near Moscow was in progress the kind-hearted Gaisberg was appalled by the poverty and lack of housing in the capital:

"I remember driving to the outskirts of the city where we were shown a loft. On opening the door we were nearly knocked over by the stench. Lying body to body were two rows of snoring droshky-drivers. There was no ventilation, and no light of any kind except our torches which revealed walls crawling with vermin. Bad as it was and badly though we needed the premises, I declined to give the word to the agent which would have sent the occupants packing."

Even for so seasoned a traveller as Gaisberg the itinerary of his second trip was extremely daunting. From St. Petersburg in the north he went via Moscow to the southernmost parts of the country where in Tiflis (Tbilisi) and other major cities of the Caucasus he made a large number of recordings of local artists. On completion of the project the records and equipment were sent off by rail to Moscow; somewhere *en route* they vanished, never to be seen again by the Gramophone Company. It was an ominous portent of what was to befall the Russian branch itself some two years later.

Gaisberg had long been convinced that revolution was inevitable and, having done all in his power for the Company, he was glad at the end of his third trip to start the roundabout return to London in November, 1915. The war had halted the ferry services across the Gulf of Bothnia to neutral Sweden and he had no option but to go by rail from Moscow via Finland to the nearest point to the Swedish border. The last twenty miles were accomplished in stages by horse-drawn sleigh with Gaisberg wrapped in layers of furs to protect him against the freezing temperatures. It was by any reckoning a bizarre conclusion to what had been the most challenging missions of his career thus far.

48

English Columbia's list for March, 1917 included the well-known baritone Thorpe Bates singing *Heroes of the Dardanelles*. When this record was issued the Dardanelles episode was already a matter of history. The British and French fleets in February and March, 1915 attacked the straits that were the key to Constantinople (the then Turkish capital) beyond which lay the Black Sea, a much needed supply route to Russia. The narrow waterway was heavily guarded on both sides by a series of forts and shore batteries; seapower alone proved insufficient to gain the Allies' objectives and the ships withdrew. Some weeks later the operation was reopened with landings by British, Australian, New Zealand, French and Indian troops on the Gallipoli peninsula. Thoroughly alerted by the naval attempt on the straits the Turks had had plenty of time to deploy their men on the strategic high ground. For the attackers the terrain was inhospitable in the extreme and, as the year went on, the summer heat brought with it the torment of hosts of flies and the attendant dysentery. The fighting at Gallipoli had much in common with that on the Western Front: attack and counter-attack succeeded each other with massive loss of life but, despite the exceptional bravery of the opposing armies, neither side made any decisive progress. In sharp contrast, Allied submarines were roving the Dardanelles and the Sea of Marmara like latter-day buccaneers, some even penetrating to the harbour at Constantinople itself where surprise attacks were made on shipping and dockside installations. British army reinforcements were sent out and a further landing took place at Suvla Bay in early August, but again stalemate ensued. The men pinned down at Gallipoli could not be spared indefinitely just to sustain a state of deadlock and in December/January, 1915/1916 the Allied soldiers were evacuated.

In London there had been serious military, naval and political repercussions throughout the campaign which had been championed by the First Lord of the Admiralty, Winston Churchill. The First Sea Lord, Admiral Fisher, resigned over the matter of naval reinforcements, Asquith's Liberal government was forced into a coalition with the Conservatives and Churchill was relegated to the Chancellorship of the Duchy of Lancaster. Had the Dardanelles operation succeeded Germany would have lost her Turkish ally and the war might well have been brought to a much speedier conclusion. At the outset press coverage was sparse and, with virtually no personal contact between those at home and the men battling far away on the very edge of Asia, it was some time before a true picture of events in this new theatre of war began to emerge.

Amongst those who later wrote accounts of their Gallipoli experiences was Compton Mackenzie, established novelist and future founder of *The Gramophone*. At this stage of his career, though, the only records that occupied his attention were those he compiled as an Intelligence officer on the staff of General Sir Ian Hamilton. Music, however, was liable to come to his mind at some unlikely moments. The Allies' large-scale attack of fourth June, 1915 was preceded by a heavy artillery barrage which gave way to the lighter sound of machine guns and small arms fire when the troops began to move forward. From his observation post Mackenzie could see little of the action but the noise reminded him of "a change of orchestration in a symphony, as though after a heavy and almost dull opening the strings were leading to a breathless finale of the first movement." On another occasion close personal involvement brought with it less exalted musical thoughts. He was on board a motor launch that was to pick up an Allied agent from a rendezvous on Turkey's Asiatic coast. The agent did not appear and in waiting beyond the arranged time the launch was stranded by the falling tide on a sandbank close in-shore.

> "As the first beams of the sun came winking over the mountain tops, somebody pointed to what looked very like the winking of bayonets among the trees. A Turkish patrol? I tried to remember the tune of that favourite ... composition; but I could only remember another one called the Turkish Retreat, which I learned to play on the piano in early youth."

Fortunately by now the tide had just turned and, to everybody's relief, the boat was able to slip discreetly away from the impending danger.

The British world of entertainment's reaction to the Dardanelles was, not surprisingly, somewhat guarded. The rumblings in Westminster and Whitehall had indicated all along that the subject was a contentious and risky one. For the actual participants, especially the Australians, the campaign immediately took on something approaching epic status, but for the record companies it would have been commercially and patriotically imprudent to associate themselves too conspicuously with a military failure, even so honourable a one as Gallipoli. Edward Dwyer's disc about Mons was not a comparable case since that particular retreat, unlike the withdrawal from Gallipoli, was not the end of the story. English Columbia had a highly individual approach to repertoire and a well-developed talent for identifying and filling vacant slots. It is probably no coincidence that their *Heroes of the Dardanelles* was issued in the year that was to see the publication of the government's Dardanelles Commission's reports and at a time when the earliest books relating to Gallipoli were being read. It was fitting that the gramophone should commemorate the gallant endeavour in some way and the title of Thorpe Bates's song made it clear that it was the men who had taken part who were being celebrated rather than the campaign itself. The backing was a number yearningly entitled *When the Boys Come Home*; taken in conjunction with the other side it is tempting to wonder whether there may not have been a hint of war-weariness in Columbia's offering.

Russia's exit from the war came when the Bolsheviks negotiated a peace treaty with Germany in March, 1918. For the Allies, however, the balance of fighting power had been maintained by the USA's entry in April, 1917, a move that had finally come about through Germany's policy of unrestricted submarine warfare and the resultant U-boat attacks on American shipping.

The music and record industries in the United States took immediate action. The composer George M. Cohan was well to the fore with his *Over There*, a marching song that to this day conjures up pictures of American forces fighting in wars overseas. Its popularity was phenomenal and it soon crossed the Atlantic to Britain where, amongst others, HMV's Walter Jeffries and Columbia's Jamieson Dodds recorded it. Without a doubt the most surprising performance of all was the version made in America for Victor in 1918 by Enrico Caruso. The great tenor was in boisterous form, singing first the original words then repeating the lyric in French, thus neatly addressing the song to the Allies on both sides of the English Channel.

Because of the late stage at which the USA entered the war the American record companies had been able to monitor and assess the commercial viability of the various types of patriotic material issued in large quantities since 1914 by their Canadian neighbours. In both countries the male voice quartet was a highly esteemed

51

entertainment and the American and Peerless Quartets were constantly in the studios recording war-related pieces. Amongst the output of the latter group was Von Tilzer's song *What Kind of an American Are You?*, a broad hint to those of German extraction that their adoptive country expected their loyal backing in the war. This Victor disc also circulated in Britain on the HMV label, one example amongst many of the interchange operating between the major companies and their affiliates abroad. In this way gramophone owners in America, Canada, Britain, France and Australia enjoyed access to recordings from or about each others' countries. Thus Canadian HMV's catalogue included not only a descriptive of the *Landing of the Australian Troops in Egypt* but also Australian patriotic songs performed by the British baritone Stanley Kirkby. The same industrious singer (this time under the pseudonym Lloyd Johnson) also publicised the Australian contribution to the war for English Columbia.

It was inevitable that in the United States there should be descriptives of the *Departure of the American Troops for France* and *Arrival of the American Troops in France*; the Peerless Quartet performed this service for American Columbia and the recording was belatedly issued in Britain in November, 1918, a delay brought about by a fire that seriously damaged Columbia's London factory. For the same reason a descriptive by a Canadian officer, Lieutenant Gitz-Rice, dealing with *Life in a Trench in Belgium* was similarly late in reaching the British record shops. Gitz-Rice knew his subject well for he served with the artillery on the Western Front until he had the misfortune to be gassed. After being invalided back to Canada he was placed in charge of entertainments for the troops in that country. Show business came naturally to him and he was involved in the composition of several war songs including *Keep Your Head Down, Fritzie Boy*, a hit number that was recorded by both the American and Peerless Quartets.

From its quarters in New York and elsewhere the American music industry turned out songs that often combined optimism and belligerency to a remarkable degree, as in the long-forgotten *We're Goin' to Knock the 'Hel' out of Wilhelm and It Won't Take Us Long*. It is doubtful whether such facile sentiments were shared by the doughboys experiencing the carnage in northern France. Perhaps the most authoritative Allied voice preserved on disc in the course of the war was that of General John J. Pershing, the American Commander-in-Chief in Europe who, in Paris in March, 1918 was recorded by Nation's Forum in *From the Battlefields of France*, an address which gave the American public a short but altogether truer view of the situation than anything the popular entertainment sector might be expected to produce. The abundance of the patriotic output from this latter source may be gauged from the more than one hundred sides of war-related material issued between them by just two companies, Victor and Columbia, during the year and a half the Americans were fighting in Europe.

At last, an exhausted Germany was obliged to admit defeat and on 11th November, 1918 at 11 a.m. the guns fell silent. The gramophone came out of the war well with its credentials as an influential and responsible medium established beyond all doubt. It had helped recruit and even train men for the armed forces. It had cheered and diverted civilians and for the services it had been a favourite form of relaxation. In particular, in France and Belgium it had brought great comfort and pleasure to men whose brief life expectancy in the front line could be forecast with almost actuarial precision. For the connoisseurs of vocal art it had continued to bring out recordings by the world's finest singers and a select number of documentary discs confirmed its value as a historical archive. These were achievements of which the record companies could be justly proud.

Now the record industry everywhere had to face the problems posed by a world at peace for the first time in four years. Something had to be found to replace the patriotic recordings which had been a staple of the companies' lists of new issues. The ragtime music which grew up in the United States around the turn of the century had been extremely popular on both sides of the Atlantic and by 1917 adventurous American musicians were putting their own stamp on it with improvised solos. In this way ragtime gradually developed into jazz, the craze for which in North America and Europe was so great that it supplied the record makers with an immediate and highly profitable substitute.

For the Gramophone Company, however, the decisions on new repertoire were a simple matter compared with the difficulties arising from their wartime losses. The Russian branch, annexed by the revolutionary government, was acknowledged to be irrecoverable, but there were high hopes that when a peace treaty was signed the Hanover factory would revert to its original owners. It was not to be, for this valuable asset had been liquidated by Germany in 1916 and bought up the following year by Polyphon Musikwerke. The long struggle to reclaim their property was unsuccessful and it was not until 1926 when they set up the Electrola company that HMV re-entered the German market.

★ ★ ★

EPILOGUE 1920

Britain's war dead were honoured by the nation with the tomb of the Unknown Warrior in Westminster Abbey and Sir Edwin Lutyens's Cenotaph in London's Whitehall. Standing in the bustle of a public thoroughfare in the heart of the capital the Cenotaph with its austere lines and surfaces speaks as eloquently of the sacrifices made as any more ornate statuary. It was here, on the morning of 11th November, 1920 that King George V and the Prince of Wales awaited the arrival of the procession that accompanied the remains of the unknown British soldier. The body had been reverently brought to London from France and, when the cortège halted at the Cenotaph, the King laid a wreath of laurel leaves and crimson flowers on the coffin. As eleven o'clock struck, the crowds in Whitehall stood motionless and silent in the late autumn sunshine. The coffin was then taken on the last, short stage of its journey to the Abbey where the Band of the Grenadier Guards had been playing solemn music by British, French and Belgian composers to the packed congregation before the funeral service began. The coffin was borne into the Abbey and laid in the grave at the centre of the nave and the King scattered earth from a French battlefield upon it. Prayers were said and the whole congregation, led by the Band, sang *Abide with me* and a setting of Kipling's *Recessional.* After the service had ended with the Blessing and the sounding of Reveille vast numbers of men and women from all walks of life began filing past the grave in a remarkable act of public yet personal homage to the dead.

This day of mourning was the first occasion when, by permission of the Dean and Chapter, recordings were taken of a ceremony in the Abbey; what is more, those sound documents were made

54

electrically. The process used had been devised by an Englishman, Lionel Guest, a younger son of the first Baron Wimborne, and Horace Owen Merriman, a Canadian engineer. They had met during the war in which they served as flying officers and after demobilisation began testing the ideas they had discussed about new recording techniques. For a year they experimented in a less than ideal laboratory set up in a London garage and were convinced their system would be a great advance for the gramophone industry. A vital factor in their negotiations with the Abbey authorities for permission to record part of the service was that their technology was unobtrusive. There would be no unsightly acoustic horn and recording equipment with its attendant engineers to distract the congregation. Instead, a microphone was discreetly located in the Sanctuary, two more were fixed on the choir screen and a fourth was placed in the nave near the Unknown Warrior's grave. From these points cables ran out of the building to the mobile studio in a lorry parked between the Sanctuary and the Chapter House. The studio contained all the bulky electrical equipment, the turntable and cutting head, a heating stove and an oven in which to keep the blank wax discs at the correct temperature.

With their microphones Guest and Merriman believed they could blend the choral and instrumental strands of the music to produce an effect far beyond the capabilities of the acoustic method and it was agreed that *Abide with me* and *Recessional* would be the most suitable parts of the service to record. The pressing was done by Columbia and the disc was sold at the Abbey and by mail order from *The Times* newspaper; it was priced at 7s.6d. (37½p) and the proceeds were donated to the Abbey's restoration fund. The very nature of the recording ensured that what was in effect a limited edition would soon be sold out. Unfortunately the sound quality failed to come up to expectations and the British gramophone industry did not feel impelled to build on the pioneering work of Guest and Merriman.

On the other side of the Atlantic, however, research into electrical recording had been going on since 1915 and in 1924 and 1925 the Autograph, Victor and Columbia companies began marketing records that proved to all other major producers that the electrical process was the key to survival.

Dictators and Wars, 1919-1939

DURING THE TWO decades that separated the signing of the Treaty of Versailles and the outbreak of the Second World War the European democracies watched with mounting concern the rise of four dictatorships which threatened the political stability of the continent. The Russian revolution of 1917 brought in its wake civil war and eventually the emergence of the Union of Soviet Socialist Republics (the USSR). Until the death of Lenin in 1924 and then under Stalin the enormous empire that extended from the Arctic Ocean to the Black Sea and eastwards almost to Alaska was ruled by an ideologically-based system that permitted no departure from rigid communist norms or from the lines laid down by its leaders in the pursuit of their political ambitions.

Next to succumb to totalitarianism was Italy where Mussolini, once a Marxian socialist, dedicated himself to nationalist policies and founded his Fascist movement in opposition to what he saw as the ineffectual socialism of post-1918 Italy. Mussolini's party gathered popular support and on the last day of October, 1922 he became the country's head of government. There was now a gap of eleven years until in Germany Adolf Hitler and his Nazi party, capitalising on the discontent generated by the Treaty of Versailles and the economic disasters that dogged the Weimar Republic, swept into power in 1933.

Geographically, democratic Europe was now almost divided into two parts by the German and Italian dictator states between which there remained only the corridor formed by Switzerland and Austria. By 1938 Switzerland alone remained, for in March that year Hitler's long-term programme for the expansion of the Third Reich had begun with the annexation of Austria.

Finally Europe's western flank was put at risk by the upsurge of fascism in Spain where, in 1936, the right wing General Francisco Franco led a revolt by the Army against the socialist government

56

of Manuel Azana. Germany and Italy sided with Franco who benefited greatly from the men and aircraft sent to Spain by Hitler and Mussolini, both of whom were eager for their forces to gain battleground experience. Russia did not intervene in the war, but contented herself with advising and equipping the Azana regime. In April, 1939, after three years of bitter fighting, Franco was victorious. Europe's fragile peace, however, did not last long; a mere five months later the Second World War began.

⋆   ⋆   ⋆

The revolution in Russia which Fred Gaisberg had predicted with such certainty erupted in February, 1917, when the pent-up resentment expressed itself in strikes and demonstrations by the working classes and in mutinies by the armed forces. The Tsar, Nicholas II, was forced to abdicate and the administration of the country was taken over by liberal and socialist politicians in conjunction with representatives of the workers and the army. This uneasy partnership lasted only until October when the Bolsheviks toppled the provisional government and replaced it with a body of People's Commissars headed by Lenin. The Tsar, who was arrested in March, was moved around from one place of confinement to another until at Ekaterinburg (later Sverdlovsk), on the orders of Lenin, the royal family together with their doctor and servants were shot by the Red Guards on 16th July, 1918. The cold-blooded and crudely performed execution took place in a cellar and those unfortunate enough to survive the bullets were killed off with bayonets and rifle butts. When the news eventually reached the outside world Fred Gaisberg's memories must surely have taken him back to his Russian visit at the beginning of the century when he had hoped to record the Tsar's voice for the gramophone, a cherished project that regrettably came to nothing.

During the period 1914-1918 the Russian record companies experienced the same shortages of manpower, machinery and materials that beset their counterparts in the western European countries involved in the Great War. The market leader, the Gramophone Company's thriving Russian branch, suffered most of all on account of the serious disruption of the manufacturing process when it twice became necessary to move the plant out of the path of the advancing Germans. The transfer from Riga to St. Petersburg bought only a short breathing space before safer quarters again had to be found. Aprelevka became the branch's final

57

base but operations had scarcely been resumed there when the Bolsheviks came to power.

Regardless of the civil war the revolutionaries quickly set about implementing their policy of nationalisation and continued systematically with the programme until the Russian economy was totally under state control. The turn of the music industry came on 20th August, 1919 with a decree nationalising shops, warehouses and workshops manufacturing and selling keyboard and other musical instruments. The draft document had been submitted to the Council of People's Commissars in early June and was scheduled for ratification by the executive committee on 12th August but as the Moscow Soviet's representative failed to attend the meeting the matter had to be deferred. A week later the decree was ratified by Lenin himself in his capacity as Chairman of the Council and, amongst others, A. V. Lunacharsky, the People's Commissar for Education.

This new law specifically included gramophones, phonographs and recordings, all of which now came within the remit of the Music Department of Lunacharsky's directorate. The property, stock in trade and capital of the Russian gramophone industry were taken over by the state and the employees of the former companies were transferred to the Music Department. The cut-throat competition, sharp practice and downright piracy rife in the Russian industry from its early days were now things of the past; and, sadly, the old vitality and enterprise soon started to decline when deprived of their former commercial incentives by the dirigiste policies of the Communist regime.

The first step towards politicising the recorded output came with a series of discs made by leading figures of the revolutionary movement, most notably Lenin himself who had used the gramophone for political purposes as early as March, 1919, some five months before the nationalisation decree was enacted. Russia's new masters exploited all available ways of spreading the Communist message and saw the gramophone as a convenient and effective supplement both to the packed columns of *Pravda* and *Izvestiya* and to the constant public meetings throughout the country. It cannot be claimed that a relatively small number of recordings was as influential as the official press or the party machine but in the pre-radio age in a country where standards of literacy were low, the voices of famous activists, women as well as men, lent authority and a sense of purpose to the rapid changes taking place in the wake of the revolution.

These short speeches, comprising some forty titles, were issued over the period 1919-1921 by the Soviet Record division of the Central Agency of the All-Russian Central Executive Committee for the Distribution of Publications. The political correctness of the speakers and the content matter was ensured by the presence on the editorial board of Lenin, M. I. Kalinin and Alexandra Kollontay; soldiers, politicians, writers, poets and actors were carefully chosen so that the records should appeal to as wide an audience as possible. The studio sessions were carried out not by Russian engineers but by two Germans, Oscar Blösche and August Kibarth of the Metropol Record company of Moscow and the pressings were made at Metropol's Aprelevka factory. This latest form of Bolshevik propaganda was available throughout the country and, in the hands of dedicated party workers, was put to highly productive use, especially amongst army units and at political centres. Considering that Soviet Record was concerned exclusively with the home market and taking into account the language barrier and Russia's isolation from the international community it is not surprising that the recordings were (and have remained) little known in the West.

The revolutionaries whose voices were preserved by the gramophone were almost entirely Russian, but a notable exception was a German woman, Clara Zetkin, a close friend of Lenin's and a tireless advocate of socialist and communist principles. She was held in such regard in Russia that in 1921 she was brought on to the standing committee of the Third International (the Comintern) which had been set up by Lenin two years earlier. Some of the Bolsheviks on these recordings have now faded into the historical background. One such was Nikolay Podvoisky whose post-1919 responsibilities ranged from military matters to physical culture and sport. Podvoisky, who lived from 1888 to 1968, survived the dangerous political environment of the Stalin years as did the more famous Mikhail Kalinin, the Soviet head of state from 1919 until his death in 1946.

Other speakers were less fortunate. Trotsky was ideologically at odds with Stalin for which apostasy he paid the penalty with a period of internal exile and, in 1929, expulsion from Russia. He finally settled in Mexico where he continued to promote his doctrine of permanent revolution, in the process of which he went into the studio once again in 1938 to record (in English) his *Speech on Occasion of 10th Anniversary of the Left Opposition*. His constant criticism of Russian-style Communism was silenced in 1940 by Stalin's hired assassin. Lev Kamenev was at the height of his power in 1922 when, because of Lenin's illness, he, Stalin and Zinoviev took over the government of the country. Thereafter he increasingly experienced Stalin's enmity until in 1936 he was put on trial accused of plotting to kill the dictator and was shot. Execution by firing squad was also the fate of Nikolay Bukharin in 1938 when the former editor of *Pravda* and *Izvestiya* was tried and declared guilty of crimes against the state.

The subjects covered by the speeches offer few surprises. N.V. Krilenko announced *We have begun to build our State* and G.I. Petrovsky spoke *About Vladimir Ilyich Lenin*. Alexandra Kollontay's *To the Workers* introduces the present day listener to a remarkable personality - heterodox daughter of a Tsarist family, propagandist, minister, diplomat and feminist who preached (and practised) the creed of free love. "I was", she wrote proudly, "appointed People's Commissar ... of Social Welfare. I was the only woman in the Cabinet and the first woman in history who had ever been recognized as a member of a government." One of her many passionate affairs almost brought about an early downfall when she was denounced for failing in her official duties. There was probably more to it than just that for Kollontay believed strongly in a democratic Communist movement in which workers should be given the opportunity to help shape party policy, an idea that was unpalatable to power-hungry members of the governing hierarchy. In the end it was only through Lenin's intercession that she did not join the ranks of those executed for political reasons by the Soviet state. Lenin's act of clemency seems to have accorded her lasting protection for she went on to a successful career in the Russian Foreign Service which lasted until she was well into her seventies.

Anatoly Lunacharsky's contribution to the series was a disc entitled, perhaps a shade optimistically, *The Masses are thirsting for Knowledge*. It may be that indirectly Lunacharsky was cannily buttressing his department through his recording in order to offset the risk of any future radical downgrading of the government's education policy. Whether this was so or not, there can be no doubt that Lunacharsky was genuinely concerned to improve the educational condition of the Russian proletariat and as a first step towards this goal he brought in a law to simplify the alphabet and the principles of spelling. The man whose volume of *Three Plays* was shortly to be familiar to customers of the more intellectually-inclined British bookshops, had his darker moments however. Louise Bryant, an eye witness of the Revolution's early days related how

"when he heard that the Kremlin was razed to the ground he took to his bed and resigned his position. He appeared at his post a few days later when he found that it was a false report."

Lunacharsky's wish to see Russia's cultural heritage made accessible to the people was at least partially fulfilled when music and the theatre ceased to be the recreations exclusively of the privileged and the wealthy. In 1920 Mrs. Philip Snowden, the wife of the British Labour politician, published an account of her visit to Russia as a member of a joint Labour Party/TUC delegation. If he read the book Lunacharsky would have been gladdened by her praise for the way Art was now "within the reach of the poorest classes in the community" and her approval of the system by which "Certain nights at the opera and theatre are reserved for soldiers and sailors, certain others for Trade unionists and other workers, and the remainder are for the general public."

The lion's share of the Bolsheviks' recording programme fell to Lenin. In the main, the twelve speeches he put on disc over the years 1919-1921 were *ex cathedra* statements of Communist aims and policies which, in cold print, are somewhat turgid; but the actual recordings, despite their technical deficiencies, conveyed enough of Lenin's powerful personality to make the desired impact on his listeners. It is soon clear that the audience Lenin envisaged was "those who are now leading millions of working people and who, with the greatest zeal, march in the front ranks of the army of labour!" The mass of the workers and the peasants are more often spoken about than directly addressed. The peasantry in particular was the object of almost missionary attention and Lenin reminds the party activists that

"we must know, remember, and put into practice the rule that when Communist workers go into rural districts they must try to establish comradely relations with the middle peasants, it is their duty to establish these comradely relations with them; they must remember that working peasants who do not exploit the labour of others are the comrades of the urban workers and that we can, and must, establish with them a voluntary alliance inspired by sincerity and confidence."

The importance of not antagonising the nation's food producers could hardly have been more emphatically expressed.

The briefest item Lenin recorded (less than a minute and a half's duration) is an eulogy *In Memory of Comrade Yakov Mikhailovich Sverdlov*, the recently deceased Chairman of the All-Russia Central Executive Committee. The longest, lasting for four and a half minutes, is *An Appeal to the Red Army*, made while the Bolsheviks were still at war with the counter-revolutionary forces. Significantly, in this instance Lenin speaks on a much more personal basis to the soldiers on whom the success of the uprising depended. He stresses the gains already made and assures the Army it is invincible; united with the workers and peasants, "A little more effort, a few more months of fighting the enemy, and victory will be ours." Occasionally the perilous state of the Russian economy is graphically described, as in the short speech entitled *Work for the Railways*:

"We have a lot of grain, and now we have coal and oil. We are being held up by transport. The railways are out of action. Transport must be rehabilitated. Then we can bring grain, coal and oil to the factories, then we can deliver salt, then we shall begin to restore industry and put an end to the hunger of the factory and railway workers."

Yet despite the tremendous difficulties at home Lenin still kept a close watch on the fortunes of the Communist movement elsewhere in Europe.

Communications on the Wireless Negotiations with Béla Kun is, perhaps, the most vivid of all Lenin's recordings. It throws a revealing light on the political turmoil in the newly founded Hungarian republic where the Russian leader's protégé, Béla Kun, was head of the Communist party. On his return from Russia where he had been a prisoner of war Kun was soon gaoled again, this time by the Károlyi government, for his subversive activities. He was released in March, 1919 and joined a Communist/Social Democratic coalition of which the Communists rapidly took control. The Armistice was not the end of the fighting in central Europe and in the same month that Kun came out of prison Hungary went to war with Czechoslovakia and a few weeks later was invaded by Romania. Internal matters had not gone smoothly either and Kun forfeited the support of the Hungarian peasantry when the great landed estates were taken into national ownership. Lenin was anxious for first-hand information about the true state of affairs in Hungary and Kun's own position there. On the recording he tells how

"... I sent a wireless message to Budapest, asking Béla Kun to come to the apparatus, and I put a number of questions to him of such a nature as to enable me to make sure that it was really he who was speaking. I asked him what real guarantees there were for the character of the government and for its actual policy. Comrade Béla Kun's reply was quite satisfactory and dispelled all our doubts... Long live Soviet power in Hungary!"

The confidence was misplaced; the revolution lost all impetus and in August, 1919 Kun hurriedly left Hungary for Vienna. From 1920 he made his home in Russia where later he was yet another victim of Stalin's purges.

Photographs of Lenin addressing large audiences, often in the open air, show him at ease with his attentive listeners, but in one taken in the studio in March, 1919 he looks slightly wary and self-conscious as he speaks into the impersonal recording horn. If he had any problems in adapting to the techniques required by the unfamiliar process they were soon resolved. In the United States between 1900 and 1923 the Democrat William Jennings Bryan and the Republican William H. Taft frequently made commercial cylinders and discs to promote their parties' views and policies, but it was Lenin, together with his chosen colleagues in their supporting roles, who put the gramophone to the most calculated and concentrated political use thus far in its forty year history. Lenin's own recordings established a positive bond between the leader and the masses; in this way the gramophone was the earliest medium other than the press to help in creating the cult of personality that was to become such an integral feature of the inter-war European dictatorships.

Within a few years, however, the gramophone's political applications in Russia were largely superseded by the cinema and radio.

The Music Trust of the Supreme Council of the National Economy was responsible for record production from the 1920s until 1933 when its work was transferred to the Record Trust which, in its turn, gave place to the All-Union Recording House for Record Production in 1938. During this period there was virtually no formal contact between the Russian gramophone industry and the companies operating in the rest of the world and for this reason Russian recordings in the era of electrical 78s lacked the technical refinement that had developed elsewhere in the 1930s. As far as repertoire and artists were concerned the emphasis was primarily on Russian music and, of necessity, on Russian artists. Paradoxically, it was not until after the Soviet Union was invaded by Hitler in 1941 that a trickle of Russian recordings at last began to reach the West.

★   ★   ★

Fired by the political and social changes set in motion by Lenin in Russia, Benito Mussolini cast himself as the saviour of Italian socialism and, by extension, of the nation itself. Italy entered the Great War on the side of the Allies in 1915 but fared badly in the fighting on its north-eastern frontier with Austria. The Caporetto campaign, fought in appalling weather in the last three months of 1917 against combined German and Austrian forces, resulted in a demoralised Italian army retreating to the Piave river. After the Armistice a series of administrations struggled without success to overcome Italy's internal problems until, in October, 1922, Mussolini and his Fascist party decided to show their strength and marched almost unopposed on Rome; on the last day of the month Mussolini was asked by King Victor Emmanuel III to form a government.

Mussolini's political philosophy was formed largely on the 'pick-and-mix' principle from a wide variety of sources. Some ideas came from his blacksmith father for whom politics was a consuming interest; others stemmed from his extensive reading of Marx, Nietzsche, Hegel and Kropotkin, to name only a small sample. The heady concepts he absorbed were well matched by his confident, aggressive nature and his way with words, both written and spoken. With his contempt for Italy's lack-lustre post-war performance on the one hand and his opposition to Bolshevism on the other, Mussolini appeared to offer the country an acceptable middle way and his leadership was enthusiastically acclaimed. However, even before he came to power the nationalist element in Mussolini's brand of socialism had begun to be a major ingredient of his ideology following Italy's failure to win any territorial rewards at the Paris Peace Conference. In due course the Italian corporate state, created and presided over by Mussolini, was the instrument through which Fascist policy and propaganda were to be channelled from 1923 until the dictator's overthrow in the palace revolution of July, 1943.

The Italian musical profession was automatically sucked into the political system. Harvey Sachs in his *Music in Fascist Italy* describes a world of

"workaday infighting and intrigue in abundance, much grotesque opportunism, occasional examples of naive good faith in the government, and very little real political opposition. Through it all, there flowed an endless torrent of fluctuating government directives on musical education, the management of opera houses, the formation of innumerable musicians' unions, corporations, councils and committees, and the organization of festivals, congresses, competitions and musical show-cases - all brainchildren of various party Excellencies or of musical personalities who had ingratiated themselves with the fascists. Some of the ideas were good, others absurd; all but a few remained partly or wholly unrealized."

At the top of the bureaucratic pyramid Mussolini, himself an amateur violinist, frequently aired his views (and therefore the gospel) on what was or was not desirable musically in the Fascist state. He enjoyed Beethoven, some Wagner and was particularly fond of Puccini and Mascagni, but disdained dance music. His supposed love of Palestrina may well have been voiced just to add weight to the official policy that encouraged the promotion of the important, but at that time neglected, composers of pre-nineteenth century Italy.

Government ministers such as Nicola de Pirro in the field of the theatre and Giuseppe Bottai with his responsibility for national education were often the originators of musical policy the administration of which fell to men like Adriano Lualdi, Giuseppe Mulè and Alceo Toni, all composers and practising musicians. Lualdi and Toni constantly paraded their loyalty to the Fascist regime and

65

all three were in frequent correspondence with Mussolini on musical matters, usually with an eye to personal advantage.

Within the corporativist framework the gramophone came under the direction of a body set up to control the radio and musical appliances industries. In 1927 this organisation joined with a number of other groups to form the National Fascist Federation of Theatrical, Cinematic and Related Industries. The sponsorship of musical works was a regular feature of the Mussolini years and the Italian record companies had the problem of balancing what might be expected of them by the state against what was likely to be commercially viable. Works which quickly gained wide public approval or which had become an integral part of life under Fascism posed little difficulty. The prime example of the latter category was the party's patriotic song *Giovinezza*. It was not until 1946 that Italy adopted an official national anthem and prior to Mussolini the *Marcia Reale d'Ordinanza* was used on most state and public occasions. However, with its constant repetition by the Fascists, *Giovinezza* soon pushed the *Marcia Reale* into the background. Up until the time he left Italy in 1929 and on his return visits before the outbreak of World War II the great conductor Arturo Toscanini, an outspoken anti-Fascist, flatly refused to play *Giovinezza* at any of his performances and suffered many indignities as a consequence. Perhaps the most commanding recorded version of *Giovinezza* was made not in Italy but in the United States by Giovanni Martinelli in 1926 for the Victor company. The world-famous tenor had made his American debut in 1913 at the Metropolitan Opera House, New York where audiences were to revel in his singing for the next thirty years and more. The disc was published at a time when Mussolini's reformist programmes still seemed preferable to the rudderless efforts of his predecessors and Victor's decision to make the recording was no doubt influenced not just by the certainty of its success in Italy but also by the anticipated volume of sales amongst the large Italian section of the American population. Presumably at this stage Martinelli was favourably impressed by the new developments in his homeland; whatever the motivation, he put his heart into *Giovinezza* which was well suited to his ringing voice, although not even his artistry could disguise the threadbare nature of the piece.

Under Fascism the most eminent Italian composers produced political anthems or secular hymns in celebration of the new era; naturally, the more illustrious the composer the more willing the Italian companies were to commit such music to disc. Pietro Mascagni, who moved to La Scala, Milan when Toscanini left for America, had made his name in Italy and abroad with the première of his masterpiece *Cavalleria Rusticana* in Rome in 1890. His music had Mussolini's commendation and by currying favour with the dictator he established himself as composer laureate to the Fascist movement. One of his products of this period was a hymn for the party's youth movements, but if there was a significant recording of the work it is not listed in Clough and Cuming's *World's Encyclopaedia of Recorded Music* (WERM), the first volume of which covers historic acoustic discs and the electrical output up to 1950. On the other hand, his *Canto del Lavoro*, the work hymn, achieved a wispy immortality through the recording made by the chorus of La Scala for Italian HMV. Sadly, Mascagni was only rarely able to recapture the sureness of touch that had endeared *Cavalleria Rusticana* and, to a lesser extent, *L'Amico Fritz* to opera lovers internationally. When in 1935 his classical Roman opera *Nerone* (in blatant flattery of Mussolini) was staged at La Scala the record companies steered clear of the work deterred, perhaps, by what the *New Grove* calls its "empty rhetoric". Despite the resurrection of so much little known music by the gramophone since the advent of the LP disc *Nerone* has remained in almost undisturbed obscurity, although one aria, *Perchè dovrei tremare*, was salvaged by the soprano Renata Scotto for inclusion in a recital given in Paris in 1983 and recorded live by the Etcetera company.

Mascagni's career in the recording studios extended from the acoustic days, when he made an abridged set of his opera *Parisina* with the original cast for Fonotipia, up to the early 1940s. In the concert hall he was well-known as a conductor of non-operatic music, one of the favourite items in his repertoire being Tchaikovsky's *Pathétique* symphony, but when it came to the gramophone what the companies wanted from him was operatic music, and that mainly his own. On disc Mascagni enjoyed a successful partnership with the orchestra of the Berlin State Opera with whom in 1927 he made a series of recordings for Polydor and also a similar group of short pieces with the same orchestra for the Odeon label. With the exception of one Verdi and two Rossini overtures

67

these two selections comprised some of his most popular music interspersed with extracts from the less familiar *Guglielmo Ratcliff, Le Maschere* and *I Rantzau*. Although in recent times the specialist Italian operatic label Bongiovanni has brought to light a performance of *Cavalleria Rusticana* conducted by Mascagni and recorded live in Holland in 1938, the most historically significant items in his legacy of commercial discs came during the Second World War when *Cavalleria Rusticana* and *L'Amico Fritz* reached their fiftieth anniversaries.

Puccini's *Inno a Roma* of 1919 pre-dated by three years the Fascists' takeover of power but thereafter it effortlessly achieved the prominence that, in the main, eluded the works which his contemporaries specifically tailored for the Mussolini regime. For Puccini, to whom music was all-important, patriotism and politics were of lesser concern and during the Great War there were even suspicions that his sympathies were pro-German. The Hymn to Rome, a setting of words by the poet Fausto Salvatori may, perhaps, be construed as Puccini's reply to such rumours, although the composer himself regarded it as a trivial thing. Harvey Sachs recounts how

> "its bombastic nationalism and implicit imperialism appealed to fascist leaders ... so much so that Mussolini eventually made the anthem part of the patriotic hymnal to be learned by school children throughout the country. In 1936, when the dictator proclaimed the birth of the Italian Empire, Puccini's hymn became a sort of third national anthem ..."

Not surprisingly, such strong official endorsement resulted in the issue of numerous recordings. Italian HMV brought out discs by two famous tenors, Beniamino Gigli and the sumptuously named Apollo Granforte and supplemented these performances with an orchestral arrangement played by the Milan Symphony Orchestra. Odeon contributed versions for chorus with and without orchestra and Fonit aimed at a different sector of the record buying public with a chorus accompanied by the Milan Military Band.

Amongst the bureaucrats of the Italian music world during the Fascist period Adriano Lualdi's reputation as a composer stood high and his influence as an administrator undoubtedly helped in his being well represented on disc. The number of entries under his name in WERM (vol. 1) indicates, moreover, that the record companies considered him to be a paying proposition. A song with orchestra and extracts from three operas rub shoulders with his *Inno all' Aviatore*, a typical response to the musical requirements of Fascist ideology, played by the Italian Air Force Band and recorded on the domestic Columbia label. Lualdi's research into Italy's musical heritage also resulted in recordings of arrangements of concertos and other works by Durante, Paisiello, Pergolesi and Porpora. Giuseppe Mulè was less generously recorded although, predictably enough, his *Marcia Trionfale* appeared on Italian HMV played by the Italian Guards Band. It would seem that the music of Alceo Toni only scraped into the record catalogues by virtue of his edition for piano of a keyboard toccata by the seventeenth century composer Michele Angelo Rossi which occupied one side of an Italian HMV twelve-inch disc.

Viewed in retrospect, Mascagni's recordings with the Berlin State Opera Orchestra may be seen as a prelude to the Italian-German musical exchanges that later were a prominent feature of cultural life in the two countries following Hitler's assumption of supreme power on the death of President Hindenburg in 1934. The Augusteo Orchestra of Rome under its conductor Bernardino Molinari toured Germany in 1937, the same year in which Victor De Sabata was there at the head of the complete company of La Scala, Milan. De Sabata was no stranger to Germany for he had already conducted the Berlin Philharmonic in the mid-1930s. In 1939 he was back again, this time in response to the greatest honour Germany could bestow on a foreign conductor, an invitation to direct performances at the Bayreuth Festival. That same year *The Gramophone* reviewed his idiosyncratic reading of Brahms's Fourth Symphony which formed part of a famous group of recordings he made for Polydor with the Berlin Philharmonic; the sessions encompassed a wide range of music that took in Richard Strauss's *Tod und Verklärung*, Resphigi's *Feste Romane*, the Vorspiel and Liebestod from Wagner's *Tristan und Isolde*, and a fiery account of Kodály's *Dances from Galanta* in which even the Berlin Philharmonic was hard pressed to satisfy De Sabata's demands. The strong element of "anything you can do I can do better" that pervaded the Hitler-Mussolini relationship ensured that their two countries enjoyed the finest music-making each had to offer; thus, Italian audiences flocked to performances by such renowned German artists as the conductor Wilhelm Furtwängler and the pianists Walter Gieseking, Wilhelm Backhaus and Edwin Fischer. So great was the importance attached to these cultural links by the dictators that the exchanges continued well into the Second World War.

Italy's Fascism was glorified in every possible way, not least through works of music. If composers were not coming forward unprompted with suitably triumphalist scores, then the state would induce them to do so by means of competitions. Even if the music was unremarkable - and it usually was - an aspiring composer chosen as a winner would have his moment of glory; and if there was a large number of entries the state could point with pride at the way composers were inspired by Fascism's progress.

Sachs gives an illuminating account of these competitions in which the requirements ranged from the general (a "symphonic or choral composition of a heroic nature") in 1937 to the specific (a "symphonic poem for large orchestra, on the subject of 'The March on Rome'") in 1928. Some were so prescriptive that only a composer of genius could have breathed life into the topic as, for instance, in 1930 when the organisers asked for "an anthem whose subject will be the battle for wheat production", adding informatively that "the text has already been written". The latter two competitions suggest that the Fascists were trying to match in music the cinematic propaganda of the Russian communists. The March on Rome orchestral work may be seen as the counterpart of S. M. Eisenstein's impressive retelling of the 1917 revolution in his film *October* which also came out in 1928, whilst the wheat cantata reminds one of those scenes in Russian films where sturdy peasants harvest bumper crops from fields of grain stretching away to the far horizon. Despite the copious publicity that attended the competitions the quality of the winning pieces clearly failed to impress the commercial record companies as none of the larger-scale works for which Sachs gives details of composer and title is to be found in volume one of WERM.

Amongst Mussolini's many grandiose plans was one in which Italy would take its place alongside Britain and France as a great colonial power. The vast empire acquired by ancient Rome through conquests in Europe, North Africa and the Middle East was the obvious spur to such thinking, especially as, when Mussolini came to power, Italy already had a nucleus of overseas possessions to which others might be added. In eastern Africa Eritrea had become a colony in 1890 to be followed in 1905 by Somalia. Then, after a brief war with Turkey, Tripolitania and Cyrenaica (together now Libya) entered the Italian fold in 1911. It was in 1935 that Mussolini's quest for empire changed from a political aim to harsh reality when a disagreement over frontiers was used as an excuse to attack Somalia's neighbour Abyssinia (now Ethiopia). The outcome of the staged war was a foregone conclusion for, bravely as they fought, the primitively equipped forces of the emperor Haile Selassie were no match for Italian land and air power. With the exception of French and British Somaliland the rest of the Horn of Africa was now Italian territory.

The hollow victory was proclaimed to the nation on 9th May, 1936 by Mussolini speaking from a balcony of the Palazzo Venezia, his political headquarters in Rome; as well as being covered by newsreel cameras and the press the occasion was both broadcast and recorded by Italian radio as a matter of course.

Once radio came to be accepted as an important medium for information, education and entertainment it followed that the most significant broadcasts should be preserved in recorded form. The commercial recording companies' system of cutting wax matrixes (the first stage in a sequence of processes leading to the pressing of shellac discs) was one of the available options but it was expensive, time-consuming and uneconomic when quantity production was not required; clearly, a simpler alternative had to be found. Taking Britain as an example, the BBC was looking at the possibility of recording on iron wire as far back as 1927, the same year in which they had used Dictaphones (originally designed for dictating office letters) to record two national sporting events. Four years later in its search for a recording system more suited to radio's needs the BBC began using the Blattnerphone machine of the late 1920s which recorded on to steel tape. Although a bulky piece of equipment and not particularly easy to operate it had three crucial advantages: the recording could be played back immediately, the tape could be edited by cutting and splicing and, moreover, could be wiped for re-use. A few years later a more traditional style of recording was pioneered in London by Cecil Watts whose innovation was to cut directly on to aluminium or zinc discs coated with lacquer (i.e. acetates). These metal-based 78 r.p.m. discs fitted in well at the BBC which, since its early days, had been geared to the regular playing of commercial gramophone records. The development of a tone arm that moved laterally and incorporated a finely calibrated gauge made it possible to edit and play extracts from recordings on acetate discs with remarkable accuracy. The Blattnerphone, however, was by no means superseded and the BBC continued to record on both systems.

As more economical recording methods became available to them broadcasting organisations began to build up historical sound archives, concentrating at first on the spoken word then, in due course, widening their scope to take in music. Beyond the world of radio the arrival of acetate discs enabled more well-to-do recording enthusiasts to indulge their special interests and a number of unique sound documents survive from the later 1930s as a result.

Thanks to the technological advances of the inter-war years we are able to hear not just the words themselves but the verbal nuances and emphases that went into such public statements as Mussolini's proclamation of the Italian empire. On the Pearl company's 1992 CD compilation *The Rise of Fascism* the recording of that broadcast of 9th May, 1936 conveys the occasion with remarkable realism. The dictator's powerful and unmistakably triumphant voice presents the addition of Abyssinia to Italy's overseas possessions as the dawn of a new age. Not unexpectedly, Mussolini's message is punctuated by well-drilled roars of approval from the huge crowd assembled outside the Palazzo Venezia. The acquisition of this latest colony was also commemorated in music; at one extreme was Adriano Lualdi's "colonial rhapsody" *Africa* (a piece of orchestral bombast not represented in WERM) whilst at the other the song *L'Italia ha vinto* (Italy has won), recorded on Odeon by the light, almost weightless tenor A. Masseglia, has more than a touch of a British music hall ditty about it.

Abyssinia figured prominently in the music competitions of 1936, one of the winners being Pina Carmirelli with her song *Casetta abissina* (Little Abyssinian cottage), an unlikely-sounding work for a fine musician who, with her Carmirelli String Quartet, went on to make some well-regarded chamber music recordings for Decca in the 1950s and 1960s. The euphoria generated by the Abyssinian success was still running high in 1939 when a competition for instrument makers required a piano designed to be "as suitable as possible for transportation to the Colony and the dominions of the new Italian Empire." As it turned out, there was little time for early settlers to invest in any such pianos that may have been made for by mid-May, 1941 Abyssinia had been retaken by British forces and restored to Emperor Haile Selassie.

Before the outbreak of World War II, however, the ease with which Abyssinia had been taken encouraged Mussolini to continue with his empire-building. During the 1930s Albania had been drawn closely to Italy with financial, economic and military ties. Situated on the opposite shore of the Adriatic the country was an easy target and in April, 1939, while Europe's attention was concentrated on the German annexation of Czechoslovakia, Mussolini sent in his army of occupation. The anxiety felt by Islam's followers in the Balkans and their co-religionists in the Middle East over the imposition of Italian rule on Albania's large Moslem population was almost certainly one of the factors that later the same year placed the gramophone at the centre of a diplomatic protest.

On 20th September, 1939 Signor Crolla, the Italian Chargé d' Affaires in London, called at the Foreign Office. It had come to the notice of Italy's Consul General in Beirut that a local recording firm, Baydaphone, was proposing to bring out "a gramophone record of an Arabic poem attacking the Duce as the enemy of all Moslems and being rude to Italy generally." When Baydaphone heard that the Italians knew what was being planned the company swiftly dissociated itself from the project which, it alleged, was being undertaken by English Columbia.

The Italians could discover nothing about the originators of this propaganda exercise but nevertheless Signor Crolla had been instructed in the interests of maintaining good Anglo-Italian relations to ask the Foreign Office to intervene and prevent Columbia producing the record. The Foreign Office was privately doubtful whether there was any substance to the story; on the other hand, if a recording did actually exist, the likeliest scenario was that having cut their wax Baydaphone, who lacked their own manufacturing plant, asked for Columbia's help in the pressing and distribution of the required number of copies. This, however, does not seem to have been the case as EMI's archives contain no correspondence relating to the disc.

As a matter of form the Foreign Office agreed to make inquiries and wrote to the Board of Trade requesting any information they might have which could be used in a reply to Signor Crolla. But the Board of Trade was deeply involved in far more important work as Britain was now at war with Germany. By early December the Foreign Office was still awaiting a response and sent a gentle reminder pointing out that although "The Italian Embassy have not returned to the charge ... we should be glad to have the ammunition in case they do." If Signor Crolla had intended to keep his government's complaint alive he would have renewed his representations to the Foreign Office but when he made no further move the matter was quietly shelved just before Christmas by the Whitehall officials.

This was not the first time the Foreign Office had been faced with the problem of Arabic propaganda discs for earlier in 1939 it had received reports that recordings of anti-British songs and dialogues were available in Syria and elsewhere in the Middle East and that some had been broadcast over Iraqi radio. To their undoubted chagrin Columbia on this occasion had unwittingly played a leading part in providing this material for the militant Arab cause.

Wattar Frères, Columbia's Syrian agents, had cut a batch of supposedly harmless waxes which were to be processed and put on sale in the Middle East. Columbia manufactured these records and allotted them catalogue numbers in the ten-inch green label GTS export series. Keen to avoid aggravating the volatile situation in the Middle East and to protect their own good name, Columbia arranged for copies of the suspect discs to be assessed for their political content by an independent specialist in Arab current affairs;[3] his expert opinion was that about forty per cent of those he had auditioned were, indeed, anti-British propaganda. Wattar Frères on whom the blame lay for this serious *faux pas* engaged to recall as many of the provocative items as possible and, full of contrition, pledged to exercise strict supervisory control over the cutting of future waxes.

The message of these records was directed mainly at the Palestinian Arabs urging them to fight for their independence against the British who, under the League of Nations mandate, governed what was the Arabs' rightful territory. The Treaty of Versailles and the League of Nations as well as the pro-Zionist

British were all the subject of bitter criticism and some of the discs took a similar stance against Hitler and Mussolini. Much as these two men might be admired for the way in which they had contrived to destabilise Europe, Arab listeners were bidden to remember the dictators were rampant imperialists and that Mussolini had made it clear he was set on adding Tunisia to Italy's existing North African colonies.

By the early summer of 1940 the possible effects of insulting Arab propaganda records were consigned to the political background while Mussolini kept close watch as one European state after another fell victim to the Nazis. Conscious that if Italy was to have a share of the spoils he would have to join forces with Hitler, Mussolini declared war on Britain and France on 10th June, a week after the evacuation of Dunkirk and less than a fortnight before the armistice between France and Germany.

★   ★   ★

In 1923, only a year after Mussolini's rise to power, Spain too became a dictatorship following a coup led by General Primo de Rivera. The immediate switch to martial law did little to endear the new regime to the Spanish people generally and in 1925 Primo de Rivera was obliged to take the outwardly democratic step of changing his role to that of Prime Minister, but his cabinet was heavily weighted with army colleagues. An uprising by the Riff Arabs in Spain's Moroccan territory and persistent unrest at home posed intractable problems for the government and Primo de Rivera resigned in January, 1930.

The King (Alfonso XIII), although in favour of the army's takeover, had distanced himself from events by going to live in France. After Primo de Rivera's death in March, 1930 the King returned to Spain, but the ensuing elections were a triumph for the Republican left which demanded, but did not obtain, Alfonso's abdication; instead, the King again took up residence outside Spain. The domestic situation continued to worsen with the irreconcilable aims of the political right and left leading to strikes and revolts that threatened to reduce the country to chaos. The right began to attract a greater degree of public sympathy but a series of coalition governments failed to restore stability. The deterioration of their country became intolerable to a group of senior army officers stationed in Spanish Morocco; armed intervention, they believed,

75

was the only way of resolving Spain's problems. Their revolt of July, 1936 led by General Francisco Franco ignited the bitter civil war that dragged on until March, 1939.

The wide spectrum of Spanish political affiliations becomes apparent when one examines the composition of the opposing sides. Franco's Nationalist forces brought in monarchists, the more conservative Catholics and, from the far right, Carlists and the fascists of the Falange movement started by Primo de Rivera. The Republicans drew their support from the moderates of the centre, the socialists, communists and anarchists as well as from the people of the short-lived republic of Catalonia and sections of the Basque population. Today the complexities and historical sequence of the Spanish Civil War have grown hazy in the memories of most non-Spaniards, overshadowed by the unparalleled struggles of the Second World War that followed so soon after.

Late twentieth century perceptions of the war have been more strongly influenced by writers such as George Orwell, W.H. Auden, Ernest Hemingway, André Malraux and Laurie Lee who were there at the time than by the works of specialist historians. The visual arts furnished other enduring reference points with two startling images - Picasso's anguished painting inspired by the bombing of Guernica and Robert Capa's photograph capturing the very moment of a soldier's death in action. These rapidly became familiar and potent symbols of the war and even though doubts have been cast on the authenticity of Capa's famous shot it remains unforgettable, regardless of whether it was genuine or faked.

It was only occasionally that any products of Spain's domestic gramophone industry penetrated the European and north American markets but the cultural barrier resulting from a repertoire of mainly popular indigenous music was surmounted by a number of universally acclaimed Spanish artists of the 1920s and 1930s. The discs of Andres Segovia, the classical guitarist, the cellist and conductor Pau (Pablo) Casals and the mezzo-soprano Conchita Supervia enjoyed massive sales world-wide although, travelling as they did on the international music circuit, their recordings were not always made in Spanish studios. It was a sad blow for lovers of fine singing when Supervia died at a tragically early age a few months before the Civil War broke out.

Casals's long connection with the gramophone went back to the days of acoustic 78s and continued well into the LP age. As a political idealist and an ardently patriotic Catalan he could not bear to live in a Spain divided against itself by the savagery of civil war and he exiled himself to Prades in the French Pyrenees where his former professional career was voluntarily reduced to private music-making in the company of his closest friends. He did not play in public again until 1950.

When in 1919 he set up and funded from his own pocket the Orquestra Pau Casals it was with the specific aim of bringing great music to his fellow Catalans, particularly in the form of workers' concerts. The orchestra was based in Barcelona, the same city in which Spanish HMV had its studios and there in 1928 he made recordings of Beethoven's first and fourth symphonies which were also issued in Great Britain. The following year on the orchestra's return to Barcelona from a highly successful series of concerts in Paris Casals was joined by his chamber music colleagues Jacques Thibaud, the violinist and Alfred Cortot, the pianist. With Cortot conducting the orchestra they recorded Brahms's double concerto for violin and cello, a set the memorable qualities of which have ensured its survival through many reissues on long-playing and compact discs.

It was some nine months after the outbreak of the Spanish Civil War that Casals made the recording with which perhaps more than any other his fame as a concerto soloist is linked. In April, 1937 he was due to play the Dvořák concerto in Prague with the Czech Philharmonic Orchestra under Georg Szell. Fred Gaisberg was deeply disturbed not only by the developments in Spain, where Barcelona was now closed to British HMV as a recording venue, but also by Hitler's threat to the peace in central and eastern Europe. The fact that Casals was at the height of his powers yet proposing to withdraw from public life made it vital to seize every opportunity to record the great cellist. Apprehensive that HMV's operations on the continent might at any time be brought to a sudden halt Gaisberg arranged for a recording of the concerto to be made the day after the concert. On his miserable railway journey from Berlin to Prague Gaisberg encountered hostility from railway staff and frontier officials. Fortunately the recording session went without trouble and when he later set down his memories of the occasion Gaisberg described how Casals

"... smartly rehearsed and recorded one after another the ten sides forming the complete work... As the last record was made he collapsed completely and allowed us to take him to his hotel, where we saw that he was carefully looked after...

The records turned out to be an unqualified success, and as soon as they were published I sold the first set to a most appreciative music-lover and record collector, Jan Masaryk."

For the Spanish record industry the Civil War was inevitably a time for belt-tightening. By September, 1936 Franco was in control of most of the country west of a line from Cadiz in the south to Irun on the Bay of Biscay; the effect of this was to put EMI's Spanish branches in opposite camps. Columbia was in Franco territory at San Sebastian on the north coast near the border with France whilst the Compania del Gramofono-Odeon, HMV's Spanish affiliate comprising the Odeon and La Voz de su Amo (His Master's Voice) labels, was located in Republican Barcelona. When the war broke out the Barcelona factory was occupied by a committee of workers and turned over in part to the production of armaments. All the British technical staff were evacuated and by November, 1937 the Republican military authorities were making ready to requisition the factory. There followed a flurry of consultations involving the Gramophone Company, EMI and the Foreign Office in London and, in Barcelona, J.N. Macleod (the Compania's manager) and the British Consul-General. Macleod decided resistance would be unwise and with the Consul-General's help secured the best terms possible for safeguarding the Gramophone Company's interests.

For the rest of the war their Spanish branch raised a series of problems for the Gramophone Company with regard to both personnel and financial matters. A Spanish member of staff was tried by a Republican court on account of his Nationalist sympathies and was condemned to death. The sentence was commuted to thirty years imprisonment and in October, 1938 efforts were being made at Hayes to have the man included in an exchange of political prisoners between the warring sides but, frustratingly, the Gramophone Company was not in a position to do anything beyond offering procedural guidance to the man's family. By the end of the same year it was clear that the fall of Barcelona was imminent (it was taken by Franco's forces on 26th January, 1939) and it was important to ensure the administrative status of Macleod and his colleague C.T. Girling would be recognised by the Nationalists once the city was in their hands. In preparation for a return to normal trading conditions the Compania del Gramofono-Odeon petitioned the authorities at Burgos (Franco's temporary capital) over this matter and at the same time sought permission to collect outstanding debts from individuals and businesses in Nationalist territory and to pay the salaries of employees who now found themselves resident in areas controlled by Franco. At the same time the Gramophone Company was doing all it could to protect the assets of the Compania, not least because the Spanish branch was in debt to its British parent to the sum of £100,000 "for goods and materials supplied."

The effects of wartime economic constraints on Spanish record output were described by Eric Edney, an English volunteer with the International Brigade. Writing in *The Gramophone* of December, 1938 he told of his off-duty searches for music while he was a Republican soldier. When it cropped up on the radio his kind of music was not always appreciated by his comrades. Live performances were rare and he was only able to attend two throughout his army service, so the gramophone became his most fruitful source of musical entertainment. On an early leave at Pastraria he found an inn where there was an ancient machine and a large, mixed collection of records that yielded great pleasure. It was even better when his Battalion acquired a gramophone and Edney enjoyed a record-buying expedition in Guadalajara, returning to his unit with discs by Wanda Landowska, Leo Blech and Conchita Supervia.

Subsequently when on leave in Madrid he came across even more exciting treasures.

"I discovered H.M.V.'s showroom in the Gran Via but it was boarded and sandbagged up, as it lies in the most shelled portion of the city. However there was a notice of their temporary headquarters and I took the Metro to Goya station and bought some records, chiefly flamenco and some recordings of Anarchist songs issued by H.M.V. sung by the Orféo Catala Choir. Some minutes walk away ... I found another record shop, and what a treat met my eyes! Old stocks of classics, chiefly Columbia (which in Spain are all 'Regal') ..."

He came away with discs by such golden age singers as Boninsegna, Slezak and Zenatello, all at bargain prices. They accompanied him

> "... all through the Aragón campaign of the Autumn with the help of the cookhouse lorry, and I had hopes of bringing them back to England, but alas, they were lost in Barcelona just before I left ..."

Edney's brief article gives a remarkably informative account of the gramophone industry in the Civil War. The new issues of Columbia and La Voz de su Amo/Odeon were not available outside the territorial divisions in which the companies were based. Apart from its purely Spanish output La Voz de su Amo was unlikely to venture beyond recordings by such reliable sellers as the singers Gigli and Lili Pons. Patriotic discs abounded and Edney makes special mention of Odeon's *Joven Guardia*, "the Spanish version of St. Galles' 'La Jeune Garde'" and La Voz de su Amo's recordings of the band of the Karl Marx Barracks, conveniently on hand in Barcelona.

An advertisement put out by La Voz de su Amo/Odeon corroborates Edney's outline of the war-related material available in Republican Spain and also demonstrates the degree to which the Compania had been politicised. Against a background of fixed bayonets a grim-faced worker wears a stylised cap of liberty bearing the initials of two powerful left-wing organisations, the FAI (Iberian Anarchist Federation) and the CNT (National Confederation of Labour). He appears to be shouting an order or words of encouragement and at the bottom of the picture the reader is urged to buy the Odeon recording of the revolutionary song *Hijos del Pueblo a las Barricadas* (Sons of the People to the Barricades). As a final sales inducement the advert carries a note that the disc is a charity issue for the benefit of victims of Fascism.

Air power played a significant part in the outcome of the Civil War. At the start the air forces on both sides were ill-equipped for the tasks required in a full-scale war but aircraft sent in by the antagonists' European backers soon transformed the situation. High-performance Russian fighter-bombers flew for the Republicans whilst Franco's Nationalists were supplied with planes and pilots by Germany and Italy. There was strong popular support in Russia for the Republicans but the logistical problems of aiding a country at the opposite end of Europe coupled with Stalin's concern over

German rearmament resulted in Russia's involvement remaining relatively low key.

With Italy and Germany the case was quite different. Spurred by his success in Abyssinia, Mussolini calculated that participation in the Civil War could be a means of extending Italy's influence in the Mediterranean and, in his typically bullish style, committed Italian land, air and naval forces to the conflict. Germany's contribution, however, was the most telling of all. It began in July, 1936 with the despatch of a number of transport planes and elderly fighters; these were followed later in the year by a tank force that set about training crews from the Nationalist army. More advanced German planes swelled the numbers until when peace came in 1939 the Luftwaffe had tested under battle conditions most of the aircraft types that were brought into service at the onset of World War II. The flying and support personnel (volunteers, so-called) were the most skilled that could be drafted from Germany and were transferred to Spain together with their dismantled planes on ships sailing under South American colours. The force, which included specially trained Spanish units, earned itself a formidable reputation as the Condor Legion.

From 1937 onwards strategic air missions flown by the Legion formed an integral part of each major campaign launched by the Nationalists. Over half a century later one name in particular can still be guaranteed to recall the work of the Condor Legion: Guernica. On 26th April, 1937 German planes laden with high explosive and incendiary bombs attacked this northern town near Bilbao for nearly three hours. Guernica's river bridge was on the route of the retreating Basque army as it fell back towards Bilbao but apart from this there were no other targets of tactical importance. It later emerged that the pulverisation of Guernica was a deliberate trial of the Luftwaffe's bombing capabilities, an experiment that accounted for the lives of around 1,600 people but left the bridge more or less unharmed. Franco's military staff would have had other reasons for mounting this air strike. Guernica had always been closely associated with the Basques' movement for independence and the smashing of the town would not only be due retribution for their stand against the Nationalists but also a symbolic denial of their political aspirations.

The war still had a long way to go after Guernica and it was not until Christmas, 1938 that Franco's army began the advance in

Catalonia that led a month later to the capture of Barcelona. Valencia and Madrid surrendered in March, 1939 and the savage war gave way to the repressive peace of Franco's rule.

Once its services were no longer needed the Condor Legion was shipped back to Germany where its exploits had been widely publicised in the media. More substantial descriptions of their operations went on sale in the bookshops where the Legion's own *Deutsche kämpfen in Spanien* (Germans fight in Spain) competed with *Kampf um Spanien* (Battle for Spain) by Werner Beumelburg, a military historian and novelist highly regarded by the Nazis for his nationalistic views. For the gramophone, Telefunken celebrated the heroes' return in the most authentic way possible by issuing a ten-inch disc of the Legion's band and chorus performing their Parade March and March of the Bomber Crews. The purely instrumental sections of these two pieces are good examples of spirited martial music in the German style but the words, enthusiastically sung by the Legionnaires, give a foretaste of the mass-produced patriotic military songs that were heard incessantly in Germany during the Second World War. The Bomber Crews' march refers in passing to the Reich's Italian allies in Spain but dwells mainly on the subjects of honour, freedom and peace which, we are to believe, were the motivation for the Legion's presence.

To the relief of Britain and her allies Franco did not join the Axis powers in their bid to seize control of Europe and North Africa. The stability gained by Spain remaining neutral enabled the new government to set about rebuilding the country in both the physical and political senses. War damage had been considerable in many major cities but with the coming of peace commercial activity was soon on the increase. A rough impression of the record industry's post-war recovery in formerly Republican Barcelona may be obtained from figures relating to the Gramophone Company's Spanish branch. Discographical information compiled by the National Library of Spain shows that La Voz de su Amo/Odeon's issues with matrix numbers in their OKA and KA series fell sharply in 1936, the year the Civil War began. In 1937 and 1938 there appear to have been no issues at all bearing these matrix prefixes and in 1939, the year hostilities ceased, there were only two. By 1940, however, business was back in full swing and the National Library's record collection reveals that, overall, more than 120 KA

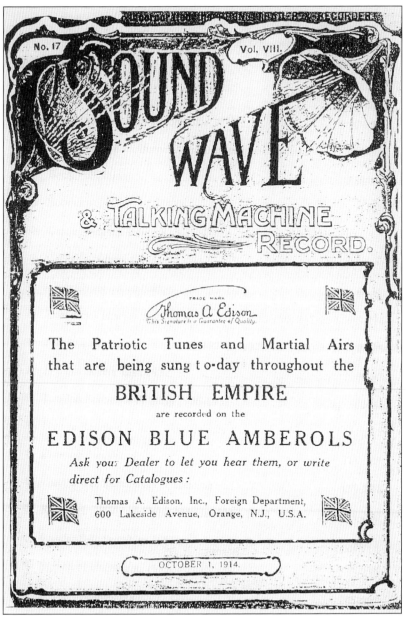

*The Edison company was quick to send patriotic cylinder recordings to its
British dealers on the outbreak of World War I.*

Columbia's distribution department dispatching cases of World War I patriotic recordings to British dealers.

(BY KIND PERMISSION OF CBS SONY).

A gramophone is well to the fore at a World War I recruiting rally in London's Trafalgar Square.

NEW RECORDS

MAGGIE TEYTE

—Our Greatest British Prima Donna Sings Exclusively for

Columbia-Rena DOUBLE SIDED **Records**

THESE—the FIRST COLUMBIA Records by Miss Maggie Teyte—are issued at standard prices by the famous singer's special request in order that these songs shall be heard by the largest possible public, the wider sales thus securing greater benefit to the Prince of Wales's Fund, to which a royalty on each record sold is paid.

10 inch 2/6
12 inch 4/-

Royalty on Each Record sold paid to PRINCE OF WALES'S FUND.

2467 { Your King and Country Want You ("Daily Mail" Recruiting Song) - - - - } 10 inch 2/6
{ The Homes they Leave Behind - - - - }

495 { Your King and Country Want You ("Daily Mail" Recruiting Song) - - - - } 12 inch 4/-
{ The Homes they Leave Behind - - - - }

Sung by MAGGIE TEYTE, Soprano.

THE SEASON'S SENSATION!

READY IN A FEW DAYS

PATRIOTIC RECORDS

A small selection from our Special Brochure bearing the flags of the Allies in colour

VOCAL

Madame CLARA BUTT (with the Guards Band)

These two records are accompanied by the Band of H.M. Coldstream Guards, conducted by Captain J. Mackenzie Rogan, M.V.O., Mus. Doc., Hon. R.A.M.

03240	God save the King 12-inch Record. 6s. 6d.	
0333	Land of Hope and Glory 12-inch Record. 12s. 6d.	Elgar

MARCEL JOURNET

03203B La Marseillaise 9s.

Mr. THORPE BATES

4-2147	The Admiral's Broom 10-inch Record. 3s. 6d.	Bevan
02228	The Midshipmite 12-inch Records. 5s. 6d.	Adams
02312	The Deathless Army	Trotère

Mr. PETER DAWSON

4-2229 The Blue Dragoons — Kennedy Russell
10-inch Record. 3s. 6d.

Mr. HARRY DEARTH

02230	A Sergeant of the Line 12-inch Records. 5s. 6d.	Squire
0.291	My Old Shako	Trotère
0.465	They all love Jack	Adams

Mr. STEWART GARDNER

0284 Danny Deever — Damrosch

Mr. ROBERT RADFORD

4-2319	Drake goes West 12-inch Record. 5s. 6d.	Sanderson
0399	When the King went forth to War	Koenemann

Mr. ROBERT HOWE

0464 A Soldier's Song — Mascheroni
12-inch Record. 5s. 6d.

Mr. R. KENNERLEY RUMFORD

0198 Three for Jack — Squire
12-inch Record. 5s. 6d.

Mr. CHARLES TREE

02507 Up from Somerset — Sanderson
12-inch Record. 5s. 6d.

CHURCH CHOIR (Mixed)

Solo by Mr. THORPE BATES

4910 The National Anthem
10-inch Record. 3s. 6d.

CHORUS OF LA SCALA OPERA, MILAN

54.54 Soldiers' Chorus ("Faust") — Gounod
10-inch Record. 3s. 6d.

HARRY LAUDER

0247B Ta-ta, my bonnie Maggie darling
12-inch Record. 5s. 6d.

LEWIS WALLER

1443 The Charge of the Light Brigade — Tennyson
10-inch Record. 3s. 6d.

BANDS

BAND OF H.M. COLDSTREAM GDS.

Conducted by Capta. J. Mackenzie Rogan, M.V.O., Mus. Doc., Hon. R.A.M.

10-inch double-sided Records. 3s. 6d.

B 105	God bless the Prince of Wales God save the King	
B 106	La Marseillaise Rule Britannia	Bixio / Arne
B 118	Trooping the Colour In a Clockmaker's Shop	
B 102	La Czarine (composed for the last ceremonial visit of the Czar of Russia to Paris) La Mattchiche	Ganne / Borel Clerc
B 112	Regimental Marches of the Brigade of Guards March Past of the Lancashire Brigade	

12-inch double-sided Records. 5s. 6d.

C 130	1812 Overture Zampa Overture	Tschaikowsky / Herold
C 297	Review of the Brigade of Guards. Part 1. Review of the Brigade of Guards. Part 2.	
C 112	(Held in Hyde Park, April 28, 1913) Land of Hope and Glory Musica Proibita	Elgar / Gastaldon

DESCRIPTIVE

GRAMOPHONE BAND

2-108 Departure of a Troopship
10-inch Record. 3s. 6d.

Get your copy of the Patriotic List

Columbia's advance publicity for Maggie Teyte's recording of the best known British recruiting song of World War I. From Sound Wave and Talking Machine Record.
(BY KIND PERMISSION OF CBS SONY).

HMV's releases for September 1914 included this list of Patriotic Records.

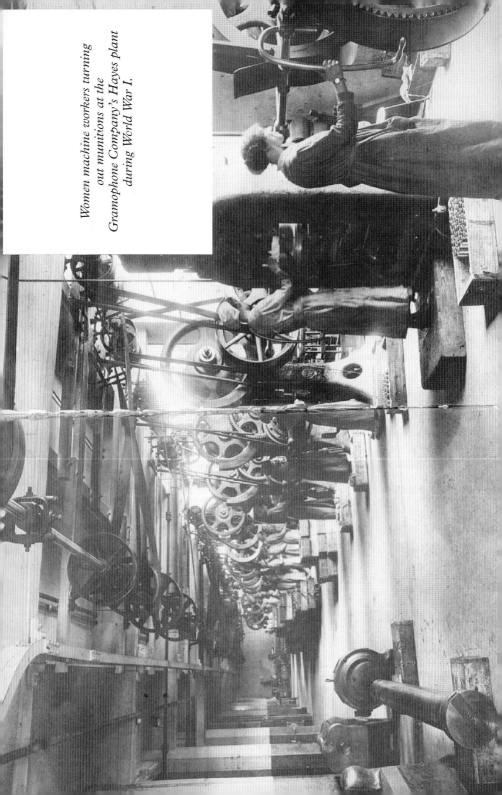

Women machine workers turning out munitions at the Gramophone Company's Hayes plant during World War I.

"The Passing Show of 1915"

SUPERB EXCLUSIVE RECORDS by ALL the ORIGINAL ARTISTS

Among the most delightful Revue Records ever issued are these sparkling numbers by Revue celebrities. The Palace Theatre Revue is easily the finest one of the season.

BASIL HALLAM
12-in., 5/6
The Constant Lover   02563

GWEN. BROGDEN
10-in., 3/6
Mr. Producer   2-3064

ARTHUR PLAYFAIR
10-in., 3/6
J. J. Juggernaut 4-2536

NELSON KEYS
10-in., 3/6
The Four-Foot ten Brigade   4-2537
(Finnikin Fusiliers)

NELSON KEYS AND GWENDOLINE BROGDEN
12-in., 5/6
The Home of the Hun   04125
(God bless old England)

BASIL HALLAM . ARTHUR PLAYFAIR . NELSON KEYS AND DOUGLAS PHILLIPS
12-in., 5/6
When the clock strikes 13   04124

Harrowing tales of what *might* happen when the clock forgets itself and performs a biker's do en instead of the conventional twelve

London's GREATEST Revue

Elsie Janis

in a **striking Fox-Trot pose**
(from a camera portrait by Hoppé)

HER NEW RECORDS

12-in., 5/6
Prudence   03403

The Fortune Teller   03402
(Adapted from " For he's a Ragpicker ")
DUETS with BASIL HALLAM

10-in., 3/6
Ballin' the Jack—Fox-Trot   2-4251
The words of the song tell you how to dance the Fox-Trot, the vogue of the day.

12-in., 5/6
Same old song   04026

A LETTER from ELSIE JANIS

who is an **EXCLUSIVE** " His Master's Voice" artist

To   April 15
THE GRAMOPHONE CO., LTD.

Dear Sirs,

Your wonderful "His Master's Voice" records, unequalled for artistic fidelity, harness to the home the world's greatest artists in Concert and Vaudeville.

You claim me to belong to the Great in Vaudeville, and have again approached me to secure records of my successes in "The Passing Show of 1915." I am delighted to agree: if your recording is as true as in my last year's records of "The Passing Show," then indeed will you secure the living personality of

Elsie Janis

"His Master's Voice" Records

A two-page spread in HMV's May 1915 list of new releases confirms the popularity of the wartime revues.

Russian Revolution. Lenin addresses the acoustic recording horn, March 1919.

Weimar Republic. Berlin street beggar, 1923. Many disabled ex-servicemen earned a living in a similar way in British cities and towns during the 1920s and 1930s.

*Under Republican control HMV's Barcelona branch advertises
a Spanish Civil War patriotic recording.*

matrix numbers were used in that year. For technical or artistic reasons it is unlikely that every matrix cut in the studio would have been passed for publication and it may be assumed that the number of discs actually issued would have been somewhat lower; nevertheless, the broad figure confirms the sudden increase in production once the fighting was over. That the Compania del Gramofono-Odeon was so quickly back in a trading position is a tribute to the skill and tact with which from the sidelines in Barcelona J. N. Macleod and C. T. Girling had helped it to ride out the war years.

⋆　　⋆　　⋆

On the morning of 30th January, 1933 the German president, General Paul von Hindenburg, conferred upon Adolf Hitler the office of Chancellor. That evening, to celebrate their leader's appointment as the country's head of government, an exultant Nazi Party marched for hours in a torchlight procession through the heart of Berlin; it was the culmination of fifteen years of political manoeuvring which, more often than not, had gone hand in hand with flagrant violence. From this time onwards the leitmotifs of night and fire recurred at various crucial moments during the twelve-year span of what Hitler envisaged would be the thousand-year Reich.

The theatrical torchlight finales to the Party's annual Nuremberg rallies were an integral part of political gatherings stage-managed with meticulous attention to detail from start to finish. Only a month after Hitler came to power the Reichstag (Germany's parliament building in Berlin) was seriously damaged by fire. Marinus van der Lubbe, a Dutch communist, was conveniently discovered and arrested when engaged in attempted arson on the premises but there is little doubt that the Nazis themselves were responsible for the main conflagration. They clamorously attributed the blame to the German Communist Party which they immediately proscribed and then went on to restrict the basic civil rights of freedom of speech and freedom of the press. Other far-reaching constitutional changes were to follow. The civil service and the judiciary became, in effect, National Socialist institutions and by mid-summer 1933 Germany was a one-party state; the following year trade unions ceased to have any individual existence after being forcibly merged to form a single Nazi-controlled labour organisation.

Culture was an early victim of Nazi ideology. The events of the evening of 10th May, 1933 set in motion the systematic destruction of books by Jews and any other writers considered to be degenerate or subversive and therefore unfit to play a part in the intellectual life of Aryan Germany. That night in the Opernplatz, Berlin and in university towns and cities throughout the country bonfires were prepared and the works of Marx, Thomas Mann, Heine, Kästner, Brecht, Remarque and many more, including undesirable foreigners like Freud, Proust, Hemingway and Jack London, were thrown into the purifying flames. As students and academics burnt the printed word they were praised in a broadcast speech by Josef Goebbels. Likewise, the music of Jewish and other decadent composers was banished from concert halls, recital rooms, opera houses and recording studios. Indeed, in Nuremberg, the Nazi political capital, measures were taken against it even before Hitler became Chancellor. The actress Gerda Redlich was there in the cast of a 1932 production of Shakespeare's *A Midsummer Night's Dream* and years later she told the historian Alex de Jonge how

> "All of a sudden we were not allowed to use Mendelssohn's music. It was no longer lovely music, it had become Jewish music ... We went through all the actions as if the music were playing. There was no wedding march, but we walked in the rhythm. The silence was uncanny, and the audience giggled hysterically. It lasted two nights, then we had stinkbombs. I had had enough and I left."

Differences over policy soon divided the highest-ranking Nazis and Hitler saw his status as Party leader threatened by men who favoured a more radically socialist restructuring of Germany than he was prepared to countenance. Hitler accused his opponents of plotting against him and the new Germany he was creating; his revenge was swift and totally ruthless. On 29th-30th June, 1934, the Night of the Long Knives, General Kurt von Schleicher (Hitler's predecessor as Chancellor), the highly influential Gregor Strasser who had charge of the Party's political machinery and Ernst Roehm, the commander of the SA, the Nazis' para-military street fighters, were murdered together with other major and minor figures in the movement. The number of those killed in the purge varies from the seventy seven admitted by Hitler to a post World War II estimate of more than a thousand.

The Party rally of September, 1935 was the occasion chosen by Hitler to give a facade of legality to the Nazis' treatment of Germany's Jewish population. The notorious Nuremberg Laws stripped German Jews of their citizenship, prevented them marrying Germans and made it illegal for them to have Germans as their servants. Inevitably, anti-Semitism now flourished without restraint. The murder of a German diplomat at the Paris Embassy on 7th November, 1938 by a young Jewish refugee from the Nazi regime was used as the excuse for the supposedly spontaneous demonstrations against the Jews throughout Germany forty eight hours later.

Once again, night was the cover for outrageous acts of violence. What happened during the hours of darkness on 9th-10th November, 1938 (known as the Kristallnacht, the night of broken glass) was not spontaneous but had been planned by Reinhard Heydrich, Himmler's second-in-command in the Gestapo. The property and persons of known Jews suffered brutal attacks; synagogues, shops and houses were smashed and set on fire; men, women and children caught up in the rampage were killed; looting was widespread. A further turn of the screw came a little later when the Jews were denied insurance payments for their losses whilst at the same time an enormous collective fine was imposed on them by the state for what Hermann Goering cynically referred to as their abominable crimes. The Kristallnacht brought Hitler's anti-Semitic policy one stage closer to its logical conclusion. This was reached during the Second World War when in January, 1942 in Berlin the details of the Final Solution were discussed and approved; from then onwards the principles of the industrial production line were applied to the existing genocide process. The Jews of the occupied countries were transported to Auschwitz and the other extermination camps in Poland. There they were either worked to death as slave labour or consigned straight to the gas chambers and thence to the crematoria, where specially designed banks of ovens reduced the maximum number of corpses to smoke and ashes in the minimum of time. Such was the totalitarian state in which the German record industry operated during the Third Reich.

When Hitler was in Berlin waiting for the call from Hindenburg at the end of January, 1933 he stayed at his favourite hotel, the

Kaiserhof. Ernst (Putzi) Hanfstängl, Hitler's one-time press officer and private pianist, remembered how the Führer would sit in the palm court enjoying the music of Barnabas von Geczy's "pseudo-Hungarian" orchestra, the reputation of which was by no means restricted just to Berlin or Germany. Parlophone's British catalogue for 1934-1935 contained a considerable number of von Geczy's recordings which give some idea of what Hitler found so attractive about the orchestra. Light music was represented by *Country Wedding in Hungary* and *At the Vintage in Tokaj* by a composer named Por, but more durable works appeared in the form of selections from Lehár's *Merry Widow*, Kálmán's *Gipsy Princess*, Romberg's *Student Prince* and Richard Strauss's *Der Rosenkavalier* as well as the predictable medley of Johann Strauss waltzes. Many more discs were listed in the dance music section of the catalogue where von Geczy's orchestra rubbed shoulders with a similar central European group, the Dajos Bela Orchestra. Other far more familiar bands providing dance music for Parlophone were those of Duke Ellington and Bix Beiderbecke but the company's British main stay was the band of Harry Roy which recorded prolifically. Roy's American-style bouncy rhythm was particularly suited to jazzy numbers, although the band was equally at home playing the sweeter music of the day. The titles of von Geczy's recordings, however, show that his repertoire concentrated on the more sentimental type of popular music. This tendency is clearly seen amongst the foxtrots and waltzes where titles like *You are my Dream*, *My Song of Love*, *When the Lilac blooms again* and *When you've gone* predominate. The current taste for sham-Hawaiian music was catered for in such pieces as *Greetings to Hawaii*, but it was the tango, which reached Europe around 1910 and had grown in popularity from the 1920s onwards, that made up the largest group of the orchestra's offerings in the 1934-1935 catalogue. Obviously the patrons of the Kaiserhof must have been very keen on this impassioned dance but some decidedly odd titles (*Oh! Mr. Leader, Erica, don't you want a Boy Friend?* and *Hawaiian Stars are gleaming*) suggest that, musically, Latin American authenticity was not of the essence.

The orchestra, like all others in the country, had to comply with the Nazi embargo on Jewish music. It is a chastening thought that the light-hearted melodies on two of von Geczy's discs in this catalogue, waltz sequences from Offenbach's *La Belle Hélène* and Kálmán's *Gypsy Princess*, would qualify for inclusion on the index of prohibited music in Germany merely because of the composers' Jewish ancestry.

EMI made generous provision for von Geczy's British fans as in addition to the recordings that appeared on Parlophone those made for Electrola were issued by His Master's Voice. The HMV catalogue for 1939-40 listed all the company's recordings available at June, 1939, amongst them a block of twenty nine discs by von Geczy. As on Parlophone, there was again a stable companion, this time Marek Weber's orchestra, arguably the most accomplished of the many light music ensembles of the inter-war years. Sadly, both Marek Weber and Dajos Bela were to appear on the official Nazi black list of Jewish musicians.

Whereas von Geczy's Parlophone titles comprised mainly music from the dance floor the HMV issues reflected the palm court side of the orchestra's work. Such was their range that it is now difficult to detect any strong orchestral character emerging from the profusion of pieces on offer. Cradle songs by Mozart, Max Reger and Järnefelt, the Hindu Song from Rimsky-Korsakov's *Sadko*, Sibelius's *Valse Triste*, Tchaikovsky's *Chanson Triste* and Francis Thomé's *Andante Religioso* hint again at a somewhat sentimental approach but this is offset by a livelier group of eight assorted serenades. One of these was the immensely popular *Donkey Serenade* from the 1937 Hollywood film version of Rudolf Friml's operetta *The Firefly*. A ten-inch disc was devoted to a *Paul Lincke Medley* and one side of another to what is perhaps that composer's best loved number, the waltz *Unrequited Love*. With Lincke, von Geczy was, politically speaking, on the safest possible ground as the music of this leading exponent of Berlin-style operetta was warmly endorsed by the chief Nazi opinion-formers. Elsewhere in the list waltzes were relatively sparse (largely because the Marek Weber orchestra seems to have been given preference in the Strauss family's music) but one of those recorded by von Geczy was English, the delightful *Destiny* by Sidney Baynes. Also calculated to attract British record buyers was Noel Gay's *The Lambeth Walk* from the long-running musical *Me and My Girl*. The very last item was that old favourite *The Teddy Bears' Picnic*, seemingly so English though actually written by an American, John W. Bratton.

British sales of von Geczy recordings did so well that even during the Second World War HMV's 1942-43 catalogue still listed a surprising twenty three discs. By 1947, however, deletions had taken their toll and only seven discs remained, amongst them *Destiny* and *The Teddy Bears' Picnic*. The staying power of these two recordings was remarkable with the latter making its final appearance in the 1955-56 catalogue where, though not for much longer, the dwindling number of 78s shared the pages with HMV's early LPs and 45s.

Superficial though they were, Adolf Hitler's musical interests extended far beyond what he listened to with such pleasure at the Kaiserhof Hotel. Whether pontificating on the cultural significance of Wagner's works for the new Germany or putting his personal stamp on the militaristic music that was part and parcel of Nazi ceremonial Hitler's opinions were inevitably accepted as gospel by the Party. Thus it was that in July, 1937 the Reichsmusikkammer (the organisation in charge of all musical matters) decreed that by order of the Führer the *Nibelungen March* which was played for the entry of the standards at the beginning of the annual Nuremberg rally and again at the close of proceedings was, from that date onwards, to be reserved solely for these two rituals. On 1st December, 1938 another official announcement restricted the use of the *Badenweiler March* to occasions graced by the Führer's presence, a telling illustration of Hitler's manipulation of the cult of personality surrounding him. A further edict came in February, 1939 when the Reichsmusikkammer published Hitler's instructions on the precise tempo at which the *Deutschlandlied*, the German national anthem, was to be performed. It was also laid down that the *Horst-Wessel-Lied*, the most hallowed of the Nazis' marching songs, was always to be taken at a speed befitting a revolutionary call to arms.

Horst Wessel was born in 1907 and in due course joined the SA, opportunely combining his paramilitary activities with the time-honoured profession of pimp. His enthusiasm for the National Socialist movement was so great that he was inspired to write some fiery verses which Goebbels published in the Party's newspaper *Der Angriff* in 1929. The following year Wessel died after being shot by a rival member of Berlin's vice network who was connected with the Red Front communists. Goebbels immediately capitalised on the death of this ready-made martyr. Wessel's link with the prostitution racket was totally ignored and the propaganda machine set about honouring the hero's name in a variety of ways, most notably with the *Horst-Wessel-Lied*, a musical setting of his short poem.

Opinions have differed widely on the origin of the tune the Nazis chose to go with Wessel's words. The modern German reference book *Das grosse Lexikon des Dritten Reiches* describes it as a sailors' song but Putzi Hanfstängl was equally certain it was a piece of Viennese turn of the century cabaret music. Part of the real answer is to be found on the label of Telefunken's 1934 recording by a band and chorus of Nazi storm troopers; here the composer is given as Méhul, the Etienne Méhul who had written patriotic songs during the French Revolution and whose seldom heard operatic music was much admired by Sir Thomas Beecham. David Mason's notes to the Pearl/OPAL *Rise of Fascism* CD complete the picture by tracing the tune to the opera *Joseph* that had its première in 1807.

With its words translated into English the *Horst-Wessel-Lied* was taken into service as a marching song by Sir Oswald Mosley's British Union of Fascists, a party which paraded its anti-Semitic credentials at provocative, often bloody demonstrations in the Jewish East End of London. In 1935 a performance by the Union's Male Voice Choir (sounding a touch more inhibited than their Telefunken counterparts) was recorded by Decca in their SP series of special discs which, until the Second World War, was used for privately commissioned work that did not appear in the company's commercial catalogues. At a time when only a few British firms had the means both to record and press shellac discs to special order it is a fair assumption that Decca would have charged handsomely for their services in producing what must have been a relatively small run of copies for Mosley's blackshirt followers. By the end of the decade, however, the mounting alarm over the actions of Hitler and Mussolini had seriously eroded what little credibility the British Union of Fascists had achieved as a political movement. Even so, during the Second World War the government wisely took no chances and in May, 1940 Mosley was arrested and placed under detention in the interests of national security. In prison his health deteriorated and as in the official view he then no longer posed any great risk he was released on humanitarian grounds in November, 1943.

Considering their wholesale appropriation of radio, film and press it is at first sight surprising that the Nazis did not exploit the gramophone more as a mass communication channel, particularly in view of Hitler's compelling oratory which regularly brought his audiences to the verge of frenzy. Curt Riess's explanation of this apparent neglect is that once records were sold to the public in quantity through the normal trade outlets they ceased to be under full Party control; films, the discs cut by broadcasting stations and the Party's own recordings could be rapidly withdrawn should the need arise, but commercial records were a latent political hazard. In his conduct of affairs Hitler was capable of seizing upon anything which at the moment was advantageous to his personal image or to the government's standing: to have in general circulation recordings of declarations or promises that later might be jettisoned would imperil the Führer's aura of infallibility by revealing the gulf between rhetoric and reality.

Riess's interpretation is convincing enough as far as it goes but other factors must also have influenced the decision to steer clear of the gramophone. Hitler's style of oratory in which he would introduce his subject at some length, move on to a detailed exposition of his ideas and then conclude with a rabble-rousing peroration required plenty of time, on occasion as much as two hours, to achieve its intended cumulative effect. Reckoning the duration of a twelve inch 78 r.p.m. record side at four minutes, an hour-long speech would take up seven or eight double-sided discs; this would not have been a very enticing prospect for any commercial record company since the spoken word recordings in those days were rarely so lengthy. Even if the content of a speech offered no particular hostages to fortune, once market forces came into play there was the worrying possibility that record buyers (including the most faithful Party members) might decide there were more essential or attractive goods on which to spend their hard-earned money. It was therefore prudent of Hitler to distance himself from a medium in which recordings of political speeches would be competing for mass sales with the latest popular hits.

Nevertheless, thanks mainly to recordings made for German radio archives and by foreign monitoring stations the voices of Hitler and other leading Nazis survive in sufficient quantity to form a valuable oral supplement to the printed documentation of Nazism's rise and fall. From the end of the Second World War to the present day many of these speeches have been dubbed and marketed by small independent firms or individual traders to cater for the enduring (perhaps sometimes unhealthy) interest in the Third Reich. The July, 1959 issue of the American *Schwann Long Playing Record Catalog*, for instance, gave prime advertising space to a new LP entitled *Hitler's Inferno* issued by the New York company Dauntless International. It was, according to the copywriter, "The record that Germany is trying to suppress!!!". Its contents included extracts from speeches by Hitler and Goebbels and from proceedings at the Nuremberg War Crimes Trial together with numerous marching songs sung by Nazi storm troopers. The advert went on to state:

> "Never before has this shocking material been heard in the United States. The joyous quality of the music is frightening when one thinks of the destruction that occurred during this period of time!"

The appearance of *Hitler's Inferno* in the record shops in the summer of 1959 may not have been entirely fortuitous since in the previous year George Lincoln Rockwell had founded his American Nazi Party which matched Hitler's ruthlessness in its attitude towards Jews and blacks. Dauntless International presumably meant their disc to be a salutary reminder to decent Americans of the evils of Nazism; on the other hand, there can be little doubt that the recording would also have sold well, though for less wholesome reasons, amongst Rockwell's obnoxious followers.

Over the years there have been other more extensive collections of Nazi spoken word recordings, notably the audio cassette series *Sounds of Our Times* produced by a specialist British dealer for mail order customers. Covering the period 1930 to 1945 these dubbings constitute an effective survey of landmarks in the history of European fascism, as does the previously mentioned *Rise of Fascism* compilation in its more concise format. In the section which follows, recordings contained in these two sources are indicated by (ST) or (RF) respectively.

Well before the Third Reich came into being Goebbels was the speaker (RF) on a disc recorded by the Party's Propaganda Department in 1930. The already familiar litany was delivered with chilling conviction. The Weimar Republic had been a total failure and the nation was now suffering the disastrous effects of galloping inflation; Germany must be restored to its rightful position where it would no longer be subject to the corrupting influence of the English, the French, the Jews and the League of Nations. Economic and political stability were the prerequisites for full employment, fair wages and proper housing: all these National Socialism would provide as well as finding a solution to the problem of "Raum" for the people of Germany.

1932 brought two Presidential elections in which Hitler stood unsuccessfully against Hindenburg and two Reichstag elections, neither of which gave the Nazis an overall majority. A recorded version (ST and RF) of Hitler's all-purpose manifesto, his *Appell an die Nation* (Appeal to the Nation) was issued on the Party's own label, Die Braune Platte (The Brown Disc), a name that unmistakably associated the records with that ever-present manifestation of organised Nazism, the brown-uniformed SA. The eight-minute speech covers much the same ground as Goebbels had done two years earlier and starts with the dramatic announcement that the great time for decision had come. In this plea for all Germans to unite under his leadership Hitler constantly uses the politician's stock device of repetition, referring time and again to the workers, the agricultural community, the middle classes, the intellectuals, the Protestants and the Catholics and clearly has to hurry to complete the latter part of the speech before time runs out.

With the help of recordings from 1933 (ST) the progress of the Nazis in that momentous year can be followed in considerable detail. There is Hitler's first speech after his appointment as Chancellor at the end of January, followed by his address the next month to a massive gathering at Berlin's Sportpalast(ST). Another Reichstag election had Hitler again canvassing for national support in his *Aufruf an das deutsche Volk* (Call to the German People) (ST). After the Reichstag fire of 27th February the Nazis gained sufficient backing from the remaining deputies (the Communists having been ousted for their alleged involvement in the fire) to pass legislation suspending the Weimar Republic's constitution and conferring Draconian powers on the government for the next three years; part of a Reichstag speech by Hitler (ST) on this Enabling Act still survives. Having secured their parliamentary base the Nazis immediately set about creating the new Germany in their own image, a process that continued without further political hindrance after the Reichstag election of 12th November in which they were returned unopposed.

As well as Hitler's voice that of Goebbels was increasingly heard during 1933, the year that the Party recorded and sold in aid of its own funds a eulogy by the now Minister for Public Enlightenment and Propaganda in memory of Horst Wessel. His broadcast speech in praise of the burning of the books in Berlin on 10th May was preserved in radio archives (ST) and affords another grim example of Goebbels's dedicated anti-Semitism. Perhaps the most significant recording to come down from 1933 is that of Hitler on 14th October announcing Germany's withdrawal from the League of Nations. This intergovernmental organisation, the forerunner of the United Nations, had its origins in the Paris Peace Conference held at the end of the Great War. The creation of a body designed to settle future international differences by amicable means was successfully advocated by Woodrow Wilson, the American President. Germany eventually joined the League in September, 1926, more or less the half way mark in the short life of the Weimar Republic. Hitler, however, regarded the League as an ineffectual talking shop and knew perfectly well it had only very limited means with which to enforce any stern resolutions it might pass on matters of deep international concern. When Germany cut its links with the League the Nazi dictatorship was free to threaten the stability of Europe with little likelihood of being faced with strong counter-actions, a situation that Hitler repeatedly exploited to his advantage until the outbreak of the Second World War.

In 1934 Rudolf Hess, a devoted member of the Nazi movement from its earliest days, was appointed the Party's deputy leader in which post as well as his public role he played a key part in the discussions and decision-making of Hitler's inner councils. Recordings (ST) of Hess taken from radio broadcasts give some idea of the work entrusted to him as a political presenter. It was Hess who spoke to Germany on 2nd August, 1934 on the death of President Hindenburg and in December, 1936 he broadcast the Party's Christmas greetings to the nation, displaying the benevolent image so assiduously cultivated at this time of year when high-ranking Nazis would show how much they cared for the German poor by being photographed on the streets of Berlin shaking collecting boxes in aid of charities. Hess's services were later lost to the Party when in 1941, just before the German invasion of Russia, he flew off alone to Scotland. Motivated by the irrational belief that the power and influence he wielded in Germany would be universally respected, he made the hazardous solo flight to enemy territory with the intention of negotiating a peace settlement with Great Britain. For his pains he spent the remainder of the war in British custody, was subsequently tried at Nuremburg and imprisoned for the rest of his life at Spandau gaol in Berlin, where he died in 1987.

Hitler's vision of the reborn Germany's future was conveyed in 1937 to district and area officials of the Party through secret speeches, extracts from which may still be heard today (ST). During the next two years Hitler made it painfully obvious that Germany intended to be the dominant power in Europe, taking whatever it wanted by force if blustering diplomacy failed to produce the required outcome. On the excuse of protecting the interests of the country's allegedly oppressed National Socialists Austria was invaded on 12th March, 1938; a plebiscite on union with Germany was held the following month and, true to form in a dictatorship, the result was that 99.75% of Austrian voters were in favour. To coincide with the plebiscite a recording was made by the Deutsche Grammophon Gesellschaft for the Party on which the speaker was the Nazi Food Minister and Farmers' Leader, Richard-Walther Darré. His widely publicised views on the heroic nature of the Nordic races, the inherent nobility of the German peasant farmer, Germany's need for Lebensraum and the worthlessness of the Jews earned him political office when the Nazis came to power. Darré, though, was essentially an ideologist rather than a planner and when his handling of Germany's wartime food supplies failed to match Hitler's expectations he was rusticated in May, 1942.

Darré's brief address (RF) used the 1938 plebiscite as a convenient starting point for a survey of the achievements of the German farming community during the five years that Hitler had been the country's leader. Back in 1927 in the bad old days of the Weimar Republic 35% of the nation's food had to be imported but now, despite enormous difficulties, that figure had been reduced to 19%. When Germany no longer had to rely on these remaining outside sources its freedom and the success of the Führer's foreign policy would be ensured. The homily was rounded off with Darré urging his listeners at this important moment in German history to think back gratefully on all that the Führer had already done for them.

With Austria firmly welded to the Reich, the next objective was Czechoslovakia. By means of brinkmanship involving threats and overt preparations for war Hitler successfully engineered an international agreement in September, 1938 which granted the transfer to Germany of some 10,000 square miles of Czech territory; six months later in March, 1939 when Slovakia declared its independence Hitler sent his army into the Czech provinces of Bohemia and Moravia, proclaiming them a German protectorate. Throughout these troubled times Hitler and Goebbels were regularly making speeches designed to keep the political situation in a state of flux; many of these tirades (ST) were recorded and are still capable of making the listener feel in uncomfortably close contact with the Nazi dictatorship in full cry.

Further documentary recordings from 1939 (ST) punctuate the grim sequence of events that led to the Second World War. On 30th January Hitler yet again aired Germany's grievances in a two-hour speech to the Reichstag delegates and it was the same sycophantic audience that on 28th April heard his rejection of President Roosevelt's efforts to obtain assurances that Germany and Italy would respect the sovereign status of thirty one European and Near Eastern countries. Then at Kassel in early June Hitler addressed the German armed forces - this at a time when the Nazis were deliberately bringing the dispute with Poland over the free city of Danzig (Gdansk) to crisis point. Incidents during the summer in the German-Polish border area were excuse enough for Hitler to profess that his patience was exhausted. His broadcast speech to the Reichstag on 1st September was received ecstatically by the delegates (RF) and with foreboding by the world's democracies. In it he denounced the Poles for their acts of provocation and atrocities committed against German nationals: he had therefore decided that Poland must be treated in the same way that Poland had treated Germany. Hitler's army invaded without any declaration of war being made and Poland became the next victim of Nazi aggression; two days later Britain and France were formally at war with Germany.

While the Axis dictators pursued their expansionist programmes their British acolyte, Sir Oswald Mosley, worked hard, though with limited success, to convince his fellow countrymen that the way of fascism was the road to Utopia. A recording (ST) originally issued on flexible Durium 78 r.p.m. discs of a rally at the Royal Albert Hall, London in 1934 conveys the atmosphere of the occasion remarkably well. Before the main event the orchestra plays a march that is followed by great applause from the large audience and concerted shouts of "We want Mosley". The speech echoes those being made in Nazi Germany: there was a vital need for "a policy in accord with the new economic facts of the modern age"; they must "build a Britain worthy of the sacrifice our generation made', and thus "move into the new civilisation of fascism". Mosley then plays up to his audience by criticising in mock-sorrowful tones the apathy of politicians such as Stanley Baldwin at a time when "you want a movement that represents England awake". In conclusion he praises the men who created the British Empire and asserts that their spirit lives on in the Blackshirt movement. As a token of solidarity with their Italian comrades the band strikes up *Giovinezza*, but clearly not many of those present knew the words. The proceedings are then brought to an appropriately patriotic close with the playing and singing of *God Save the King*.

A more intimate side of Mosley's political style is revealed in the two short speeches recorded in the mid-1930s by Decca for the British Union of Fascists' own Greater Britain Record label (RF). The theme of *Comrades in Struggle* is the importance of keeping up the momentum of their revolutionary movement in its fight to save the soul of Britain. *British Union* concentrates on one of the main ingredients of Mosley's policy, the menace of Jewish-dominated international finance, which he denounces as the force responsible for flooding the country with cheap foreign merchandise turned out by sweated labour. British industry stood no chance against this unfair competition which undercut our own prices so drastically that British goods were in danger of being squeezed out of the market. Fascism, he claimed, was the only system capable of uniting the country and fighting this deadly threat to the economy.

Despite the occasional trace of crescendo, Mosley's smooth, carefully modulated voice in the Greater Britain Record speeches contrasts sharply with Hitler's rasp and Mussolini's roar. The demagogue of the London mass meetings gives way to a speaker who has for the moment forsaken large-scale effects and instead is putting over his message almost as if he were chatting to friends around the fireside. Yet however persuasive Mosley may have sounded on disc, his man-to-man attempt to present himself as the epitome of sweet reasonableness was effectively discredited by the violent conduct of his own followers in their marches through the streets of London.

From 1933 onwards the virus of anti-Semitism attacked the German commercial record companies in a variety of far-reaching ways; hitherto dormant cells of Nazi sympathisers emerged from the shadows and flourished; Jewish employees from blue-collar workers to senior executives were forced out and left to survive as best they could in a country where their only hope of work was with their co-religionists; music by Jewish composers was withdrawn from the catalogues and banned from the repertoire; and Jewish recording artists, no matter how famous, became non-persons save for the occasions when they served as the butt of racist abuse.

The Lindström company which controlled German Columbia, Parlophone and Odeon suffered particularly badly at the highest administrative level from the immediate campaign against the Jews. Richard Seligsohn, an important board member and internationally respected figure in the gramophone industry, was obliged to resign, but the Nazis had an even more crucial target in their sights, the head of the company himself, Max Straus. Curt Riess describes the humiliations suffered by Straus who entered his office one morning to find his role had been taken over by an ambitious engineer, Dr. Kepler, whose main qualification for this meteoric promotion was that his Nazi Party membership dated back to the movement's earliest days. Kepler's unsuitability was soon apparent and Straus was asked to resume his position - as a temporary measure. It was during this distressing time that Riess witnessed a chance meeting on Berlin's Unter den Linden between Straus and Hjalmar Schacht, the banker who was shortly to become Hitler's economics minister. Straus asked Schacht what he thought of the present state of affairs in Germany and the latter grudgingly conceded that it was an awkward situation for Straus as a Jew; the brief conversation came frigidly to a close with Schacht recommending Straus to reconcile himself to the fact that he was, in a manner of speaking, a casualty of war. With Lindström being part of the EMI organisation and therefore British-owned, the reinstated Straus had some reason to hope that the Nazis would now leave him alone. His optimism, however, was unfounded and in mid-1935 when in

London on business he read a newspaper report stating he had asked to resign from the company and that his request had been granted. In this malevolent fashion the Nazis rid themselves of the man who, with his partner Heinrich Zunz, had bought up the original small Lindström workshop in 1904 and transformed it into one of Europe's major record producers. Understandably, Straus never returned to Germany.

Presumably because he was a businessman rather than a musician, Max Straus did not feature in the *Lexikon der Juden in der Musik*,[4] the official blacklist published in 1940 as part of a series of books produced by the Nazi Institute for Research into the Jewish Question (Institut der NSDAP zur Erforschung der Judenfrage). The record industry itself, as opposed to its recording artists, did not provide many candidates for the *Lexikon* although Ernst Viebig, a conductor, composer and writer on music was noted as being a producer for HMV's German label, Electrola, from 1925 to 1928 and subsequently for Orchestrola Vocalion-Berlin. Despite the turgid prose style of Nazi bureaucracy it is clear from their preface that for the editors, Theo Stengel and Herbert Gerigk, compiling the *Lexikon* had been a labour of love. Similar listings had appeared in the past but these were all superseded by their *Lexikon* which, they said, was now the definitive source of information for all those responsible for protecting the Third Reich from the contaminating influence of Jewish music, music making and musicology. The book codified what needed to be known and was, in effect, the Nazis' justification for the persecution visited upon the German music world since 1933.

The diligence of the research workers was remarkable, resulting in minutely detailed entries sometimes as brief, yet sinister, as that for the emigré

ELKAN, Josef. Born Wesel 9.1.1885. Singer and dentist. Since 1937 living in Southampton (England).

The 1943 issue of the *Lexikon*, which brought the number of copies printed up to 14,000, made the point that the editors had been greatly assisted in their task by the registers of births, marriages and deaths and other documents now open to them in the occupied countries of Europe. It is almost a relief to find that so rigorous a guide was not infallible for there was no entry for Solomon, the renowned British pianist, whose recordings and public performances had earned him an international reputation.

98

With inadvertent omissions of this sort in mind the editors cordially welcomed for inclusion at a later date any additional names the *Lexikon's* users might be able to supply. To complete the identification process, long lists of rank and file Jewish professional musicians not important enough to qualify for the *Lexikon* were published as part of the official announcements (*Amtliche Mitteilungen*) of the Reichsmusikkammer, from which organisation they were henceforth excluded and therefore no longer eligible for employment in the Third Reich.

No distinction was drawn in the blacklist between composers of popular and serious music. At one extreme were Irving Berlin, George Gershwin and Jerome Kern, though the editors had to admit that watertight proof of these American songwriters' assured Jewishness was not at present available to them; in complete contrast at the other end of the musical spectrum were figures like Mahler, Mendelssohn and Meyerbeer whose racial status was not in the slightest doubt. The ideologues of the Nazi Party had no hesitation in denying German audiences and record buyers access to music that was freely enjoyed elsewhere in the world. If, as the Führer declared, Germany was to be cleansed of all things Jewish, it was a simple, logical consequence that Jewish music must be consigned to oblivion. Nevertheless, it was not until near the end of 1937 when the German press informed its readers that from the new year onwards, in accordance with government regulations (the Schallplattenverordnung), gramophone companies would no longer record works by Jewish composers or performances by Jewish musicians.

At first sight it may seem surprising that this latest act of cultural vandalism was so long in coming, but the Nazis had their reasons for proceeding cautiously. Reduced to its simplest terms the attack launched on the Jewish printed word in 1933 succeeded so well at home because Hitler, even at that early stage, was completely confident he had all the backing he required, for the vast majority of his most fervid supporters came from sections of society where literature and scholarly studies were dispensable commodities. Outside Germany the proscription was publicly condemned but, due to the language barrier, the enormity of the crime was only imperfectly understood.

In the case of musical censorship, however, matters were complicated by the very nature of an entertainment form capable of transcending social, educational and national divisions; because of this, the Nazis waited until they were absolutely certain they commanded mass public support. Since 1933 Hitler's policies had been achieving a steady economic recovery in which, most importantly, the scourge of galloping inflation was brought under control. In the recovery process rearmament and a huge public works programme were, significantly, crucial elements in the provision of work for the jobless. Self-respect gradually took the place self-pity as the German man in the street began to glimpse and believe in a brilliant future for his country. Following the death of Hindenburg in 1934 Hitler became the *de facto* supreme ruler of Germany and barely a year later the Nazis' shameless use of the Reichstag as a rubber stamp sped the anti-Semitic Nuremberg Laws to the statute book. As Germany's fortunes rose those of the Jews plummeted and the non-stop Party propaganda saw to it that nobody was unaware of this correlation. In March, 1936 Hitler's reoccupation of the demilitarised Rhineland met with only verbal opposition and in the following August Germany showed its confident new face to the world when, in spectacular style, the Olympic Games were hosted in Berlin. By the time the Schallplattenverordnung came into force in 1938 the combination of Hitler worship and rampant nationalism had made conditions perfect for the next assault on Jewish culture.

The heart of the problem facing the would-be censors was the sheer diversity of the music they were planning to suppress. Some was of minority interest which meant that the banning of many German contemporary composers would arouse the minimum of dissent. Another category of which few would feel deprived was serious American music which, in the 1930s, had little appeal for German (or indeed European) audiences and record buyers; the loss of works by George Antheil, Marc Blitzstein and Aaron Copland would thus go unnoticed. Amongst British exclusions from the world of Aryan music were no less than three knights of the realm, Sir Julius Benedict, the German-born composer of the once-famous opera *The Lily of Killarney*, Sir Frederic Cowen, now almost completely forgotten and Sir Landon Ronald who is remembered more as a conductor and musical adviser to the Gramophone Company than for his numerous compositions. Once again, the

100

non-availability of music by these three would have had no serious repercussions for German programmers.

Some of France's Jewish composers, however, were trickier propositions. Of least concern was Charles Alkan whose virtuoso works for solo piano were little known except by specialists and it was not until after the Second World War that they gained a wider public and a place in the record catalogues. The Nazis were lucky, too, with the operas of Jacques Halévy which had long since declined in popularity although a few arias (mainly from *La Juive*) remained in the repertoires of international singers during the inter-war years. But Paul Dukas, Darius Milhaud and Emil Waldteufel could not so easily be made redundant.

Like Alkan, Dukas was denoted in the *Lexikon* as a composer whose Jewish origin still awaited full confirmation. It is possible, though unlikely, that Friedrich Herzfeld in his biography of Wilhelm Furtwängler (published in 1942) was allowing Dukas the benefit of the doubt when he included the orchestral piece *The Sorcerer's Apprentice* amongst the list of works most frequently given by the conductor. Furtwängler is credited with a dozen concert performances, although he never made a commercial recording of the *Apprentice*. Even though Dukas's inspiration was a ballad by Goethe this would scarcely have influenced the censors in the Frenchman's favour; a more probable reason for the composer's appearance is that Herzfeld, like the music world in general, would undoubtedly have had difficulty keeping abreast of the steady flow of information from the Reichsmusikkammer and other sources. The problem would have been especially acute for an author when a publisher's deadline was imminent. This is well illustrated by a note at the end of Herzfeld's book where it was felt advisable to point out that a number of the persons mentioned in the text, for instance Bruno Walter, Otto Klemperer, Darius Milhaud, Kurt Weill and Arnold Schoenberg were all logged as Jews in the *Lexikon*.

Milhaud's music had its admirers on both sides of the Atlantic and from the late 1920s onwards gramophone companies (particularly French Columbia and Polydor) produced a generous selection of recordings, some of them featuring the composer himself. Nazi ideology and propaganda were brought to bear on Milhaud's reputation which offered some easy targets for racist ridicule. Anybody who wrote in the jazz idiom as Milhaud had done in his ballet score *La Création du Monde* was automatically a pariah. A po-faced bureaucracy was naturally delighted to condemn as decadent the Frenchman's tongue-in-cheek settings of a *Catalogue des Fleurs* and a list of *Machines Agricoles*, whilst the opera *Christophe Colombe* - a monstrosity, according to the *Lexikon* - additionally served to expose the shortcomings of the Weimar Republic's musical Establishment. In 1930 at the Berlin State Opera Erich Kleiber had conducted the première, the preparation for which had entailed twenty five orchestral and one hundred chorus rehearsals. Stengel and Gerigk were scandalised by the money, time and effort invested in the staging of Milhaud's opera when the work of so many deserving German composers was waiting to be heard.

Because it was lighthearted and specifically designed for popular consumption Waldteufel's music reached a larger public in Nazi Germany than that of any of the other blacklisted French composers. His finest waltzes, polkas and galops were seemingly permanent items in the treasury of European dance music written from around 1830 to the end of the nineteenth century and beyond. Waldteufel was regularly played by bands in the parks and orchestras in hotels, cafés and theatres; moreover, waltzes such as *The Skaters*, *The Grenadiers*, *España* and *Estudiantina* had sold well in the record shops from an early stage in the gramophone's development. The *Lexikon's* editors implicitly acknowledged the difficulties that beset the eradication of Waldteufel's music by devoting nearly three columns to a register of the most well-known pieces under both their French and German titles. To appreciate the deadening effect of the Schallplattenverordnung on the German domestic gramophone industry one needs look no further than the Waldteufel entries in the first volume of Clough and Cuming's *World's Encyclopaedia of Recorded Music*. The output by major and minor companies over the years had been so large that the editors decided to produce no more than a selective listing in which Polydor, Odeon, Electrola, Telefunken and Austrian HMV discs crop up with great regularity. With the suppression of the music came the banishment of all recordings, whether by favoured artists like Barnabas von Geczy or the banned Dol Dauber, Marek Weber, Paul Godwin and Dajos Bela; versions played by symphony orchestras conducted by Frieder Weissmann (Jewish) and Alois Melichar (Aryan) were likewise fated to disappear.

Clough and Cuming's discography is also an invaluable source of information on the German companies' recordings in the 1920s and 1930s of works by three of the most eminent serious composers to be proscribed by the Nazis - Mahler, Mendelssohn and Meyerbeer. It was not until after the Second World War that Mahler started to attract the international audience that nowadays takes for granted live and recorded performances of all the symphonies and song cycles. Considering the first recording of a major Mahler orchestral work was the acoustic version (on 22 sides) of the *Resurrection* symphony by Oskar Fried for Polydor, it comes as rather a surprise to find how sparsely this composer had been represented on record in Germany since that ambitious early venture. What did find its way on to disc was essentially vocal music and almost entirely thanks to the efforts of Polydor where there would seem to have been a keen Mahlerian in a position to influence choice of repertoire. In 1928 this company issued a four-sided set of the *Kindertotenlieder* sung by Heinrich Rehkemper with the Berlin Philharmonic conducted by the young Jascha Horenstein, but Polydor's other contributions were shorter pieces. Another famous baritone of the time, Heinrich Schlusnus, coupled *Rheinlegendchen* with *Der Tambourgesell*, both settings of words from *Des Knaben Wunderhorn*, whilst from its roster of women singers the company was able to call upon the contralto Lula Mysz-Gmeiner, a lieder specialist, for a third *Wunderhorn* item, *Wer hat dies' Liedlein erdacht*. Electrola edged into the picture when they recorded the same song with Elisabeth Schumann as the soloist. By the standards of our own day this selection seems positively minute, but in 1938 the paucity of Mahler discs was a useful bonus as far as the work of the Nazi censors was concerned.

In Mendelssohn's case the vocal works were largely ignored by the German companies and his instrumental and chamber music fared little better. The *Scottish, Italian* and *Reformation* symphonies were left strictly alone, but that well-loved masterpiece the E minor violin concerto mustered a performance on Telefunken by Georg Kulenkampff with the Berlin Philharmonic directed by Hans Schmidt-Isserstedt in addition to HMV's 1926 recording of Kreisler with the same orchestra under Leo Blech. Mendelssohn's short orchestral pieces were clearly what German record buyers most wanted and the overtures *The Hebrides, Ruy Blas* and *A Midsummer Night's Dream* (together with its most familiar incidental music) generated a host of discs played almost entirely by the Berlin Philharmonic or Berlin State Opera orchestras. The impressive array of conductors included Wilhelm Furtwängler, Otto Klemperer, Erich Kleiber and the composer-conductor Hans Pfitzner, as well as the now only dimly remembered names of men like Leo Blech, Artur Bodanzky, Joseph Rosenstock, Fritz Zweig, Julius Prüwer and Frieder Weissmann, all of whom worked industriously in the studios in the late '20s and early '30s.

If the spectacular grand operas of Giacomo Meyerbeer were less frequently to be found on the stage, individual arias were still greatly cherished by star singers of the inter-war years. Amongst the artists who dipped into the German language texts of this repertoire were some of the most illustrious vocalists of the period. To name each singer listed by Clough and Cuming would be tedious but prior to the Nazi clampdown the output of the German companies had embraced discs by Elisabeth Rethberg, Hans Hermann Nissen, Joseph Schmidt, Helge Roswaenge, Franz Völker, Marcel Wittrisch, Margarete Teschemacher, Lauritz Melchior, Max Lorenz, Adele Kern and Gitta Alpar. Meyerbeer's overtures and ballet music were issued on a similarly generous scale with more or less the same orchestras and conductors being employed as for the Mendelssohn recordings. Even the non-operatic *Fackeltanz* (Torch Dance) no. 1 was so popular that by the mid-1930s it had appeared four times on domestic labels.

When it came to banning Jewish performing artists the Nazis' audacity was just as breathtaking as in their suppression of Jewish music. For the present day serious collector accustomed to the enormous range of historic twentieth century recordings available in modern transfers it is almost beyond belief that the *Lexikon* blacklisted (amongst many others) the conductors:

Jascha Horenstein, Otto Klemperer, Serge Koussevitzky, Eugene Ormandy, Fritz Reiner, Georg Szell, Bruno Walter

the violinists:

Jascha Heifetz, Bronislaw Huberman, Fritz Kreisler, Yehudi Menuhin, Nathan Milstein

the cellists:

Emanuel Feuermann, Gregor Piatigorsky

the pianists:

Vladimir Horowitz, Artur Rubinstein, Artur Schnabel, Rudolf Serkin, Wanda Landowska (harpsichordist/pianist)

104

and the singers:

Alexander Kipnis, Selma Kurz, Joseph Schmidt, Friedrich Schorr, Richard Tauber.

To prepare the way for the eventual ethnic cleansing of German musical life the Nazis had actively encouraged the production of books, articles and speeches on the pernicious effect of non-Nordic influences and races (especially Jews) on Aryan culture. The sub-literature that sprang up consisted of supposedly scientific research decked out with windy rhetoric and pseudo-philosophy, its constant theme being the imperative need to preserve Germany's racial and cultural purity. The psychological power of repetition was exerted as ruthlessly in Nazi musicology as in every other area of state propaganda and the sinister message was endorsed time and again in public pronouncements by Goebbels and Hitler himself. The process of indoctrination worked so well that Mozart was in danger of being denounced by ultra-zealous Party members because of his association with his Jewish librettist, Lorenzo da Ponte; and bigotry was so widespread that Beethoven and Schubert, whose looks did not conform with the clear-cut Germanic ideal, were categorised respectively as Nordic and Sudeten-German to remove them from the shadow of suspicion.

Ideology also played an integral part in the glorification of outstanding Aryan musicians. It comes as no surprise, therefore, to find Friedrich Herzfeld's biography of Furtwängler opening with a chapter solemnly entitled Blut (Blood) which celebrates at some length the conductor's spotless lineage on both his father's and his mother's side. The book could not have been easy to write for although he was publicly idolised Furtwängler had declined to conduct at overt party-political events such as the Nuremberg rallies and had championed the music of Paul Hindemith. The latter, though an Aryan, had earned the Führer's deep disapproval mainly on account of the scene in the opera *Neues vom Tage* (News of the Day) which featured a nude soprano in her bath. By adopting the policy of least said soonest mended, Herzfeld contrived to skirt round such awkward topics as the uneasy relationship which existed between Furtwängler and Germany's rulers; the end-product was a highly selective account of the conductor's life coupled with hymns of praise for his artistry - a mixture admirably in keeping with the requirements of the Nazi dictatorship.

As part of their campaign against what they called "cultural Bolshevism" the Nazis heavily publicised exhibitions of degenerate art (Entartete Kunst) consisting of what, to them, were the most outrageous examples of twentieth century art that could be appropriated from German museums or private collections. The organisers cunningly ensured maximum interest in the exhibition held at Munich in July, 1937 by refusing to admit young people lest German youth should be contaminated by the alleged obscenities displayed on the walls. In 1939, after Hermann Goering had annexed for himself paintings by Van Gogh, Gauguin, Cézanne and others, the most valuable works from the exhibitions were sold on behalf of the Nazis by a leading Swiss art dealer. The fate of the remainder recalls the Burning of the Books for on March 20th, 1939 Berlin's central fire station was the scene of the ritual incineration of nearly five thousand works of art.

Exhibitions were such a regular channel for Nazi propaganda that it was probably with a certain malicious pleasure the German tourist and information offices abroad urged people to "Come and see Germany's Homes and Gardens at the great Düsseldorf Exhibition 'A Nation at Work', May-October 1937". Advertisements placed in British women's magazines exultantly referred to it as "the most inspiring, thrilling and entertaining exhibition the world has ever seen ... it is the unique record of a great nation's stupendous reconstruction." The majority of foreign visitors would have been unaware they were making an involuntary pilgrimage to a city emotively linked with the Party's early days as it was here in May, 1923 that one of Nazism's honoured martyrs, Albert Leo Schlageter, was shot in a brush with French occupying troops.

Düsseldorf was also the chosen venue for the week-long Reichsmusiktage (National Music Conference) of May, 1938 which incorporated the infamous Entartete Musik (Degenerate Music) exhibition. On the purely musical side of the proceedings Richard Strauss conducted his opera *Arabella* but local press reports leading readers to believe Furtwängler would direct Beethoven's *Choral* symphony at the closing concert proved to be unfounded; Furtwängler did not attend the festival. On the final day a speech by Goebbels laid down the "Ten Principles of German Musical

Creativity". The latter part of the Third Principle enshrined the anti-Semitic doctrine that

> "Jewishness and German music are opposites, which due to their nature, grossly contradict each other. The battle against Jewishness in German music, which Richard Wagner, in solitude and solely relying on himself, had once taken up, is, therefore, still our primary duty at present, never to be abandoned. Today the battle is no longer being fought merely by a knowing and lonely genius, but carried out by a whole people."

The Entartete Musik exhibition visually and aurally complemented the policies set out by Goebbels. The music so viciously disparaged was not exclusively Jewish and individual sections were given over to Hindemith, Stravinsky and Jazz, the latter being condemned both for its debased musical content and the black (therefore equally debased) composers and musicians associated with it. Amongst schools of composition Schoenberg and the atonalists were singled out for special attention, likewise the "petty Bolshevist giants" whose ranks included Franz Schreker, Alban Berg and Ernst Toch. The report in the July, 1938 issue of *Musical America* helps us to visualise the lay-out of the exhibition which was housed "in a room partitioned off into a series of open alcoves, each equipped with a gramophone playing one of the exhibits, which could be turned on simply by pressing a button."

The generally conservative tastes of German audiences and record buyers had, understandably, resulted in only a relatively small amount of new, adventurous, avant-garde or otherwise "degenerate" music appearing on domestic labels and after Hitler came to power the trickle of such issues dried up completely. In the case of the despised Stravinsky, Erich Kleiber had recorded *Fireworks* with the Berlin Philharmonic for Telefunken but this was scarcely an assault on the listener's ears. Oskar Fried (on Polydor) and Kleiber (this time on Odeon) had each made a set of the 1919 Suite from *The Firebird*, now a well established score in the international concert repertoire. Significantly, no German company had been bold enough to tackle *The Rite of Spring* which still conveniently conjured up memories of the disorders that marred the ballet's première in Paris back in 1913.

The exhibition was so hurriedly assembled that there was not time enough to prepare a catalogue. Our sketchy knowledge of the musical examples furnished by the push-button gramophones comes mainly from the recollections of actual visitors many years after the event, but by checking this information against *The World's Encyclopaedia of Recorded Music* (WERM) it is possible to gain a rough idea of the discs that were, or might have been played.

Stravinsky was represented by *The Soldier's Tale*, a work which the composer himself had recorded for Columbia and which was marketed by that company's French, English, Italian, German and American branches. Although the choice was ideologically fault-less the organisers made an error of judgment when they selected Kurt Weill's *Die Dreigroschen Oper* (The Threepenny Opera) from which visitors recalled hearing Jenny's pirate song. Since it was first staged in 1928 *Die Dreigroschen Oper* had always drawn the crowds; it continued to do so at the exhibition, though not for the reasons (Jewish composer, jazz-influenced music, libretto by the Marxist Bertolt Brecht) the Nazi musicologists would have wished. Telefunken's 1930 abridged recording - the obvious choice for the exhibition because of its authentically "decadent" style - was an extremely popular set, the cast of which included Weill's wife, the incomparable Lotte Lenya, in the role of Polly. Hanns Eisler's *Solidaritätslied* (Song of Solidarity) served to show how this half-Jewish composer prostituted his music in the cause of Marxist pol-itics; WERM, unfortunately, gives no clue as to the recording used at Düsseldorf for Clough and Cuming found nothing to list under Eisler whose agitprop pieces (as opposed to his 12-tone works) would probably have fallen outside their terms of reference. Ernst Toch was another whose music is known to have been played, but pre-Second World War German recordings were sparse, consist-ing of Polydor's three Burlesques, op. 31 for solo piano, an acoustic made by Toch's one-time teacher, Willy Rehberg, and the same company's later issue of *Le Jongleur* (one of the Burlesques) by L. Dymont.

A little more information is contained in a letter written by Hans Severus Ziegler, the director of the National Theatre in Weimar, who devised the exhibition. He, too, mentions Toch and Weill and also refers to music by Krenek, Schoenberg and Hindemith but the only title specified is the latter's *Neues vom Tage*; although WERM has a sizeable group of entries for Hindemith the editors discov-ered no recordings from this work. There are several ways in which the gap might have been filled if WERM's nil return is correct. It is conceivable that a German company may have recorded an extract but, mindful of Hitler's opinion of the opera, wisely decided not to publish it. If this were the case, to produce special pressings for the exhibition would have been a well-nigh inescapable public duty. Alternatively, the officials responsible for selecting and obtaining the musical examples may have found suitable material in the archives of the German radio network. If nothing was forthcoming from these sources one may assume that a specially commissioned disc was custom-made for the occasion.

What was chosen to represent Schoenberg can, once again, only be a matter of speculation. By 1938 relatively little of his music had been explored by the record companies and most of the activity was confined to America where Victor had brought out Stokowski's classic pioneering set of the *Gurrelieder* (Songs of Gurre) on fourteen discs and Eugene Ormandy, with the Minneapolis orchestra, had introduced *Verklärte Nacht* (Transfigured Night) to the Columbia catalogue. For the exhibition a more appropriate choice than either of these pieces of ripe, post-Wagnerian romanticism might have been the two songs from the cycle *Das Buch der hängenden Gärten* (The Book of the hanging Gardens) recorded by the soprano Erica Storm as part of English Columbia's multi-volume *History of Music*. Prior to Hitler, Ernst Krenek's music, especially the 1927 jazz opera *Jonny spielt auf* (Jonny plays on), had a hugely appreciative German following that was well catered for by the domestic companies. A selection from *Jonny spielt auf* played by the Dajos Bela orchestra appeared on the Odeon label as did the *Blues* and *Triumphal Song* sung by the baritone Ludwig Hofmann. These vocal excerpts were also to be had in an arrangement for violin and piano on Electrola. An acoustic Polydor had supplied record buyers with the waltz movement from the String Quartet Op. 20, whilst more recently the Dol Dauber orchestra had made the March No. 1 for Austrian HMV. As with Weill's *Dreigroschen Oper*, it is quite probable that anything from these commercial discs of Krenek's music would have run the risk of attracting the wrong sort of attention from exhibition visitors.

After a lapse of more than half a century the chances of identifying with certainty all the recordings heard at Düsseldorf have grown increasingly remote. The Nazis would undoubtedly have used any suitable "degenerate" music in the back-catalogues of the German companies which were now in no position to question the actions of their political masters. The only commercial recording of Stravinsky's *The Soldier's Tale* was Columbia's, but it is unlikely that Ziegler or anyone else observed the niceties of international copyright by applying for permission to play in public a recording that was the property of a multi-national corporation. Even if this had been done it is equally unlikely that Columbia and its parent body EMI would have agreed to their product being treated as an example of musical depravity. Given the Nazis' single-minded pursuit of an ethnic and cultural nirvana it seems safe to assume that Columbia's discs were played regardless of possible legal consequences.

Despite the calculated use of the gramophone as a channel for its ideological message the Entartete Musik exhibition did not turn out to be the success the Nazis had anticipated and problems of musical censorship, particularly with regard to jazz, continued to arise throughout the remaining years of the Third Reich. Liberal-minded German music lovers with catholic tastes may well have tended to avoid the dismal affair altogether; others with little or no intellectual interest in the subject probably did not feel urgently impelled to attend unless they were from the more fanatical ranks of the Party. Whatever the reasons, low attendances can certainly be inferred from the fact that by mid-June, 1938 the exhibition was dismantled and sent on its travels to Munich, Vienna and Weimar where, presumably, it was hoped to attract larger numbers of more impressionable visitors.

Even though with the passage of time the details of the exhibition itself have been largely forgotten, the piece of art work that publicised the event still has the power to give a disturbing jolt to the memory. It took the form of a caricature of a black saxophone player in full musical flow. He is wearing a top hat and evening dress and the cynical glint in his eye hints unmistakably at the jazz-fuelled pleasures, especially the lurid night life, inherited from the Weimar Republic and which the Nazis were determined to stamp out. The jazz band had long been a stock-in-trade image in advertising and to that extent there was nothing particularly original in Düsseldorf's solo saxophonist; indeed, if one discounts his top hat, he bears a strong resemblance to his bandsman counterpart in an Art Deco advertisement used in 1933 by La Voix de Son Maître

(French HMV) to attract custom for recordings of "Le Hot Jazz". The distinctive feature of the German player is the flower in his button-hole, for at its centre is the Star of David, the Jews' religious symbol which they were compelled to wear in Nazi Germany to distinguish them from the Aryan population; what at first sight seems to be a standard advertising image thus turns out to be that detestable hybrid from the Nazi demonology: a performer of decadent music who is a Jew into the bargain.

As the increasingly restrictive laws together with overt persecution removed Germany's Jews from the country's commercial, professional and cultural main streams those who did not have the means to escape were forced into a ghetto-style existence. The bloodletting of the Kristallnacht was followed only two days later on 12th November, 1938 by Goebbels's decree making it illegal for Jews to attend any German cultural occasions, a catchall term that was flexible enough to take in everything from concerts and lectures to vaudeville shows and circuses. Because for the last five years the National Socialist state had enabled the Jews to create their own self-contained cultural life there was no longer any reason, Goebbels argued, for them to share the same intellectual milieu as Aryan Germans.

Although the local authorities were empowered to ensure that no Jewish or un-German works intruded into public music making this still did not satisfy the Nazis. Since at least 1932 musicologists like Karl Blessinger had advocated (doubtless with an eye to future advancement) that music making in the home should also conform as a matter of course with the norms of National Socialism. The documentation prepared for the reconstruction in London in 1995/96 of the original Entartete Musik exhibition stresses that

> "The totalitarian state did not tolerate any nonsanctioned free space. Even music played in the family circle by amateurs was declared to be 'a concern of the movement'."

By the end of the decade anyone in the Aryan household rash enough to play or sing in private any music that did not have the Party's approval risked being accused of disloyalty to the Third Reich. Hitler's Germany, like all totalitarian regimes, was a natural habitat for the informer and music lovers who overstepped the mark might, if unlucky, find themselves reported to the Gestapo by neighbours, relatives or even their own brainwashed children.

111

Gramophone enthusiasts had their special problems. Dyed-in-the-wool Nazis may well have voluntarily purged their personal record collections of offending material, but there is little hard evidence of how less politically dedicated record owners may have reacted. Proscribed music on disc (provided it was not too well known or aggressively modern) was probably relatively safe from the suspicious ears of the Party faithful; and when it came to performances by banned artists only the most expert informer would have been able to distinguish between, say, Beethoven's violin concerto played by the impeccable Kulenkampff or the discredited Kreisler without reference to the record labels. The restrictions imposed on live and recorded music by the Nazis' warped political philosophy were both wicked in conception and illogical in practice. They were, however, an inescapable fact of life and it was not until the downfall of Hitler in 1945 that freedom of musical choice re-emerged in Germany.

During the early 1930s the major record companies became concerned over the increasing use of their copyright products not just in public places such as theatres and restaurants but also (in America and Europe particularly) on the radio. The International Federation of the Phonographic Industry which was set up to represent the interests of record companies worldwide held its inaugural congress in Rome in November, 1933 and a number of legal test cases were initiated in an effort to protect its members from the unregulated broadcasting of gramophone records. Switzerland, Denmark and the then Yugoslavia were amongst the countries taken to court and in early April, 1935 it was Germany's turn. *Das Dritte Reich*, an annual survey of current affairs, reported in language remarkably akin to the vocabulary of Communist Russia that although the German broadcasting system wished to reach an amicable agreement it would not submit to the monopolistic manoeuvres of international cliques.

In response to the Federation's legal challenge the Nazis banned the broadcasting of all records made by firms that were not in a contractual relationship with German radio and the network's record libraries were sealed off pending a settlement. Both parties were, of course, perfectly aware that this move deprived the companies of a valuable showcase for their recordings. The radio, meanwhile, made up for the temporary loss of this very popular programme material by simply increasing the number of exchange broadcasts on the network. The law case did not last long and on 28th May the Berlin court gave its judgment which banned the radio from using spoken word recordings but reaffirmed its right to broadcast commercially made music recordings as before.

The adversaries, however, were not satisfied and each decided to appeal, the Federation in the hope of securing a better deal for its members' music output, German radio in a bid to sweep the board and add the spoken word to its previous winnings. The ensuing legal argument went on until February, 1936 but failed to change the original judgment. Spoken word recordings which, in any case, were not a major ingredient of the programme format might only be broadcast if licensed by the manufacturers but music recordings could continue to be played over the air free of charge and without a special licence. Goebbels immediately gave instructions for the reopening of the record libraries and, to the undoubted delight of German listeners, gramophone companies' music discs returned to the studio turntables. Well though the radio had fared in the test case, the creeping censorship of music and musicians that culminated in the Schallplattenverordnung and Stengel and Gerigk's *Lexikon* ironically entailed a corresponding reduction in the number of ideologically acceptable commercial recordings available for broadcasting.

By the end of the 1930s the twin elements of anti-Semitism and aggressive nationalism had effectively brought German musical life to a state of near self-sufficiency. The liberal attitude of the Weimar Republic towards music of all kinds was a thing of the past, replaced by an almost incestuous devotion to the Austro-German musical heritage. One of the main reasons for the abject acceptance of the Nazis' racist policy by classical music lovers was that even with Mendelssohn and Mahler out of the reckoning there was still free access to the works of Bach, Handel, Mozart, Haydn, Beethoven, Schubert, Weber, Schumann, Brahms, Wagner, Bruckner and Richard Strauss. When to this pantheon could be added such non-German composers as Verdi, Puccini, Chopin, Liszt, Dvořák, Tchaikovsky and Sibelius the Nazis knew full well there was no shortage of repertoire with which to satisfy the needs of traditionally inclined concert-goers and record buyers.

Even though the stock of native talent was severely reduced from 1933 onwards by the emigration or summary removal from

113

public life of Jewish musicians, Germany could still produce its own impressive array of Aryan recording artists. Amongst orchestral conductors whose working lives spanned both the pre- and post-World War 2 periods were Wilhelm Furtwängler, Karl Böhm, Clemens Krauss and Hans Knappertsbusch and their discographies shed an interesting light on the effect the coming of the Nazi government had on the classical output of the German gramophone industry. All four men had been active in the recording studios in 1933 but 1934 appears to have been a barren year for them, reflecting not only the new political, economic and social uncertainties that had abruptly replaced those of the Weimar Republic but also the disruptive influence on policy exerted by hard-line Nazi employees within the companies. A handful of sessions allocated to Furtwängler and Böhm in 1935 shows the first signs of a return to more settled commercial conditions and in the following year Krauss was recording a series of excerpts from operas by Verdi, Mozart and Richard Strauss for Polydor. Furtwängler's contributions for 1936 and 1937 to the same company's catalogue included Mozart's *Eine kleine Nachtmusik* and Johann Strauss's *Fledermaus* overture. By late 1937, however, he had gone over to HMV/Electrola for whom he made a classic account of Beethoven's Fifth Symphony to be followed the next year by his equally famous version of the Tchaikovsky *Pathétique*. The international circulation of these two sets revealed more tellingly than any of his earlier recordings Furtwängler's interpretative powers and the closeness of the bond that existed between him and the Berlin Philharmonic Orchestra.

Regrettably, this memorable partnership was used by the Party's propagandists as an exemplar of how healthily the arts flourished under National Socialism. The problems that bedevilled Furtwängler in his ambiguous relationship with the Nazis were solved after a fashion when he persuaded himself it was his moral duty to continue in his post in order to ensure that Germany's finest musical traditions were upheld, even if in so doing he was reluctantly obliged to comply with the debased ideological requirements of the state.

The malicious treatment of Furtwängler's contemporary, Hans Knappertsbusch, is less frequently referred to, but its long-term effects were considerable. When Hitler came to power Knappertsbusch, who was closely associated with the music of

Wagner and Richard Strauss, was director of the Bavarian State Opera House in Munich and shortly came into conflict with the Nazis who disapproved of the non-German content in the company's repertoire. In 1936 his outspoken criticism of the regime and his refusal to become a Party member led to his dismissal; he moved to Vienna where he worked with the State Opera and the Philharmonic Orchestra but his career was once more in danger when Germany annexed Austria in 1938. After his sessions of 1933 he was excluded from the recording studios and it was not until the Second World War, when there was a rapprochement of sorts between himself and the Nazis, that he again began to record for Electrola in Vienna and Berlin.

The ranks of Aryan pianists included Walter Gieseking, particularly admired for his recordings of Debussy and Ravel, and Wilhelm Kempff, whose first Beethoven sonata cycle for Polydor was brought to a premature end by the war. Another revered Beethoven interpreter was Elly Ney who recorded for Electrola and Polydor. Outside Germany her reputation was clouded by her enthusiastic endorsement of Nazism which, no doubt, was as influential as her musicianship in winning the dubious honour of being named the Führer's favourite pianist. Wilhelm Backhaus, who excelled in the music of Brahms, was perhaps the most internationally famous German-born pianist of the period but in 1930 he settled in Switzerland and took Swiss nationality. He still played in Germany, however, and though practically all his discs had been made in London for HMV (some, even, for its ancestor, the Gramophone and Typewriter Company) it was at Dresden in June, 1939 with Karl Böhm conducting the Saxon State Orchestra that he made the first of his three commercial recording of Brahms's B flat Piano Concerto. At this late stage of the European political crisis it is not surprising that the Dresden discs were cut by Electrola for HMV; only a few weeks later a shocked world learned that Hitler had invaded Poland but by this time, fortunately, HMV's factory at Hayes had the means with which to produce pressings for the British market.

Save for the violinist Georg Kulenkampff (who was forced to leave Germany in 1943 and take up residence in Switzerland) there were few outstanding string soloists left in the Third Reich by the end of the 1930s. Nevertheless, those remaining were highly accomplished musicians who could be relied upon to give their audiences perfectly satisfying, but not necessarily deeply inspired accounts of the classical masterpieces.

Provided they were ethnically sound and observed their hosts' ground rules when planning their programmes, distinguished foreign musicians were welcome visitors to the Third Reich. For propaganda purposes they were valuable plus points, tangible proof that Germany was, as always, a leading member of the international cultural community; and for true music lovers they frequently brought not only fresh insights to well known standard works but also variety to an otherwise rather predictable musical diet.

Italy, Germany's Axis ally, was well to the fore where cultural exchanges were concerned. Victor De Sabata's celebrated Polydor recordings in early 1939 with the Berlin Philharmonic had been preceded by his concerts with that orchestra in its 1935/36 season and, in 1937 by the triumphant tour in which he had headed the complete company of La Scala, Milan. Also in 1937 another eminent Italian conductor, Bernardino Molinari, who recorded for Cetra and Columbia, was playing the role of musical ambassador, whilst the following year the momentum was maintained with more Italian opera, this time by a group that featured amongst its famous names the tenor Giacomo Lauri-Volpi and the conductor Antonino Votto. The parade of Italy's musical talents came to an impressive climax in 1939 when De Sabata conducted *Tristan und Isolde* at the Bayreuth Festival; even Mussolini's vanity could hardly have been more gratified than when the director of La Scala appeared at the Festspielhaus, Wagner's own theatre, where the performance of his operas had assumed the nature of a Germanic quasi-religious rite.

Soon after Hitler took command an unlikely-seeming friendship sprang up between Germany and Japan; despite geographical distance, the racial divide and disparate cultures they tacitly acknowledged that in the context of power politics their two nations had much in common, namely rapacious imperialist ambitions. Both saw Communist Russia as a potential enemy and in November, 1936 they strengthened their links by signing the Anti-Comintern Pact. By 1938 Japanese and German youth leaders were paying official visits to each other's countries which, in the same year, entered into a cultural agreement. In view of these diplomatic and other high level activities it is natural enough to find Viscount Hidemaro Konoye, a member of a Japanese princely family, conducting and recording in Germany during the mid-1930s. He was,

116

in fact, no stranger to Europe and had made his German debut with the Berlin Philharmonic Orchestra as early as 1924.

Although not particularly large, Konoye's recorded output was not lacking in variety. Long before his German sessions Japanese Parlophone had issued in 1930 what was probably the first recording of Mahler's Fourth Symphony in which Konoye conducted Tokyo's New Symphony Orchestra - a reminder that the intense interest shown by the Japanese in western music is not a recent phenomenon. His three Berlin Philharmonic recordings comprise Mozart's Sinfonia Concertante in E flat for wind soloists, K 297b on Columbia and, for the Polydor catalogue, Mussorgsky's *Night on the Bare Mountain* together with a pioneering set of Haydn's Symphony No. 91 in E flat, this at a time when record companies seldom ventured on any Haydn symphony which did not have a nickname they could use in their advertising. At one stage, perhaps out of genuine admiration, perhaps as a gesture of courteous flattery, Konoye asked if he might be given a personally signed photograph of Hitler and, after passing through the senior bureaucracy, his request was granted. The high regard the Nazis had for Konoye is apparent in an official letter in which he was described as the Japanese Furtwängler and the finest non-German interpreter of Richard Strauss. Konoye could not have been unaware of the extent to which anti-Semitism had permeated life in Germany but his exposure to it seems to have had little effect on his choice of repertoire when at home for on a post-1936 Japanese Polydor disc he can be heard conducting an orchestral suite from Weill's *Dreigroschen Oper*.

Sir Thomas Beecham, a more internationally celebrated conductor than Konoye, took his recently formed London Philharmonic Orchestra to Germany in November, 1936. The opening concert in Berlin set the tone for the rest of the tour. The audience included Hitler and Goebbels as well as many other members of the Nazi government and, as the *Daily Telegraph* reported:

"Every seat had been sold a week before. Sir Thomas and the orchestra were given an enthusiastic reception. After each piece in the programme there were cries of 'Bravo!' and loud and prolonged applause. Herr Hitler, who was in a box, appeared to be enjoying himself immensely and joined in the applause heartily ..."

When the programmes for the tour were being planned Beecham had reluctantly taken the advice of his organising manager Berta Geissmar (who had worked in a similar capacity for Furtwängler before fleeing from Nazi persecution) and substituted non-Jewish music for Mendelssohn's *Scottish* Symphony. This may have been what prompted Beecham to seek permission to lay a wreath on Mendelssohn's memorial at the Leipzig Gewandhaus when the orchestra reached that city. The Bürgermeister gave his consent but his deputy, a dedicated Party man, was of a different mind and, when his superior was away in Sweden on official business, ordered the memorial to be removed and destroyed. Thus Beecham's hope of paying public homage to a composer whose music he loved and at the same time displaying his implicit contempt for the Nazis was frustrated.

The concert at Ludwigshafen on 19th November, 1936 was memorable not only musically but also as a landmark in the history of sound recording. At the 1935 Berlin Radio Show the electrical concern AEG had unveiled its new Magnetophon recorder which used magnetic tape as the encoding medium. Further research and development were needed before the tape could be marketed commercially and this work was entrusted to the Ludwigshafen-based BASF, a member of the vast chemicals cartel, IG Farbenindustrie. The venue for the concert was the company's leisure centre which included a hall blessed with fine acoustics; here the orchestra was seated on a platform decorated, after the custom of the time, with a lavish display of flowers and potted palms. It had been arranged that Beecham's visit with his acclaimed London Philharmonic should be the occasion for the first recording on magnetic tape of a full symphony orchestra and two movements from Mozart's Symphony No. 39 in E flat were chosen for the experiment. British collectors had to wait for forty three years until 1979 when EMI's World Records label published a multi-disc album to celebrate the centenary of Beecham's birth before they were able to hear one of these, the Minuet and Trio.

Anthony Griffith's LP transfer of Beecham's robust reading of this movement is a fascinating aural experience. Judging by a photograph taken at the concert BASF probably used only one centrally placed microphone, just in front of the platform. The tape system, of course, had the immediate benefit of doing away with the surface noise that was inevitable in the finished product of the 78 r.p.m. disc recording process, but nevertheless there is still an audible (but not unduly distracting) steady background noise; the quality of the orchestra, however, is immediately apparent even though the woodwind section sounds recessed and the timpani uncomfortably prominent. Obviously there were still plenty of problems to be solved but once these were overcome it was clear there would be a great future for the new technology. In the studio it would release engineers and musicians from the tyranny of the four minute 78 r.p.m. side and when live recordings were being made it promised an end to those anxious moments when one cutting head was faded out and another brought into action as each wax was completed. As a carrier of recorded sound the magnetic tape held out to listeners the desirable prospect of long stretches of uninterrupted music, a continuity many collectors had aspired to either by playing their sets of classical 78s in auto-coupled sequence on noisy and slow-working record-changers or, more satisfactorily, by using twin turntables. Due to the Second World War events followed a rather less direct course. On the return of peace magnetic tape soon became the accepted format for the gramophone companies' master recordings but in 1954 when pre-recorded reel to reel tapes were first sold commercially in America and Britain they attracted little interest as extended play (45 r.p.m.) and long playing (33⅓ r.p.m.) discs had already captured the market.

A year later in November, 1937 Beecham was once again in Berlin, this time to record Mozart's *The Magic Flute* with the Berlin Philharmonic and a slightly uneven array of mainly German singers. The producer was Walter Legge whose task it was to add this opera to Fritz Busch's Glyndebourne performances of *The Marriage of Figaro, Così fan tutte* and *Don Giovanni* which had already been recorded by Fred Gaisberg for HMV's Mozart Opera Society subscription series. It was Legge's first complete opera project and there were initial difficulties over casting as Richard Tauber and Alexander Kipnis, whom Legge would have preferred for the parts of Tamino and Sarastro, were now ineligible to sing these roles in Germany since both were Jews. Likewise, Herbert Janssen would have been first choice as the Speaker but he too was, in Legge's words, "a political refugee". Their replacements were respectively the Danish tenor Helge Roswaenge, Wilhelm Strienz and Walter

Grossmann who, with the debatable exception of Roswaenge, were artists of a lesser order. The women singers, Tiana Lemnitz, Erna Berger and Irma Beilke posed no such problems, nor did the baritone Gerhard Hüsch in the important role of Papageno. Despite critical reservations from its first appearance onwards Beecham's *Magic Flute* has stood the test of time well enough to be frequently reissued on LP and CD and on each reincarnation reviewers have been unanimous in their praise of Hüsch's masterly interpretation. He was one of the foremost Lieder singers of his day and had recorded Schubert's *Die schöne Müllerin* and *Winterreise* cycles as well as a selection of songs by the Finnish composer Yrjö Kilpinen in special limited editions for HMV. It is sad to recall that so sensitive a singer should in 1934 have been drawn into recording two bombastic Nazi anthems, *Deutschland erwache* (Germany, awake) and *Das Hakenkreuz* (The Swastika) for Telefunken, a company that lost no opportunity to ingratiate itself with the Hitler regime. But even so early as this in the Third Reich nonconformity was an option few Aryan Germans mindful of their future prospects were willing to risk.

The European democracies' ineffectual attempts to curb the excesses of Nazi Germany between 1933 and the outbreak of the Second World War merely resulted in constant anxiety, unfulfilled hopes and diplomatic crises that recurred at ever shorter intervals. Bruno Walter, who had taken Austrian citizenship in 1911, was just one of the many distinguished Jewish musicians whose careers and lives were at stake, but his recorded legacy from this period is unique in the way it reveals a great conductor's inmost thoughts and documents their public expression in music.

When Hitler came to power Walter was conductor of the Gewandhaus Orchestra at Leipzig where he had succeeded Furtwängler; Nazi persecution made it impossible for him to stay and he took refuge in Austria despite the country's (and especially its capital's) reputation for anti-Semitism. There he became head of the Vienna State Opera and the Vienna Philharmonic with which orchestra he made a notable series of recordings for Columbia and HMV between late 1934 and January, 1938. Two or three of these such as Johann Strauss's *Emperor Waltz*, Brahms's *Academic Festival Overture* and some of Mozart's *German Dances* were at the light-hearted end of the repertoire. Various other more substantial works including Brahms's First and Haydn's *Military* Symphonies have been criticised as lacking due weight, but the warmth and lyricism that characterised Walter's conducting at its finest are splendidly displayed in such classic 78s as Wagner's *Siegfried Idyll*, Brahms's Third and Beethoven's *Pastoral* Symphonies.

However, it is in certain large scale works recorded by Walter during these years that the listener becomes aware of something that transcends even such deeply felt performances, something which takes the mind back to Elgar's programme notes for his *Enigma Variations* where he wrote: "... through and over the whole set another and larger theme 'goes', but it is not played." What the inward ear discerns is Walter's threnody for an age in which stability and civilised values were on the verge of collapse.

In June, 1935 HMV recorded his thrilling account of Act I of Wagner's *Die Walküre* (The Valkyries) with Lotte Lehmann, Lauritz Melchior and Emanuel List as Sieglinde, Siegmund and Hunding respectively. At the end of the act when the ecstatic lovers (brother and sister) make their escape they are at the mercy of unstoppable forces which, at the conclusion of the *Ring* cycle, will have combined to bring about the total destruction of the old world of the gods.

Eleven months later in May, 1936 Walter and the orchestra embarked on a highly concentrated week's activity. For three days they worked under normal studio conditions to record (again for HMV) Brahms's Third Symphony, the sombre two movements of Schubert's *Unfinished* and Beethoven's dramatic *Leonore* Overture No. 3 in which the composer portrays justice, courage and love conquering political tyranny. While rehearsals went on over the next two days the EMI team prepared its equipment for a live recording of the public concert in the Musikverein at which Walter was to conduct Mahler's *Das Lied von der Erde* (The Song of the Earth) with the American tenor Charles Kullman and the contralto Kerstin Thorborg as the soloists.

Ever since he conducted its first performance in Munich in 1911 this song symphony had been close to Walter's heart and modern transfers show that the microphones picked up the unmistakable sounds of his emotional involvement in this performance. Despite the occasional technical and musical imperfections the intensity of the music making was so compelling that, with Walter's

121

approval, Columbia issued this first ever recording of *Das Lied* in a seven-disc album which in Great Britain was limited to one thousand copies and available on subscription only.

Walter, like his friend and colleague Fred Gaisberg, was appalled by the extent to which ideological and political considerations were now affecting the playing and recording of great music by great artists in the dictator states. Walter's Vienna performances of works by his mentor and fellow Jew Gustav Mahler can without a doubt be construed as his own protests against musical racism. The unnamed writer of the sleeve notes for Walter's post-war Decca mono LP recording of *Das Lied* aptly summed it up as "a long, impassioned, lingering farewell to earth and earth's joys". It is difficult to think of any work more subtly critical of a Germany that prided itself on its great cultural heritage yet was willing to treat masterpieces now judged to be un-German as if they had never existed. The feelings of sadness, resignation and world-weariness which are at the core of *Das Lied von der Erde* were also to be found at the same concert in one of Mahler's most delicately wrought songs, *Ich bin der Welt abhanden gekommen* (I have lost track of the World). Kerstin Thorborg's beautiful performance was also recorded for Columbia and issued on a separate ten-inch disc in which accessible format it helped to serve as an introduction to the treasures awaiting adventurous collectors if they subscribed to the album.

In the course of their 1937 tour Walter and the orchestra together with a quartet of eminent soloists (Elisabeth Schumann, Kerstin Thorborg, Anton Dermota and Alexander Kipnis) and the chorus of the Vienna State Opera gave an unusual concert in Paris on 29th June at the Théâtre des Champs-Elysées. Instead of the showpieces we have come to expect nowadays from visiting ensembles the programme consisted of settings of three religious texts, Pergolesi's *Stabat Mater*, Bruckner's *Te Deum* and Mozart's *Requiem*. Pathé-Marconi, EMI's French affiliate, recorded the concert in its entirety with a view to producing discs for commercial release, but after listening to the test pressings Walter and Gaisberg concluded that the overall quality (especially with regard to the vocal contributions) was too uneven to warrant their issue. Nearly fifty years later in 1986 EMI relented sufficiently to bring out an LP transfer of the *Requiem* to which *Gramophone's* reviewer gave an unenthusiastic welcome. French collectors for whom, perhaps, the concert would have had greater archival interest than for their British counterparts, were duly catered for by a CD transfer of the *Requiem* in EMI's *Références* series of historical recordings.

The solemn programme was undoubtedly another instinctive artistic response to the seemingly insoluble problems of the times. Jewish though he was, one has the impression Walter was purposely using familiar components of Christian worship to stress the need for spiritual as well as diplomatic initiatives in the arduous quest for a more harmonious Europe. The *Stabat Mater* in the Roman Catholic church's Passiontide observances recounts the sorrows of the Virgin Mary as she stands at the foot of the Cross on which hangs her Son, Jesus Christ; the light of the world, it seems, has been extinguished. The miracle of the Resurrection is to follow, however, and in the *Te Deum* man affirms his faith in the infinite wisdom and mercy of Almighty God, Father, Son and Holy Ghost. Finally, when man's earthly span is over, the *Requiem* prays for his soul on its journey to the promised eternal life and peace in the hereafter. Through the medium of these three works the Parisian audience was taken on what, in essence, was a spiritual pilgrimage.

Walter's time in Vienna was fast running out when the recording sessions of January, 1938 took place. Austria's Nazi movement had grown apace in the 1930s and, inspired by the phenomenal rise of Adolf Hitler, it intervened with growing confidence in national affairs. 1934 witnessed an unsuccessful coup against the government; it was put down rapidly but not before the Austrian Chancellor, Engelbert Dollfuss, had been shot and killed. Dollfuss was succeeded by Kurt Schuschnigg who, for a short time, managed to calm matters slightly between Austria and Germany but by the beginning of 1938 relations had deteriorated to crisis point.

It was at Fred Gaisberg's suggestion that HMV recorded the public performance of the then seldom heard Ninth Symphony of Mahler that Walter (who had conducted its première in 1912) gave at the Musikverein on the morning of Sunday, 16th January in the presence of Schuschnigg and other leading members of the government. Five rehearsals had given the engineers ample time to set up their equipment to maximum advantage for preserving what, to quote Gaisberg, was to be "the swan-song of the Vienna Philharmonic Orchestra under their old conductor... because from then on until the Germans overran Austria two months later political upheavals absorbed all social life and made music-making impossible. (In fact all the orchestra leaders ... disappeared from the scene shortly after this concert, and the next time I saw them was in Paris or London.)"

Throughout the concert Gaisberg was seated on the platform next to the timpani from which vantage point he signalled to the engineers when each movement was about to begin or was nearing its end. Behind the scenes an assistant followed the full score and warned the senior engineer in advance of all dynamic extremes in the music where adjustments to the recording level were likely to be necessary; switching from one cutting head to the other at previously agreed points in the music the engineers required a total of twenty waxes before the final hushed notes died away and they could at last relax after a tense morning's work.

At so critical a stage in Austria's political troubles the long, little known symphony did not make comfortable listening for the audience in the Musikvereinsaal. The first movement in which hope and potential happiness are constantly assailed by tragedy and despair is followed by a scherzo where elements of popular music are cynically travestied. The ensuing Rondo-Burleske is more brutal still in its portrayal of Mahler's disillusionment and it is only in the fourth movement (another extended farewell) that there can eventually be found some measure of emotional relief and comfort to alleviate the anguish of what has gone before.

Gaisberg went on to describe how, not long afterwards,

"... Walter turned up a bewildered refugee in Paris, where I met him to play over and obtain his approval of the ... records recorded that Sunday. So delighted was he with the results that his usually sober face brightened up considerably."

The Mahler Ninth was issued by HMV in a limited edition for subscribers only and, as with Columbia's *Das Lied von der Erde*, a single disc of one of the composer's shorter pieces was put out on general release to whet the appetites of interested collectors. This time it was a studio recording of the Adagietto from the Fifth Symphony made the day before the Musikverein concert. Under Walter's eloquent direction the strings of the Vienna Philharmonic caress the poignant music which is all the more moving for being played without resort to an ultra-slow tempo or lush sentimentality.

Relations between Austria and Germany worsened to such an extent that Schuschnigg resigned in March and was replaced by Artur Seyss-Inquart. The latter, the country's leading Nazi, asked for Hitler's help in subduing the unrest and the waiting German army marched into Austria. On 14th March Hitler was in Vienna and his imposing motorcade drove through streets packed with cheering crowds already celebrating the union with the Third Reich that would be ratified so overwhelmingly by the plebiscite held the following month.

Once settled in Paris Walter became a French citizen and Gaisberg arranged for a series of recordings to be made with the Orchestra of the Paris Conservatoire for issue on HMV. Weber's *Der Freischütz* and Johann Strauss's *Die Fledermaus* overtures enabled orchestra and conductor to get to know each other; Haydn's Symphony No. 92, the *Oxford*, was typical Walter repertoire but an unexpected item cropped up in the form of Handel's Concerto Grosso Op.6, No. 12.

The most substantial set produced during this brief partnership was Berlioz's *Symphonie Fantastique* which might possibly have been looked on by Walter as representing the rebirth of his career, for this work had figured in the programme of his very first symphony concert given in Berlin at the beginning of the century. Like the Mahler performances in Vienna, the *Symphonie Fantastique* could also have been another oblique commentary on the age. Berlioz's music depicts the fevered mind of an artist as, waking and sleeping, he seeks his beloved, an ideal being always just out of reach. The centrally placed Scène aux Champs is a peaceful interlude but even this is disturbed by the ominous rumblings of thunder. Dreams give way to nightmares as the artist imagines himself being marched to the scaffold for execution and further horrific visions end the symphony when he sees his loved one, grotesquely transformed, taking part in the obscenities of a witches' sabbath.

Walter was not destined to stay long in Paris. Germany's ever more insistent claims on Czechoslovakia led to a frantic round of shuttle diplomacy in September, 1938 as the British and French prime ministers strove to resolve the crisis. On 29th September

Neville Chamberlain and Edouard Daladier met Hitler and Mussolini at Munich where an agreement was secured at the cost of Czechoslovakia's predominantly German-speaking Sudetenland being ceded to the Third Reich. Chamberlain flew back to London the following day and the media were at Heston Airport in force to report his words when he stepped off the plane. On the recording of the occasion issued by HMV he can be heard buoyantly declaring that "The settlement of the Czechoslovakian problem which has now been achieved is in my view only the prelude to a larger settlement in which all Europe may find peace." This statement was cheered by the crowd but the reaction was warmer still when he went on to say what everybody had wanted to hear: "We regard the agreement signed last night and the Anglo-German Naval Agreement as symbolic of the desire of our two peoples never to go to war with one another again."

Whether Chamberlain genuinely believed he had achieved an enduring settlement or was desperately buying time to allow the western democracies to prepare themselves for an inevitable future conflict is still the subject of debate. HMV's disc remained in their catalogue for several years perhaps because, when the Second World War erupted less than a year after the speech was delivered, the record then had a certain propaganda value in that it clearly demonstrated the treachery of Adolf Hitler.

In 1939 Toscanini invited Walter to New York to conduct a number of concerts with the NBC Symphony Orchestra; other American engagements followed but when the Germans occupied France in 1940 he was deprived both of his home and his French citizenship. From then onwards Walter lived in the United States and, in his old age, enjoyed a glorious Indian summer the abundant fruits of which were harvested by the gramophone companies for the lasting benefit of music lovers throughout the world.

The Second World War, 1939-1945
I – The Phoney War

THE EASE WITH which he had annexed Austria and acquired Czechoslovakia sharpened still further Hitler's appetite for empire and at first light on the morning of lst September, 1939 German forces invaded neighbouring Poland: the next stage of the planned eastward drive for Lebensraum was under way on a front that ran from the Baltic Sea in the north to Silesia in the south.

Prior to the Treaty of Versailles the entire Baltic seaboard from Schleswig-Holstein to East Prussia was Germany's, thus making Poland a land-locked country. The Paris Peace Conference decided that part of Germany to the west of Danzig (the so-called Polish corridor) should be transferred to the new republic, so enabling the Poles to develop the port of Gdynia. At the same time Danzig was accorded the status of a free city. As a result of these redrawn boundaries the province of East Prussia was isolated from Germany itself and this geographical divorce gave Hitler the pretext he needed for demanding the restoration of one-time German lands, particularly Danzig, which became the focus of his claims.

When, after the usual staged border incidents and reports of atrocities against German nationals, the Wehrmacht advanced into Poland that country's allies, Britain and France, could no longer pursue the policy of appeasement without losing every shred of credibility as major European powers. Their joint call for a German withdrawal was predictably ignored and on Sunday, 3rd September they declared war against the Third Reich.

Archival recordings vividly convey the stylistic gulf which existed between Hitler and the British Prime Minister, Neville Chamberlain. On the day of the invasion the Reichstag was the scene of Hitler's announcement that Poland was paying the price for trifling with Germany. The speech was given maximum publicity by German radio which relayed it throughout Europe and to

127

North America. Pearl/OPAL's CD *The Rise of Fascism* includes part of the speech with its simultaneous English translation as heard by listeners in the USA. At one point there was a dramatic interruption when an American announcer broke the news that the French Council of Ministers was holding an emergency meeting to discuss the deepening crisis.

Hitler's oratory that day followed the familiar pattern of an almost off-hand delivery at one extreme leading gradually to fanatical ranting at the other with the well-drilled delegates raucously voicing their agreement at every appropriate moment. The gist of the speech was that Germany had stood by long enough watching Danzig being abused and led down the road to economic ruin by the Poles. Germany was the victim of all the provocations about which there had been so much argument, not Poland. In a show of injured virtue Hitler asserted it was he who had striven for a diplomatic solution and he who had waited two whole days for a response from the Polish ambassador to his proposals. Hitler then went on to deliver the ominous warning that (in the words of the English translator) "No one should confuse my patience with cowardice." When Poland's answer came, he said, it took the form of general mobilisation and more atrocities against Germans. There could be no turning back and (to quote the translator again) "I therefore resolved to speak to Poland in the same language in which Poland has addressed us for such a long time" - a decision which brought shouts of approval from the assembly.

Within a few hours Danzig was reunited with the Reich and Hitler spoke there to an enormous public gathering that could scarcely contain its enthusiasm. As a recording from the BBC's archives demonstrates, the roars of Sieg Heil unambiguously endorsed the Führer's actions.

Compared with Hitler's histrionic excesses Chamberlain's address to the British people on 3rd September was a dignified, low-key affair. The solemn statement that Britain was at war with Germany was recorded by the BBC and we hear a voice that is uniformly quiet though not lacking in determination; the tired, almost resigned tones tell of the strain Chamberlain had been under during the preceding months as he struggled to preserve the peace in Europe. It was not the kind of voice one could imagine inspiring a nation to give of its utmost in wartime but it was, nevertheless, the voice of a man who knew where his duty lay. Because of its historical significance the recording has been used, almost since the day it was made, in a multitude of feature films, documentaries, stage plays and radio and television productions to epitomise this fateful turning point in world affairs.

The events of the next six months came misleadingly to be known as the phoney war; there was, however, nothing phoney about what happened in Poland. When in August, 1939 Germany and Russia took the totally unexpected step of entering into a non-aggression pact the two ideologically opposed powers secretly agreed that if Germany were to attack Poland, Russia would be entitled to a share of the gains. Uneasy at the speed with which the German army was engulfing Poland, Russia invaded the stricken country on 17th September. Hopelessly under-equipped and outnumbered the Poles were forced to give up the struggle on their home soil and by the end of the month the republic was summarily dismembered.

Germany's first action was to incorporate a wide swath of westernmost Poland into the Third Reich, divide it into two and appoint an autonomous Gauleiter to each part. The brief given to these officials was to Germanise the new territories by whatever means they thought fit; as long as the aim was achieved no questions would be asked about the methods employed. In the north the simplest option was chosen: all Poles there were decreed to be Germans, a demoralising blow to a highly patriotic people. In the south, resident Germans took precedence over native Poles who were forced to leave their homes and businesses. The policy of ousting the Poles also enabled large numbers of ethnic Germans who, in the past, had formed their own communities in areas of eastern Europe to be brought back into the new Fatherland.

The displaced Poles were transported to the Generalgouvernement, the German-occupied zone that separated the enlarged Reich from Russian-occupied Poland. Here the brutal administration (headed from November onwards by the rabid anti-Semite, Hans Frank) found an economic role for non-Jewish Poles who were sent in their thousands to Germany to be ruthlessly exploited as forced labour in agriculture and industry. From the very beginning, the Nazis' hatred for the Jews was given full rein in the well-guarded privacy of the Generalgouvernement where mass murders were committed as early as September and October, 1939 and where, later, many of the death camps needed for the Final Solution were located.

For Britain and France there was, indeed, a deceptive calm as far as land warfare was concerned. The French and German armies warily kept watch on each other from the fortresses strung out along their supposedly impregnable Maginot and Siegfried Lines and the units comprising the British Expeditionary Force took up their supporting positions. The RAF did, however, carry the war to the enemy, though at this stage it was propaganda leaflets, not bombs, that were dropped on Germany.

A series of disastrous British losses inflicted at sea by German submarines dispelled any illusions the Allies may have had that the war was anything other than deadly serious. Within hours of Chamberlain's broadcast the passenger ship *Athenia* was torpedoed with a loss of over a hundred lives, many of them American. In the middle of September the Royal Navy suffered its first major casualty when the sinking of the aircraft carrier *Courageous* cost the lives of some five hundred men. Worse still was to come when on 14th October a U-boat found its way through what were believed to be the impenetrable underwater defences of the naval base at Scapa Flow, sank the battleship *Royal Oak* at its anchorage and escaped unscathed. Over eight hundred members of *Royal Oak's* crew died in this attack.

As 1939 was drawing to its close it was, appropriately, the sea war which provided the first cause for British celebration. On 13th December the German pocket battleship *Graf Spee* which had been raiding merchant shipping in the South Atlantic was engaged by three Royal Navy cruisers in the Battle of the River Plate and damage to the *Graf Spee* was serious enough for her to seek temporary refuge in the neutral port of Montevideo. The three British vessels had also suffered badly but with reinforcements on the way there was no hope of the German ship surviving another encounter and on 17th December her captain, Hans Langsdorff, took the *Graf Spee* back to sea and scuttled her.

But the loss of one battleship did nothing to deflect Hitler from his plans for German expansion and with the launch of the Blitzkrieg against the countries of western Europe in the spring of

1940 there could no longer be any doubt that total war had begun in earnest.

*   *   *

The commercial record companies quickly adapted themselves to the new conditions when hostilities broke out in September, 1939. The likelihood of war had so dominated the European political scene in the later 1930s that there had been ample time for them to prepare their contingency plans. It was inevitable that, as in the First World War, shellac for 78 r.p.m. discs would again be in short supply and difficult decisions needed to be taken over how best to allocate this vital manufacturing ingredient between the various types of repertoire.

The Nazis attached great importance to the provision in depth of the aggressively patriotic marching songs used by Party organisations and the many branches of the armed services, together with other non-vocal military music. Naturally, it would have been unthinkable to push the great Austro-German musical heritage into the background so, in this sector of the market, volume of output was sacrificed in order to concentrate on recording major works in performances of commensurate quality. This approach to the classical repertoire carried its own propaganda pay-off since it served to show the outside world that Germany had lost none of its pre-war reputation for musical excellence.

Norway, Denmark, Holland, Luxembourg, Belgium and France fell with bewildering speed into German hands. By the end of June France had signed armistices with Germany and Italy, after which the country was divided into two zones, one occupied and controlled by Germany, the other unoccupied but with a collaborating government led by Marshal Pétain, the renowned defender of Verdun against the Germans in 1916. In this unnatural situation the French companies had no choice but to follow as best they could the broad pattern of pre-war issues, whilst at the same time having to comply with the policy of cultural anti-Semitism imposed by their Nazi overlords.

As far as the changed conditions allowed, the British companies likewise aimed to supply their customers with a range of choice similar to that which had been on offer during the inter-war years. A degree of preferential treatment was given to popular dance music which, with its often humorous and highly optimistic lyrics, helped

131

to enliven the winter of 1939-40, especially the nights when, as a precaution against air raids, there was no street lighting and the windows and outer doors of all buildings were subject to the black-out regulations. Moving up the scale of taste, ballad-loving record buyers continued to be catered for and the companies, sometimes drawing on unfamiliar corners of the repertoire, tried valiantly to keep pace with the growing demand for classical music which the war had generated. EMI and Decca, the two main British producers, also issued documentary recordings and gramophonic equivalents of government posters and printed information in an effort to bring the harsh realities of war to the civilian population.

Decca published this kind of material in its SP series which hitherto had been home to private recordings for organisations as diverse as the English Folk Music Society, the British Union of Fascists' Male Voice Choir and Orchestra and Guy's Hospital, the resident staff of which made discs of selections from their annual shows. Now the series provided a wider public service with records giving advice on first aid techniques, what action to take in an air raid and how to deal with incendiary bombs. Decca also took on the role of historian when it used the same series to chronicle the early stages of *World War Number Two*. With the help of authentic recordings of the leading political figures involved, the progress of the conflict was traced on ten twelve-inch discs from the European political crisis of 1938 to the fall of France in 1940, taking in on the way first hand accounts of the sinking of the *Graf Spee* and the rescue by the destroyer H.M.S. *Cossack* in mid-February, 1940 of British seamen held prisoner aboard the German merchant ship *Altmark*.

This swashbuckling incident which occurred some seven weeks before Hitler invaded Norway and Denmark immediately caught the British public's imagination. Here was the Royal Navy displaying the Nelson touch in more ways than one: not only did the rescue come in the nick of time for the 300 British seamen *en route* to prisoner of war camps in Germany but in order to bring it off the *Cossack's* captain turned a blind eye to the *Altmark's* being in what were then still neutral Norwegian waters. Decca was not alone in documenting the story for the gramophone. The original Regal company whose recording of Sergeant Edward Dwyer's recollections of Mons had been one of the most outstanding contributions to the contemporary oral history of the First World War had merged with Zonophone in 1933 as part of the rationalisation of EMI. The rechristened Regal Zonophone seized the opportunity to re-enter this specialised sector of the repertoire and on 8th March, 1940, a mere three weeks after his liberation, Second Engineer George King of the SS *Doric Star* was in the company's studio to set down his account of the events. In due course the spoken word was followed by song and *The Navy's Here* (the cry that went up as the boarding party set foot on the *Altmark*) enjoyed a brief vogue that brought dance band discs by Jack Payne from Decca and Joe Loss from HMV, though it was the boisterous Billy Cotton who took the lead when, on 19th April, he recorded the number for the cheap and cheerful Rex label.

Before the outbreak of war HMV had already been engaged in work of national importance when, for civil defence training purposes, the company produced in its bargain label BD series two ten-inch discs dealing with air raid precautions. These records reproduced the siren, whistle, rattle and handbell signals that would warn the British people of air raids or gas attacks and explained what action had to be taken in such circumstances. The risk of misuse, either in thoughtless fun or for more sinister reasons, was too great to permit the discs going on sale in the normal way, although *The Gramophone* was sent copies which were briefly mentioned in the October issue and are still preserved in the magazine's archives.

Given the advance planning needed when marketing new records each month it was probably just the result of routine scheduling that in September, 1939 HMV released *A Cavalcade of Martial Songs* played by the Bickershaw Colliery Band. The disc comprised a number of items gathered from stage revues of the 1920s and 1930s including *The King's Horses* (a song that was later "turned" by the Nazi radio propaganda service) and *There's Something About a Soldier*, both of which were associated with the vivacious comedienne, Cicely Courtneidge. To describe the selection as martial was stretching a point; these two tunes were jolly enough but they were hardly sinew-stiffening products and the same can be said of *The Toy Drum Major* and *The Toytown Artillery* which also formed part of the medley. It was a little unlucky for HMV that the appearance of such an innocuous recording should have coincided with

133

the beginning of the Second World War, yet in a way it reflected the spirit of its time. The conflict in faraway Poland was as distant from the average British citizen as the music of the *Cavalcade* was from the genuine military article and the disc can now be regarded as an apt prelude to the phoney war.

Even with modern sound effects dubbed in, the studio-made descriptives which began to appear again were of variable quality. Amongst its November releases Parlophone featured one which it advertised as:

> "Heroic War Episode. The Sinking of the SS Kensington Court (by a German Submarine and subsequent rescue by R.A.F. Flying Boats). A Reconstruction of the Episode by Capt. J. Schofield and Company. Wings over the Navy. Played by The Organ, Dance Band and Me. Intro: A Short speech of thanks by Capt. J. Schofield."

Musically as well as dramatically this was a patchwork compilation. *Wings over the Navy* was not even a British song but had been written by the Americans Johnny Mercer and Henry Warren for the 1939 Hollywood film *Wings of the Navy*. Billy Thorburn's group The Organ, the Dance Band and Me had recorded it in May that year when, prophetically, its coupling was *The Old Tin Helmet*. Having this more or less relevant piece of music readily available Parlophone economically reused it as a filler to their version of the *Kensington Court* incident.

In the two decades of uneasy peace that separated the First and Second World Wars there had, of course, been no opportunity for the British commercial record industry to develop its skills in the production of war-related discs and the pages of *The Gramophone* for the last quarter of 1939 show this lack of practical experience very clearly. If the bargain label *Kensington Court* descriptive which retailed at two shillings (10p) seems artificial by present-day standards that feeling is even more marked in another Parlophone offering, *Going up the Line* by Some of the Boys, the contents of which were summarised in the journal's Christmas number. As one reads of "marching, desultory singing, commands, and at the end machine-gun fire and the sound of shells" the years roll back and memories of descriptives from 1914-1918 irresistibly come to mind; understandably, the reviewer was not greatly impressed. It would not be long, however, before the gramophone became as distinctive a medium as the press and the newsreels for on-the-spot war reporting.

Whereas in the First World War conscription in Great Britain was not introduced until 1916, an on-going system of call-up to the armed forces had been in operation for about three months before the country went to war again in September, 1939. Because of this there was no need for the insidious moral blackmail that in 1914 and 1915 had pervaded the songs specifically designed to bring potential volunteers into the services. The RAF, though, had already indicated a lack of trained personnel when it brought out its own official recruiting song *Fall in and Fly* which the ubiquitous Billy Cotton and his band recorded for Rex in mid-February, 1939. The definitive version came a little later when HMV included it in the Royal Air Force Band's series of *Music for Service Occasions*. In keeping with their purpose and as an eye-catching publicity ploy these ten-inch discs were given distinctive Air Force blue labels and their catalogue numbers bore the prefix RAF.

★   ★   ★

During the First World War the British market for jingoistic songs which, in essence, were little more than crude propaganda set to music had begun to dry up long before the end of the conflict in 1918. The cause of this decline was that the appalling death toll on the Western Front was failing to produce any major strategic advantage for the Allies. In a war of attrition that was bloody and brutal on a scale without precedent, unadulterated chauvinism was no longer an effective means of maintaining either public or military morale. For the survivors no less than for the families and friends of those who died such songs were best ignored and forgotten since they tended merely to aggravate distressing memories of times of profound physical and mental anguish.

The best loved popular music during the Great War was of a gentler, sometimes humorous, sometimes sentimental nature and it was still strongly represented in the British companies' catalogues throughout the 1920s and 1930s, unlike the flag-waving, sabre-rattling songs which vanished from the recorded repertoire. In a totally different category, however, the archival value of Will Gaisberg's landmark documentary of the gas shell bombardment near Lille in October, 1918 ensured it would enjoy special status in HMV's No. 2 (Historical) Section for more than twenty years.

135

The enduring demand for new recordings of popular songs from the First World War was evident in 1930 when Columbia launched its mid-price DX series of twelve-inch dark blue label discs. That year's October releases included Debroy Somers and his band with the soprano Alice Lilley and a Male Quartette [sic] in a selection of *War Marching Songs*. Here was the music the fighting men had truly taken to their hearts. *Keep the Home Fires Burning, Pack up Your Troubles, Tipperary, Mademoiselle from Armentieres* and similar songs on this record had lifted their spirits in war-time and, with the return of peace, intensified memories of the comradeship which had helped sustain them through the most harrowing experiences of their lives. This disc remained on sale for well over fourteen years until its eventual deletion in February, 1945.

In passing, one notices that other war-related early DX recordings had a much shorter life-span. The Roosters Concert Party, formed during the Great War and later a well-known music hall turn, was renowned for its humorous sketches; on record, though, the *Old Comrades Re-Union* and *Tommy's Christmas* came and went within the space of seven years. *The Recruiting Office*, issued in January, 1935, departed from the catalogue exactly four years later when, with the threat of another war looming, it was inappropriate for so vital a matter as the manpower of Britain's armed forces to be treated lightheartedly. The oddest recording from this corner of Columbia's repertoire came in the initial release of the DX series in the form of *Voyage of a Troopship* with the Band of the Grenadier Guards and a Vocal Quartette [sic] conducted by Captain George Miller. Although the disc consists of a medley of mainly nautical songs its lineage clearly goes back to Fred Gaisberg and Russell Hunting's historic Boer War descriptive, *The Departure of a Troopship*. The destination of Columbia's ship was uncertain but the musical programme was highly predictable, beginning tearfully as those on shore bid farewell to their men; the perils of a storm in the Bay of Biscay are overcome and all ends happily with a Saturday night sing-song on the fo'c'sle and *Rule Britannia*. It would be interesting to know what persuaded Columbia to bring out the *Voyage* at this time for by 1930 such scenarios had already begun to seem dated. It comes as no surprise that the disc was withdrawn after being in circulation for little more than four years.

Much of the patriotic music enjoyed during the inter-war period had been familiar since the turn of the century. A. C. Benson's words to Elgar's *Land of Hope and Glory* have been sneered at by modern generations for their unashamed patriotism but they came from an age when Britain and its Empire were an enormous source of national pride and the sincerely felt lyric was superior in every way to the facile jingles of so many hurriedly concocted patriotic songs of the Great War. Elgar's immediately memorable tune had, in fact, made *Land of Hope and Glory* a gramophone favourite ever since its first appearance on disc in 1905. Numerous recordings were made in the 1914-1918 war and large numbers of new versions continued to appear in the ensuing years of peace. Gradually it took on the function of an unofficial second national anthem and in 1926 Columbia's engineers captured the voices of 14,000 community singers accompanied by the Band of the Irish Guards giving an enthusiastic rendering of it at London's Fulham Football Ground. Significantly, on this ten-inch disc it was coupled with *God Save the King*.

In contrast with the grand imperial statement of *Land of Hope and Glory* there was a large store of music the patriotic element of which stemmed from an idealised, golden view of a specifically English past often, as in various works of Sir Edward German, with an idyllic English countryside as its backdrop. Throughout the 1920s and 1930s selections from German's operetta *Merrie England* and dances from his incidental music for the plays *Nell Gwynn* by Anthony Hope and Shakespeare's *Henry VIII* were regularly played by brass and military bands and light orchestras. Meanwhile the record companies made sure that German's music was always well represented in their catalogues. By this time, though, with dance bands dominating the field of popular music, new additions to the patriotic repertoire were relatively few. As it happened, an excellent example of the genre came in early 1933 with the appearance of *Old Father Thames*. The sturdy baritone voice and impeccable diction of HMV's Peter Dawson were admirably suited to this evocation of a famous natural feature that was also a national symbol. Dawson's recording in its 78 r.p.m. format remained available for some twenty years.

Shrewd popular song writers prepared for the coming of war by building up stocks of suitable pieces ready for submission to the music publishers at the crucial moment. One of the earliest (and certainly the most durable) of the non-humorous patriotic songs to emerge was *There'll Always be an England*, which managed to combine emotive images of country lanes and fields of grain with a timely tribute to the British Empire. When HMV recorded it they had the very man in Dennis Noble, a baritone in the Peter Dawson mould, whose repertoire stretched from ballads to opera and oratorio. Noble actually recorded the song twice for the company, once with piano accompaniment and again with a vocal quartet and the Band of the Coldstream Guards. Decca had such faith in the song's selling power that it issued no less than three performances in widely differing styles by the baritone Sidney Burchall, Jack Payne and his band and, as part of a medley, by Billy Scott-Coomber and his Singing Grenadiers. It almost goes without saying that Billy Cotton was well to the fore in the race to the studios when he set down his account for Rex on 15th September, just twelve days after the declaration of war.

⋆   ⋆   ⋆

During the six months lull in the land war that followed Poland's defeat British attention focused increasingly on the massive French and German frontier protection systems, the Maginot and Siegfried Lines which, people believed, would be the setting for the next stage of the war. Deep below ground the Maginot Line comprised a string of huge fortresses capable of housing retractable artillery emplacements, all connected by a network of spacious communication tunnels, whilst on the surface tank traps and mine-fields guarded the whole length of the Line.

In addition to their own tank traps and mine-fields the Germans, on the other hand, built virtually all the Siegfried Line's fortifications above ground in a five-mile-wide zone containing over 3,000 pill-boxes. Simply expressed, the opposing defences ran from eastern Belgium to Switzerland in the case of the Maginot Line with the Siegfried Line (also known as the West Wall) extending similarly but from Holland at its northern end.

Both of the Lines gave rise to British popular songs. The Lancashire comedian George Formby, like his famous father a stalwart of the music halls, came up with *Imagine Me in the Maginot Line* which he recorded shortly before Christmas, 1939 for Regal Zonophone. *The Gramophone* in its April, 1940 issue briefly noted

138

the appearance of the disc but the song, rapidly overtaken by the course of events, was not destined to be one of Formby's greatest hits. In any case, as the Maginot Line was part of the Allies' defences it offered only limited scope to the song writers, whereas Germany's Siegfried Line was an excellent target for vocal scorn and derision. *I'm Sending You the Siegfried Line (to Hang Your Washing on)* was one of the songs to achieve several recordings but it was completely overshadowed by *(We're Gonna Hang out) the Washing on the Siegfried Line* which, either on its own or as part of a medley, received no fewer than seven dance band recordings between 15th September and 24th October, 1939. Comedians such as Arthur Askey on HMV also found it went down well with their audiences and Decca, not content with their recording by Ambrose's band alone, went on to publish discs by three highly admired music hall acts, Flanagan and Allen, Elsie and Doris Waters and Billy Russell. There could be no better illustration of how, with their wide choice of recordings of this supremely optimistic song, to say nothing of all the other brand-new euphoric numbers swelling their lists, the British companies from the very beginning played a significant part in strengthening public confidence in a speedy, successful outcome to the war.

The government recognised the importance of live entertainment as a means of keeping up the spirits of Britain's armed forces and civilian war workers and much of the responsibility for the provision of this rested with ENSA, the Entertainments National Services Association. Not unexpectedly, the quality of the fare on offer varied wildly and while some shows included stars like Geraldo and his band, Will Fyffe, the Scottish comedian and the debonair singer and dancer Jack Buchanan others were poor enough to inspire the waggish reinterpretation of ENSA's initials as Every Night Something Awful.

Thanks to the gramophone it is possible to hear some of the most popular artists of the period, often in makeshift conditions, as they contributed to the morale-boosting process. Regal Zonophone was quickly off the mark with recordings issued in December 1939 of Gracie Fields at a camp "somewhere in England" and "with the Troops in France" singing her own highly successful numbers such as *The Biggest Aspidistra in the World* mingled with a variety of current hits, amongst them the patriotic

There'll Always be an England and the comic *Run, Rabbit, Run*, a song which led a double life as *Run, Adolf, Run*.

When Arthur Askey and Richard Murdoch went on tour in France the BBC broadcast their famous sketch *The Proposal*, the script of which had Murdoch advising his diminutive partner on how to propose to his sweetheart; soon afterwards HMV issued its recording of this performance in which the two comedians and their service audience are to be heard revelling in the deliberately antique gags. Another comedian served particularly well by HMV in the early years of the war was Max Miller (The Cheeky Chappie) whose act for the forces "somewhere in England" in November, 1940 was preserved on six ten-inch sides of the company's bargain label BD series. Miller was renowned for his racy brand of humour and the set includes him telling stories from the White Book and the Blue Book; inevitably, it was the Blue Book that was most often in demand. A year later HMV rejoined Miller on the road and recorded four more sides as once again he worked his audience in his inimitable way, this time at a canteen concert for war workers.

Such discs are interesting on a number of counts. As wartime memorabilia they document the type of light entertainment that was widely enjoyed in those hazardous days. Furthermore, being live recordings they conveyed the sense of occasion, the spontaneity and the close rapport between performer and audience that could not be replicated in the studio. This immediacy increased the pleasure of contemporary gramophone listeners by helping to create the illusion of actually being present while a favourite star was on stage. For later generations they are historically valuable since they allow us to hear leading artists of a vanished age giving their utmost in the theatrical environment that supplied their greatest stimulus.

With the passing of more than half a century the humorous and sentimental wartime songs of Gracie Fields are now seldom encountered save in CD transfers of her original recordings produced by companies catering for the nostalgia market. As for the comedians, their material belonged to the robust traditions of the British music hall, an institution never noted for prudery, but even so, their acts bear witness to a less permissive age than ours. Although his signature tune included the lines "Clean if I'm not very clever/But only 'cos I've got to be", Arthur Askey's turns were

140

predominantly homely in content as, indeed, they needed to be for his regular broadcasts on the BBC which closely scrutinised its programmes to avoid any vulgarity going out over the airways. Max Miller, naturally, was not acceptable to the BBC, yet the bluest of the Cheeky Chappie's stories were mild compared with the obscenity of stand-up comedians (both male and female) of more recent times.

★   ★   ★

In Britain the war brought about a remarkable upsurge of interest in classical music. The demand for popular music was unabated but many folk began to feel the need for something more inwardly satisfying. After a brief closure following the declaration of war, the country's cinemas, theatres and concert halls were permitted to reopen and in London one of the first musicians to provide for this expanding audience was the pianist Dame Myra Hess who organised the instrumental and chamber concerts that were given daily throughout the war at the National Gallery. The Wigmore Hall was home to a long-running series devoted to French music and the Queen's Hall continued as the principal venue for orchestral concerts. It was here that Sir Thomas Beecham and the London Philharmonic Orchestra played an all-Sibelius programme in honour of Finland which, after three months of hard fighting, had been obliged to surrender in March, 1940 to its Russian invaders.

When the war came Sir Thomas was already under contract to conduct a sequence of concerts in Australia during 1940; unfortunately, by the time of his departure the future of the London Philharmonic was in jeopardy as its main backer, Lady Cunard, the London society hostess and close friend of Beecham, was herself in financial difficulties. Rescue came from an unexpected quarter when, as the September, 1940 issue of *The Gramophone* recounted, Jack Hylton, the band leader turned impresario

"... engaged the orchestra for a tour of the music halls to give twice nightly full-length orchestral concerts. He also engaged Malcolm Sargent and Basil Cameron to conduct them and Eileen Joyce to appear as a soloist...

The tour started at the Empire Theatre, Glasgow on August 12th. ... Twice nightly the theatre was filled to capacity or near it by people of all classes most of whom enjoyed for the first time the matchless stimulation of the sound of a full first-class orchestra. ... It is refreshing to think that in one week more than twenty thousand people in Glasgow paid their hard-earned money to listen to the L.P.O. playing programmes which make so few concessions to what is generally supposed to be the public's lack of taste."

Symphonies such as Schubert's *Unfinished*, Dvořák's *New World* and Tchaikovsky's Fifth adroitly mixed with attractive shorter pieces like the latter's *Romeo and Juliet* and Ravel's *Bolero* proved just how accessible classical music could be.

It was frustrating for the British companies that an increased demand for classical music should have coincided with the onset of wartime shortages and restrictions. HMV and Columbia were now unable to send their producers and technical teams to Berlin, Vienna and Prague where, in the past, they had made so many notable recordings with the great orchestras of those cities. To aggravate matters, Parlophone and Decca were respectively cut off from Odeon and Deutsche Grammophon/Polydor whose selected products the two British companies had pressed for their own classical catalogues throughout the 1930s. In passing, it is interesting to note that neither EMI nor Decca exercised cultural censorship over the new German recordings they had in their pipe-lines at the start of the war but continued to issue them a few at a time until about mid-1940 when supplies ran out.

Specialist record shops were similarly affected since they could no longer import the expensive (and often highly desirable) releases from Telefunken. By February, 1940 the London dealer Rimington, Van Wyck was advertising "Foreign Recordings. Perhaps the Last of Them" amongst which, in addition to a few remaining Telefunkens, were a number of HMV and Columbia discs not issued in Great Britain and items from the French Lumen, Pro Musica and Pathé labels. For classical collectors, especially those with esoteric musical interests, the future looked rather depressing.

As well as being deprived of front-rank European artists and advantageous franchises the British companies had many other problems in common. Unpredictable difficulties complicated the planning of recording sessions for resident British musicians who, as like as not, were busily involved in making their own contribution to the war effort; and furthermore, the companies were all suffering from the erosive effect of conscription or other forms of war service on all levels of their staff. Over and above these human factors there loomed the imminent shortage of the vital manufacturing ingredient, shellac; it was plain to see that the British gramophone industry was heading for a steep fall in output.

★   ★   ★

Shortages of one sort or another were the *raison d'être* of the many salvage drives initiated and encouraged by the government and civil organisations during the greater part of the war. When men armed with oxyacetylene torches removed the iron railings from people's front gardens, London squares and well-tended city centres the public sacrifice was, doubtless by design, a very visible one. This scrap metal was taken away supposedly to be transformed into weapons for the fighting men, though long after the war was over caches of it were discovered still in remote official stockpiles. Door to door collections of lighter products were made on a local basis by school children, Boy Scouts and other youth groups as well as by community volunteers who trundled their barrows around the streets. The appeal for old pots and pans (especially aluminium ones for the production of Spitfire fighter aircraft) was again probably intended more as a psychological boost to national morale than as a significant method of acquiring strategic metals.

The drives for paper (particularly books) and gramophone records, however, were of considerable value. Books of a recreational nature were passed on to the forces while those left over could be sent for pulping and reprocessing into new paper. In the early stages of the war the record salvagers concentrated on gathering discs that would provide entertainment in canteens and messes for service personnel in their off-duty hours. The target was therefore modern, electrical recordings as the old acoustic discs, even those of "classic" status, would hold little attraction for the average men and women in uniform. But as the war dragged on the record industry's supplies of essential raw materials ran so low that a national drive was set up to bring in discs specifically for recycling. The British (now Royal British) Legion, which since 1921 had provided social and welfare facilities for ex- and serving members of the forces, opened its record salvage campaign in August, 1942 with famous recording artists like the singers Richard Tauber and Anne Shelton queuing to hand over their surplus discs at the Legion's main office in London. Donors could leave their unwanted recordings at any of the Legion's nationwide network of branches from which they would be sold on to the needy record companies for reuse. Many of the 78s that were likely to be offered would have been issued by companies, some of them long defunct, using materials of too poor a quality for recycling; accordingly the Legion's publicity poster warned that only HMV, Columbia, Parlophone, Regal-Zonophone, Zonophone, Brunswick, Decca, Rex and Panachord discs were acceptable.

Walter Legge describes in his memoirs another salvage scheme in which the participants were the record companies, the dealers and the consumers. According to Legge

"In England records were rationed and to buy a new one the customer had to pay not only the price but give two old records as well. These were broken up and used as "filler"."

Strictly speaking, of course, records were not "rationed" in the way that food and clothing were since those necessities were obtainable by the civilian population only on production of the requisite government coupons. Under the terms mentioned by Legge a classical collector wanting a *Magic Flute* overture would have to trade in the disc equivalent of *Eine kleine Nachtmusik* and to obtain a Tchaikovsky B flat minor piano concerto would entail giving up, say, his sets of the Grieg and Schumann concertos. In other words, the more a collector bought, the smaller his collection would become, which was an unthinkable prospect. A more equitable exchange rate of one old for one new record would seem to have been adopted but even this was a deterrent to dedicated record lovers whose reluctance to trade in treasured discs would inevitably have an adverse effect on sales.

By 1939 demand for records was high and competition in the retail business was strong. Record outlets had moved a long way up market since those distant days when they had been tucked away at the back of bicycle shops. Now, in addition to shops totally given over to them, records were to be found as a matter of course in high class department stores and handsomely appointed establishments which specialised in all things musical from metronomes to grand pianos. The people who ran these outlets had to find means of protecting their record sales but just how the question of trade-in was solved is something of a mystery. Customers would soon exhaust

144

their own stock of disposable discs and the keenest of them may even have scoured their neighbourhood junk shops and sorted through the piles of hard-used ancient discs which sold for a few pence each in the hope of finding some of suitable origin for recycling. It is pure speculation but it is also possible that dealers themselves may have had private arrangements with junk shops and salvage workers in order to build up a supply of trade-in discs for use when customers were unable to produce any. The system, whatever it was, appeared to work very satisfactorily since, if a personal note may be allowed, neither the author nor any of the wartime record buyers known to him can remember ever being asked to hand in old records for new.

★   ★   ★

When it came to maintaining a wartime supply of classical music HMV and Columbia were well placed in that over the past twenty years they had developed firm ties with the most important English symphony orchestras and their associated conductors. In addition, the two companies each had another major resource: access to the transatlantic riches, popular and classical, of the Victor and American Columbia catalogues.

From the very beginning of the war there had been government warnings that hardships would have to be endured by the population at large. Austerity was to be the order of the day, a policy that rapidly made itself felt when first food and then clothing were rationed. Not surprisingly, these measures brought in their wake both informal barter and a flourishing black market that offered (at a price) goods that were in short supply ranging from whisky to razor blades and from silk stockings to elastic. For economic and social reasons the government was particularly opposed to money being spent on luxury goods, a heading under which gramophone records were later classified when purchase tax at the rate of $33\frac{1}{3}\%$ on the wholesale price was introduced in October, 1940.

With the firmly stated official position in mind and in anticipation of changing market conditions HMV and Columbia decided very early in the war to issue virtually all their new classical recordings by British orchestras and artists at mid-price. It was foreseeable that as more and more members of the armed forces left Britain for service overseas consumer numbers would drop, though to some extent this downturn would be balanced by the unavoidable fall in

145

output. In such circumstances the lower retail price would help to sustain sales amongst the regular record buyers still remaining at home and at the same time encourage the new classical music lovers to develop their interests more widely through the medium of the gramophone. Another consideration that would have influenced the decision was the (ultimately vain) hope that the availability of good music in commendable performances at a reasonable price would add weight to the industry's contention that records were not luxuries but educational, recreational and morale-boosting products.

The adoption of the mid-price policy, however, resulted in HMV temporarily losing one of its finest recording orchestras. After Beecham's departure from the London Philharmonic the BBC Symphony Orchestra was the country's one truly world-class ensemble. It had been formed in 1930 and under its conductor, Sir Adrian Boult, its performing standards were of the highest in the classics and British and foreign contemporary music. Its international status was undisputed for it was the only British orchestra which in pre-war times Arturo Toscanini could be persuaded to conduct in the concert hall and the recording studio. The BBC was unwilling to have its orchestra appear to be downgraded since from its earliest days its recordings had, with one minor exception, been issued solely on HMV's prestigious red label at premium price. It was a valid objection as the other orchestras involved, although thoroughly professional bodies, were less outstanding. When, in the national interest, everybody was being urged to pull together, it would have been invidious for HMV to single out the BBC Symphony Orchestra for special treatment while all its other British orchestras were marketed on mid-price labels. Accordingly after sessions at Bristol in April, 1940 when works by Mozart, Sibelius, Tchaikovsky and Vaughan Williams were recorded, HMV and the BBC Symphony parted company for more than four years until August, 1944 when working relations were resumed.

After the abrupt cutting of its link with Odeon, Parlophone had few resources apart from its back catalogue with which to supplement HMV and Columbia's wartime classical releases and therefore withdrew from this sector of the repertoire. Decca was a relative newcomer to the recording side of the British gramophone industry having issued its first discs only ten years before the outbreak of the Second World War. Nevertheless, it had been a quick learner and thanks to the drive and vision of Edward Lewis, the stockbroker who had floated the company in 1928 and later became its chairman, it had not only survived the Depression years but had actually expanded during the 1930s. The Edison Bell and Crystalate companies were bought up in 1933 and 1937 respectively whilst in 1934 the founding of the Decca Record Company (USA) resulted in many of the highly popular artists who had previously recorded for the American Brunswick label coming under Decca's wing.

From the very beginning Decca set out to provide its customers with plenty of modern British music and to feature British artists prominently in its output. Its initial batch of records that appeared in July, 1929 boldly included Delius's *Sea Drift* sung by Roy Henderson, a leading baritone of the day, with the pseudonymous New English Symphony orchestra and Choir; the players were actually Anthony Bernard's London Chamber Orchestra which, for contractual reasons, could not be named by Decca. Henderson recalled some seventy years after making the recording that

"No one heard a word the choir sang and hardly a word I sang - there was only one microphone ... I had to go on to ballads after that because it nearly broke them."

This was the first time *Sea Drift* had been taken up by any record company and it was followed by many other gramophone premières of British music from Decca's studios. Two outstanding examples issued in 1936 were Sir Hamilton Harty and the London Symphony Orchestra in William Walton's First Symphony (an interpretation that remained unequalled until 1966 when RCA brought out André Previn's performance with the same orchestra) and Sir Henry Wood's deeply felt reading of Vaughan Williams's *A London Symphony* with the resurrected Queen's Hall Orchestra. A steady flow of chamber music during the 1930s included major works by Alan Rawsthorne, Sir Arthur Bliss and John Ireland and, from farther afield, the String Trio Op. 20 by Anton Webern, one of the earliest examples (perhaps the first) of this composer's works to be recorded commercially - and by three British women instrumentalists into the bargain.

From 1935 until well after the end of the war Boyd Neel's String Orchestra was a prized contributor to the Decca catalogue. Neel's infectious enthusiasm for the wide variety of works available in his chosen field and for baroque and twentieth century British music in particular earned him and his fine players a staunch concert-going and record-buying public. One of the group's most influential pre-war recordings had been the complete set of Handel's Twelve Concerti Grossi, Op. 6 issued between November, 1936 and December, 1938 which set new scholarly standards for the performance of music from the baroque period.

Circumstances dictated that full scale symphonic music had to be dropped from Decca's wartime domestic recording schedules until 1944 when the company was fortunate enough to sign up Sidney Beer's recently formed National Symphony Orchestra which, to all intents and purposes, then served as Decca's house orchestra.

For its wartime issues of chamber and instrumental music Decca had a remarkable roster of artists on which it could call. The Griller String Quartet continued to support British composers with works by Bax and Bliss and the company nurtured the early recording careers of such subsequently world famous names as the violinist Ida Haendel and the pianists Moura Lympany (who between 1941 and 1943 recorded all Rachmaninov's Preludes, op. 23 and Op. 32), Clifford Curzon, the brilliant Noel Mewton-Wood who, sadly, was to take his own life in 1953 and Benjamin Britten as duet pianist, piano accompanist and conductor.

Decca may have been the new boy of the British record industry but in the space of a decade the company had acquired a large enough pool of reputable artists for it to compete with its rivals at EMI in most areas of the repertoire on something approaching level terms even under wartime conditions.

II – Total War

WHEN AT LAST the phoney war gave way to total war the transition was swift and devastating as the Wehrmacht applied its Blitzkrieg tactics to the countries of northern and western Europe. The briefest chronology is enough to convey the scale of Hitler's conquests as the spring of 1940 merged into summer. Norway and Denmark were invaded on 9th April and Denmark had no option but to yield straight away. To help in the defence of southern Norway an Allied force was sent in on 20th April but this was unable to stem the Geman advance and had to withdraw two weeks later. In the north, however, the Royal Navy had taken the important harbour and town of Narvik and it was in this area where the rest of the fighting was concentrated until on 8th June it once again became necessary to withdraw; the following day the Norwegian army surrendered.

In the meantime the Wehrmacht launched offensives on 10th May against Holland, Belgium and Luxembourg. Between the capitulation of Holland on 15th and Belgium on 27th May the Germans, having bypassed the Maginot Line, struck out across northern France to Abbeville near the mouth of the river Somme, thereby cutting off the British and Belgian armies in Flanders from the rest of the Allied forces in France. Desperate rear-guard actions were fought in the course of the retreat to the harbour and beaches of Dunkirk. From here, under constant attack during the last few days of May and up to 4th June, over 330,000 soldiers (one third of them French) were evacuated to England by naval and merchant ships and everything that could be mustered in the way of shallow draught vessels such as tugs, fishing smacks and paddle steamers capable of going closer inshore. Together with these came a great fleet of privately owned small craft sailed by men of all ages who in peacetime enjoyed the pleasures of messing about in boats and who now volunteered their services for this epic combined operation.

During the period 10th to 19th June Allied troops to the south of the German advance continued to be evacuated via the available ports on France's Channel and Atlantic coastlines; it was also on 10th June that Mussolini, with an eye as always to the main chance, declared war on France and Britain. For the French there was further humiliation when on 14th June the Germans entered Paris. The end could not be delayed much longer and on 22nd June France assented to the armistice terms laid down by Hitler. The Nazis occupied the northern part of the country and the entire French seaboard, whilst the south (except for the small areas annexed by Italy) was administered by Pétain's puppet government from Vichy. Looking ahead, France's ultimate shame was not to come for another two years when in November, 1942, following the Allied landings in French North Africa, the Germans and Italians took over the whole of Vichy France in order to guard against possible attack from across the Mediterranean.

★   ★   ★

Newsreel films of soldiers rescued from Dunkirk coming ashore in England show the faces of exhausted men thankful to be back home once more; they carried little or no equipment but their emotional burdens were heavy. It was galling to acknowledge the lamentable truth that they had been comprehensively outfought by the enemy; and memories of comrades left behind, either dead or facing an indeterminate future as prisoners of war, only added to their anguish. The impact of Dunkirk on the British civilian population was equally traumatic bringing the realisation that with only the English Channel separating them from the Germans their country would inevitably be Hitler's next target.

Alone and highly vulnerable Britain urgently needed a leader as charismatic as Adolf Hitler and it now had such a man in Winston Churchill who had for years warned of the dangers posed by the unchecked rise of Nazi Germany. Neville Chamberlain throughout his premiership had been essentially a peacemaker and lacked the toughness required by a head of government in wartime. As a consequence he inspired so little confidence that by 10th May, 1940 when Germany attacked Holland and Belgium the volume of criticism had grown so great that he was forced to resign and the post of Prime Minister passed to Churchill whose personal experience of war was considerable. During Kitchener's reconquest of the

150

Sudan he had, in 1898, ridden in the famous cavalry charge at the battle of Omdurman; as a newspaper correspondent in the Boer War he was taken prisoner but succeeded in making a daring escape from Pretoria to regain his freedom in neutral Portuguese East Africa (now Mozambique), a journey of almost three hundred miles; and when the Great War of 1914-1918 broke out he was First Lord of the Admiralty until, after the failure of the Dardanelles campaign, he went to serve with the army in France. Furthermore, he was outstandingly gifted as a writer and speaker and it was in this latter role that his voice rapidly became familiar to the people of Great Britain.

It was on 19th May, 1940, shortly after forming his coalition government, that Churchill made the first of his many broadcasts concerning the progress of the war. These historic statements, recorded as they were transmitted by the BBC, were issued by HMV on their twelve-inch, mid-price C series label. Listening to these discs one is immediately aware of Churchill's unique qualities as a public speaker. The language he used was plain and to the point but so masterfully phrased and uttered that matters of supreme importance could be dramatically imparted without recourse to high-flown rhetoric. His voice, despite the occasional impediment, was the perfect medium for his eloquent prose. Vocal colouring was perceptibly changed as he moved from serious warnings to passages of patriotic fervour and it was his own indomitable spirit that fired the passion whenever he urged his listeners to give of their utmost in the fight for democracy and freedom. The tones of greatest scorn were naturally reserved for Hitler and Mussolini; those who heard him at the time or subsequently on recordings will always remember the infinite contempt he could convey in his pronunciation of the single word 'Nazi', the printed equivalent of which might be something akin to 'Naazzee'.

Virtually every one of Churchill's wartime speeches contains phrases or sentences now to be found in any reputable dictionary of quotations. When he assumed office he told the House of Commons that "I have nothing to offer but blood, toil, tears and sweat" and the same theme ran through his BBC broadcast of 19th May issued under the title *In a Solemn Hour* as the first disc in HMV's Churchill archives He stressed the vital need to keep up the supply of armaments for the fighting men since, if France was overrun, the next battle would be the battle for Britain. Whatever the cost, Britain would not succumb to (in his graphic image) "the long night of barbarism" that was falling on the countries of German-occupied Europe.

When the evacuation of Dunkirk had been completed Churchill assured the Commons that the struggle was not over; in one of his most famous speeches of defiance he vowed "... we shall fight on the beaches, we shall fight on the landing grounds ... we shall never surrender."[5] A fortnight later, with France on the brink of collapse, people throughout Great Britain tuned in to the BBC and heard that momentous call to arms

> "Let us therefore brace ourselves to our duties, and so bear ourselves that, if the British Empire and its Commonwealth last for a thousand years, men will still say: 'This was their finest hour'."

Fittingly, these last five words formed the title of the second issue in HMV's collection of Churchill's broadcasts. Hitler, Mussolini and Stalin projected themselves as the predestined, infallible rulers of their countries but this grandiose style of leadership was totally alien to Churchill. On radio and on disc people heard a man in whom they instinctively knew they could put their hope and trust. Churchill strengthened this bond by appearing in public as often as possible and in doing so his voice and features together with his trademark hat, walking stick, cigar and V for victory sign all played their part in winning him his fellow countrymen's loyalty, respect and affection. Visually and aurally he became almost overnight the embodiment of the bulldog breed; he was familiarly referred to as Winston or even Winny and, in 1941, was celebrated in the song *The Man with the Big Cigar* which Billy Cotton recorded for Rex.

HMV performed an invaluable service by issuing this extensive sequence of live recordings. For the first time a commercial record company was proposing to mark the turning points of what would be a long and terrible war as seen and chronicled by a national leader.[6] Later generations hearing these discs share in the immediacy experienced by Churchill's original listeners. Without in any way minimising the perils ahead Churchill in these early speeches inspired the British people to fight on with renewed courage and determination. In their recorded format his words could be rebroadcast whenever required or used selectively in radio feature programmes; collectors, aware of history in the making, bought these discs to document the turbulent times in which they were living; and, perhaps most importantly of all, the copies which made their way abroad sent a clear message to the free world: Britain would never give in to the forces of oppression engulfing mainland Europe.

★   ★   ★

The fall of France had a far-reaching effect on the British popular music industry. The ultra-optimistic, comical-cum-patriotic songs pumped out by Tin Pan Alley during the phoney war understandably lost their general appeal and some, such as *Imagine Me in the Maginot Line* and *We're Gonna Hang out the Washing on the Siegfried Line* were suddenly nothing more than sick jokes. The Germans, however, realised the propaganda value of the latter song and in 1940 Deutsche Grammophon recorded an effective parody by an unnamed chorus and band. It begins jauntily with the chorus singing the English words which are interrupted by a bombing attack; the song resumes rather tentatively, only to be stopped by a second attack in which agitated cries of "Stuka, Stuka" are heard. The chorus is finally reduced to one frightened, quavery voice which fades away as band and singers (this time with a forceful German lyric) give the tune the Nazi marching song treatment.

After Dunkirk it would have made painful listening for any of the Allied forces or the civilians of occupied Western Europe who chanced to hear it. *The Siegfried Line,* as the parody was entitled, was a well crafted example of its kind and today, when it is possible to take a more dispassionate view of the disc, one cannot help but give credit to the band for its rousing performance. In Britain the memory of the original song's fall from grace still lingered on some thirty years after the end of the war when, in an episode of the BBC's much loved television comedy *Dad's Army*, there was a humorous reference to all the unsold copies gathering dust in the local record shop. In the real world of 1940, though, it is more than likely that any dealer faced with this problem would have cut his losses and passed on the shunned discs to one or other of the shellac salvage drives.

Undue optimism and ill-considered debunking of the enemy were now attitudes to be avoided by the British popular song writers who, driven by public preference, concentrated on material of

153

a more homely, often overtly sentimental nature. This was the cause of much concern to the authorities who feared that a softening of musical taste (especially amongst the Forces) would bring with it a softening of morale. In an effort to counterbalance this trend the BBC had by August, 1940 started to commission patriotic music of a high standard but failed to elicit anything of importance.

As the war continued the Germans encountered a similar difficulty as the almost non-stop diet of military music and marching songs provided by the radio proved too much of a good thing for their own armed forces. Despite the Nazis' efforts since 1933 to regulate all types of music they failed to eradicate the widespread enthusiasm for 'hot' jazz, lively dance music and the exciting new swing that was being recorded in the latter 1930s by the leading American groups. Sentimental songs, too, were just as popular with the German troops as they were with the British, especially when performed with the husky, come-hither voices cultivated by some of their women vocalists. Male singers, providing their style was manly enough, were also exponents of this type of song. One such was the bass Wilhelm Strienz who, in 1940, was Electrola's choice for *Tapfere, kleine Soldatenfrau*[7] (Brave Little Soldier's Wife) in which the nostalgic soldier, now far away, sings to his wife about their parting when he went off to the war. To give some idea of the character of this song it might well be described as a blend of those two British favourites, *Wish Me Luck as You Wave Me Goodbye* and *We'll Meet Again*.

When such strong musical preferences were held by their fighting forces it was inevitable that concessions would need to be made by British and German officialdom. Well placed observers such as Basil Dean, the head of ENSA, and entertainers like Vera Lynn and Joyce Grenfell could confirm that British troops enjoyed and wanted sentimental music and that their morale was in no danger of being corrupted by it. Reluctantly, therefore, this sort of entertainment, though not actively encouraged, was allowed to continue. With regard to the (technically) banned jazz and its 'hot' derivatives, the German solution, as so often under the Nazis, was an expedient bending of the rules. While keeping the civilian population insulated as far as possible from what were ideologically held to be the products of a jungle culture the troops were given their jazz, swing and popular British and American dance tunes via

154

armed forces broadcasting stations transmitting live performances or purpose-made German radio recordings. However, the music heard from these sources still bore the Nazi imprint for the original lyrics were replaced by new ones carrying virulent anti-British and (even before the United States entered the war) anti-American propaganda messages.

★   ★   ★

After barely more than a month's interval the evacuation of Dunkirk was followed, as Churchill had warned, by the start of the Battle of Britain in early July. At the same time as their army of occupation was settling comfortably into its duties in France the Germans had been massing a fleet of invasion barges in their newly acquired Channel and North Sea ports for a seaborne invasion of southern England. To prepare the way for Operation Sea Lion, as the Wehrmacht code-named it, Goering's Luftwaffe was instructed to pulverise the RAF's airfields and all other strategic targets, but what had been assumed would be a short and simple task turned out to be the first major setback to Hitler's war plans. Britain's recently developed radar tracking system in conjunction with Observer Corps reports enabled the RAF's Fighter Command HQ and other control centres to plot the progress of incoming German formations and set up the necessary counter-attacks. Throughout the daylight hours of the beautiful summer of 1940 the RAF was in constant action against German bombers and their fighter escorts while on the ground non-flying personnel laboured round the clock to repair the airfields and make damaged planes airworthy again. Even with the increasing flow of Hurricane and Spitfire fighters coming into service the Battle of Britain was a desperately close-run contest until by mid-September the RAF's supremacy was established beyond doubt.

Hitler postponed Operation Sea Lion and the German daylight bombing offensive was replaced by heavy night attacks as a means of reducing the losses of men and aircraft. By the end of May, 1941 when it was clear that bombing had not produced the required results the night attacks were scaled down. This was not a sign that Hitler had given up the idea of adding the United Kingdom to the Third Reich but his full attention was now devoted to the final planning stages of an infinitely more ambitious military adventure - Operation Barbarossa, the invasion of Russia, which was launched

155

on 22nd June, 1941. The clearing up of the little local difficulty on the other side of the English Channel was, Hitler reasoned, a matter that could safely be left until a later date.

Allied convoys, especially when passing through the Straits of Dover, were a regular target for the Luftwaffe and on Sunday, 14th July, 1940, when the Battle of Britain had barely begun, a BBC war correspondent, Charles Gardner, had a grandstand view of one of these attacks. He recorded his impressions on the cumbersome equipment installed in the boot of his car and the report was broadcast by the BBC the same day; the following month it was issued commercially by Decca in its SP series and the profits from sales of the disc were donated to the Royal Air Force Comforts Fund.

Gardner's account of this action was more highly charged than listeners were accustomed to hearing over the BBC whose war correspondents were directed to be serious and objective in their reporting. As the following extracts show, the sheer thrill of the air battle set Gardner's adrenalin racing as he watched ten Junkers Ju 87 dive bombers home in on the convoy. No ships were hit but a pilot baled out as his Ju 87 was shot down in flames "... slap into the sea, SMASH! ... I can see no boat going out to pick him up so he'll probably have a long swim ashore." What had happened was "... a hot little engagement while it lasted" but more was to come as a dogfight between Messerschmitts and Spitfires ensued. A Messerschmitt was hit and Gardner described it "... coming down like a rocket ... the pilot's not getting out of that one ... Oh, darn, they've turned away. I can't see ... Oh boy, look how they're going ... the RAF fighters have really got these boys taped ... I wouldn't like to be in that first Messerschmitt ... I think that first Messerschmitt has been crashed on the coast of France all right." [*Author's transcript*]

Despite the morale-boosting effect of this commentary its style did not meet with the wholehearted approval of the Establishment. Decca's recording amply confirms that Gardner's extrovert (some would have said schoolboyish) personality brought a highly partisan tone to his reporting on this occasion. His excitement, however, is readily understandable if one thinks back to the sombre days immediately after the fall of France and the evacuation of Dunkirk when Britain seemed on the brink of defeat. Given the circumstances it is not altogether surprising that, in the heat of the

156

moment, there was such gusto in Gardner's description of the punishment being handed out to the Luftwaffe by the RAF. This upbeat report actually gave British listeners something over and above the details of how two German planes were shot down in that morning's brief mêlée. Though at the time there were those who found Gardner's attitude towards the enemy too heartless for comfort, BBC colleagues John Snagge and Michael Barsley, writing long after the war was over, put the recording into historical perspective when they summed it up as the "most sensational eye-witness outside broadcast before D-Day". In early July, 1940 the British badly needed something to celebrate and Gardner's jubilant words came as a tonic which brought instant encouragement to his listeners and perhaps subconsciously also helped strengthen their sorely tried belief in their country's ability to win the war.

The recording gear available to the BBC's correspondents in the field at this stage of the war was not ideal for the purpose. It had been designed for peacetime use and comprised three separate parts: a recording amplifier, a turntable with cutting head and a battery unit to supply the power. This was satisfactory enough as long as the engineer could operate it on board the team's vehicle, but in terrain beyond the reach of motor transport it was not suitable for carrying to more advanced positions since it weighed in all about 450 pounds. The blank recording discs were acetates, preferably aluminium-based for lightness, one of the main suppliers of which from 1941 onwards was EMI. Unwieldy as it was, this recording apparatus captured eye-witness accounts of many of the war's historic moments on land, sea and in the air.

By 1943, however, Canadian and American correspondents had the advantage of portable recorders on which to make their reports. As a news provider the BBC had a high reputation to protect and could not afford to have rivals getting closer to the action than its own men. Intensive research and experiments by technical staff produced in a remarkably short time a compact machine christened the Riverside Portable, a name deceptively reminiscent of leisurely boating and picnics with music on the gramophone. But this Riverside disc recorder was made for sterner occasions. Its turntable was spring-driven and the complete recording process was entrusted to the reporter himself using a single, cleverly designed control mechanism that regulated all the

157

machine's functions. Nearly three minutes of commentary could be accommodated on each side of the ten-inch blanks and the impressive set of batteries supplied the amplifier with power for cutting up to forty discs. Weighing a mere 35 pounds the Riverside Portable could be taken into the front line where it was to be an invaluable source of news for the BBC throughout the rest of the war.

★   ★   ★

From the Battle of Britain until the end of 1940 the British record companies conscientiously maintained the flow of patriotic discs. Amongst their monthly issues for this period few were of lasting documentary importance; two, however, were royal recordings, the history of which dated back to 1923 when King George V and Queen Mary had been persuaded to make a record to celebrate Empire Day (24th May) that year. The responsibility for this and the many subsequent discs by members of the British royal family was assigned to HMV and since 3rd September, 1939 the company had already brought out King George VI's broadcast to his peoples on the outbreak of the Second World War and Queen Elizabeth's radio *Message to the Women of the Empire* of 11th November, 1939. The company's releases for July, 1940 included the King's *Message to the Empire* for that year and in December came the *Message to the Children* which had been broadcast on 13th October by the King's elder daughter, the fourteen year old Princess Elizabeth who was later to become Queen Elizabeth II. A further morale-boosting issue brought out by HMV in time for the Christmas market took the form of a special album edition of Churchill's first four wartime BBC broadcasts.

Apart from one or two other spoken word items the rest of the patriotic output during the second part of 1940 was decidedly more mundane. In the cause of good Anglo-French relations the popular comedian Jack Warner (later to achieve even greater fame as BBC television's Dixon of Dock Green) sang *Entente Cordiale* for Columbia; for the same company Debroy Somers's band played an "Allied Medley of tunes" under the title *For the Forces* and a group of British regimental marches labelled *Battle Dress*. Decca's baritone Sidney Burchall was regarded by *The Gramophone* as almost the equal of Peter Dawson, though one begs leave to doubt whether he was best served by the song *England all the Way* in the

158

course of which he recited the names of a string of the country's well known beauty spots. One notices in passing that when Columbia released Eric Coates conducting his own *Calling all Workers* the backing was his *Sleepy Lagoon* which would shortly come to be used as the signature tune of BBC radio's imperishable programme *Desert Island Discs*.

Towards the end of 1940 the review pages of *The Gramophone* were showing distinct signs of weariness with the stream of patriotic pot-boilers. Writing of a coupling by Dennis Noble and the Coldstream Guards Band of *The British Grenadiers* and *The Empire is Marching* W. A. Chislett acidly remarked "I confess that I find the older song much the more attractive, admirable though the latter is as a lesson in Empire geography!". The reception given by the same magazine to the baritone Raymond Newell's Columbia recording of *Airmen of Empire* is a clear indication of the sea-change affecting public taste. The reviewer wondered

"... who really enjoys songs such as 'Airmen of Empire.' The intention is excellent and perhaps the older generation are kindled by songs of this type, but I am assured by an airman - sitting opposite me at this moment - that 'Roll out the Barrel' is far more to the point."

In the course of 1940 *The Gramophone's* classical review section shrank considerably and by September most new British issues from EMI tended to be single discs amongst which Beecham, Boult and Weingartner performances at premium price still featured while the backlog of their recordings lasted. Fortunately, material originating from Victor continued to appear, enabling collectors to enjoy the on-going products of Serge Koussevitzky's legendary years with the Boston Symphony Orchestra as well as recordings made by Stokowski with the Philadelphia Orchestra prior to his retirement and the appointment of Eugene Ormandy in 1938. Those with lighter classical tastes benefited from regular releases on HMV's C series mid-price label by Arthur Fiedler and the Boston Promenade Orchestra[8] (the scaled-down Boston Symphony) whose lively interpretations had been relished by British record buyers since well before the war.

An off-beat September offering from Parlophone presented Richard Tauber as conductor with the Grand Symphony Orchestra (most probably the London Philharmonic) in his own four movement *Sunshine Suite* the inspiration for which came from a tour he had made in South Africa. Prudently, the three record album was available only on subscription and discs could not be bought separately; but the *Suite* failed to find a niche in the orchestral repertoire and was soon forgotten save by Tauber's most devoted admirers.

October saw HMV's initial issue in what was to be a long and famous series of Victor recordings by Arturo Toscanini and the National Broadcasting Company of America's specially formed NBC Symphony Orchestra. Beethoven's *Egmont* Overture received a thrilling reading but at the same time the disc gave a warning foretaste of the harsh, unyielding acoustic of Studio 8-H, the concert hall at Radio City, New York, where many of Toscanini's recordings of this period were to be made.

HMV, Columbia and Decca were all now trying to make good the shortfall in classical records by advertising selections from their back-catalogues under such inclusive headings as "Great Concertos", "Variations" and "Chopin" and by highlighting their foremost recording artists. HMV, however, had another resource with which to tempt collectors and in October brought out a considerable number of recordings from their *Special List*, a catalogue the existence of which was little known except to expert dealers and the most well informed buyers. *Special List* discs were pressed mainly for sale outside Great Britain and this trade, of course, had been severely affected by the war. In these circumstances it made good sense to allow the home market greater access to the *List's* intriguing contents; as a result, recordings (supplied to order only) by the Minneapolis, Boston and Paris Conservatoire Orchestras, the Pasquier Trio and singers such as Kirsten Flagstad and Tito Schipa emerged into the full light of day.

When in the autumn of 1940 the Luftwaffe turned to large scale night attacks on Great Britain the gramophone had already started to make its voice heard on behalf of both the bombers and the bombed. The Germans composed and recorded not only general propaganda pieces such as *Wir fliegen gegen England* (We're flying against England) but also songs in praise of individual planes such as the Junkers Ju 88 and Stuka bombers. A typically barbarous marching song *Bomben auf Engelland* (Bombs upon England) by an Army College chorus and orchestra came complete with simulated aircraft noises and was issued, ironically, by Electrola, HMV's pre-war German counterpart.

160

The British gramophone's reaction to the rain of high explosive and incendiary bombs being dropped on major cities and industrial areas needed to be positive and cheering, a difficult balancing act given the life and death situation. A prime example of the acceptably lighthearted approach was Florence Desmond's HMV recording of *The Deepest Shelter in Town*. This would almost certainly have been banned for broadcasting by the BBC on account of the non-stop sexual innuendo as a lady of exceedingly easy virtue compares the pleasures of her company and flat to the spartan amenities of an Anderson shelter in the back garden.

During the Blitz thousands of Londoners went nightly to the city's Underground stations where they were able to snatch a little sleep on makeshift beds during the few hours when no trains were running. To pass the time before the shut-down, anybody with a hint of talent was encouraged to provide amateur entertainment by singing, reciting or playing small musical instruments. On some occasions there were visits by professional artists and on the night of 27th November, 1940 ENSA arranged for George Formby with his ukulele to be recorded busking for an appreciative audience in the depths of the Aldwych Tube Station. Amongst the numbers he sang were one of his own specialities *With my little Ukulele in my Hand*, the wartime favourite *Bless'em All* and, considering the location, the very appropriate *Down the Old Coal Hole*.

The unnumbered discs were obviously quite an important project for the matrix numbers all bore the prefix "BBC" which suggests they were recorded for broadcasting. A further pointer to their special status is the introduction given to the little concert by Admiral Sir Edward Evans who was the Regional Civil Defence Commissioner for London throughout the war. ENSA could not have found anyone better to give the Formby discs an official cachet for Evans's bravery was renowned. He had been second-in-command of the ship *Terra Nova* on Captain Robert Scott's ill-fated expedition of 1910-1912 to the South Pole and had come near to losing his own life in the Antarctic wastes. Later, he became widely known as Evans of the *Broke*, after the name of the ship he was commanding when, during the Great War, he rammed a German destroyer off Dover in 1917. Evans was the sort of man to whom the armed forces could easily relate and, bearing in mind that ENSA circulated batches of classical music on commercial recordings for

161

recreational listening amongst the services, it is possible that the Formby discs were sent out in the same way to act as a reassurance that the people at home, particularly those in London, were facing the dangers and hardships of the Blitz with matchless spirit.

Earlier in the year the theatre had already been the source for HMV's classic six-disc set of *The Beggar's Opera* in which prominent singers like Roy Henderson and Audrey Mildmay were joined by the stage and film actor Michael Redgrave whose pleasing light baritone voice served him well in the role of the highwayman-hero Macheath. Christmas customers had an even more notable treat awaiting them in the form of extracts from J. M. Barrie's children's play *Peter Pan*. A full page advert in the December, 1940 number of *The Gramophone* carried the news that "At last, permission has been given for Barrie's most famous play to be made available on Gramophone Records and 'His Master's Voice' are proud to announce that they have been entrusted with this privileged task." An excellent cast had been assembled including Jean Forbes-Robertson, the most famous Peter of the day, and Gordon Harker (more often associated with Edgar Wallace thrillers) as Captain Hook, the pirate, whilst Nancy Evans and George Baker were the singers in the incidental music. The three mid-price, ten-inch discs could be bought either in the usual paper sleeves for 3/- (15p) each or as a complete set "in a delightfully decorated Portfolio" for 10s. 6d. (52½p), though these prices did not include the recently imposed 33⅓% purchase tax; fittingly, HMV donated all profits to London's Great Ormond Street Hospital for Sick Children. The company could, indeed, congratulate itself for rounding off 1940, the first full year of the war, by combining popular seasonal fare with a gramophone première and at the same time enhancing its good name by contributing to the funds of so worthy a cause.

*   *   *

Although in occupied Europe the gramophone industry was subject to the ideological restrictions imposed by the Nazis, means were found by which a country's patriotic feelings could still be expressed by its record companies. One of the greatest musical outpourings of national pride is Smetana's *Má Vlast* (My Country), a work venerated by all loyal Czechs but, to the Nazis, deeply suspect for that very reason. *Má Vlast* needed twenty 78 r.p.m. sides but despite the shellac shortage three complete sets appeared in

162

Czechoslovakia during the war years. The first came in 1940 from Electrola with the Czech Philharmonic Orchestra under its world famous conductor Václav Talich. When in 1941 he and his orchestra were scheduled to give concerts in Berlin and Dresden Talich insisted that *Má Vlast* should be performed in full, a stipulation to which the Nazis reluctantly agreed. Talich's brave personal stand opened the way for the completion of the cycle started in 1940 by Otakar Jeremiás and the Prague Radio Orchestra for Ultraphon. Lastly, in 1942, it was the turn of Karel Jirák and the National Theatre Orchestra to record the work for Esta. Further duplication, though of less intensely emotive music, occurred in the early 1940s when Jeremiás and Jirák both conducted complete sets of Dvořák's *Slavonic Dances* for Ultraphon (17 sides) and Esta (18 sides) respectively. There is a sardonic satisfaction to be had on reflecting that the production of all these sets of Czech national music involved German participation for not only was EMI's Electrola now under Nazi control but Esta was linked to Polydor and Ultraphon to Telefunken.

Denmark likewise successfully used the gramophone as a type of resistance movement. Between 1940 and 1943 the conductor Thomas Jensen, a noted interpreter of Carl Nielsen, made a brilliant series of recordings with the Tivoli Concert Hall Orchestra for Danish HMV and Odeon of mazurkas, polkas, waltzes and galops by Hans Christian Lumbye, a member of the family that was Copenhagen's equivalent of the Strausses of Vienna. These discs sent a clear message that when it came to jolly, nineteenth century dance music Austria did not have a monopoly. Throughout the war the tenor Aksel Schiøtz, a greatly admired Lieder specialist, made it a point of honour to sing only Danish songs at his recitals and recording sessions for Danish HMV. But undoubtedly the most overt show of defiance was made in 1944 when the baritone Einar Norby and the mezzo-soprano Else Brems were recorded singing the duet "Bess you is my woman now" from *Porgy and Bess*, not just an opera about ethnically contemptible American blacks but written, moreover, by a Jew, George Gershwin, who was on the Nazis' list of banned composers.

Having been assured by British officials that they would be in no danger in the Netherlands (even though Denmark and Norway had been invaded in April) the Sadler's Wells Ballet Company set off from London on a goodwill tour of Holland in early May, 1940. The Company at that time included virtually all the leading personalities in English ballet: Ninette de Valois, Frederick Ashton Constant Lambert, Margot Fonteyn and Robert Helpmann. From the moment they arrived the atmosphere was eerie and Fonteyn remembered in her autobiography that in the Dutch capital "... an extraordinary calm masked the tensions of a country that sensed its imminent fate and wondered only when and where the first blow would fall." After fulfilling their engagement at Arnhem the Company was rushed back to The Hague where, within a few hours, news came through that German paratroopers were landing on Dutch soil and spearheading Hitler's latest offensive. With Holland and Germany now at war it was vital that the Company should return to England without delay and, abandoning their stage equipment and music, they were taken by bus to Ijmuiden where they joined the long, slow-moving queue waiting to board a merchant ship that took them to Harwich and the relative safety of England.

Such were the combined talents of the Company that if de Valois and her colleagues had become prisoners of the Germans the effect on the future of English ballet would have been disastrous. HMV and Columbia must have felt particularly relieved at the return of Constant Lambert for the Sadler's Wells music director was a stalwart of their catalogues. It is a chastening thought that the set Lambert made for Columbia on 23rd March, 1940 of the music for the ballet *Dante Sonata*,[9] first staged in January that year, could so nearly have been one of his last wartime recordings. Listening to the Company's orchestra and the pianist Louis Kentner playing under Lambert's direction his own arrangement of Liszt's *D'Après une Lecture de Dante* is to take part in a tribute to the outstanding work and dedication of Sadler's Wells Ballet before, after, and especially during the dangerous Dutch tour in which *Dante Sonata's* famous creators (Ashton, de Valois and Lambert) and performers (Fonteyn and Helpmann) had all been at risk.

The memories Constant Lambert brought back to England were transmuted into the music of his *Aubade Héroïque* which was published in 1942. The score bears the note "This short piece was inspired by a daybreak during the invasion of Holland, the calm of the surrounding park contrasting with the distant mutterings of war". Regrettably, Lambert's beautiful little tone poem had to wait for another fifty years before it became available as a commercial recording.

When in mid-May the Dutch were forced to capitulate many made their way to England where members of the armed forces continued to take part in the war and a government in exile was set up. Their immediate concern was to establish contact with their fellow countrymen back in Holland and this was done through the new Free Dutch broadcasting service, Radio Orange, listening to which was immediately banned by the Germans, though this diktat was largely ignored whenever it was considered safe to do so. Material for Radio Orange came from a wide variety of sources among which were London's many record shops that were scoured for discs of popular Dutch songs. The original words of these were replaced with encouraging propaganda lyrics for beaming to the Netherlands and, to make the programmes as attractive as possible, it was arranged that one of the regular vocalists would be Yetje Pearl, the Vera Lynn of the Free Dutch forces.

During the inter-war years jazz had flourished in Holland both as recorded and live entertainment. The German occupiers allowed the Dutch bands, which included such celebrated groups as The Ramblers and The Moochers, to carry on performing as long as they followed the Nazis' rigid directives, the aim of which was to avoid the "decadent" style of American and some British bands. Jazz, therefore, had to be played straight which meant that no trumpet mutes or very high notes were permitted nor were musicians allowed to swing their instruments about or indulge in excessive body movement. That, at least, was the theory but in his book *Different Drummers*, a fascinating study of jazz in the Third Reich, Michael Kater argues convincingly that "... musicians in France, Belgium, Holland, and Denmark continued, after the spring of 1940, to play much as before the German conquest." For the many devotees in the Wehrmacht a posting to one of these countries was highly desirable for not only was there the chance of hearing live jazz played in more or less authentic mode but also the opportunity to do the rounds of the record shops in search of those most delicious forbidden fruits, discs that for ideological reasons could not be imported by German dealers.

The formal world of the concert hall had to comply with the Nazis' restrictions on repertoire and Willem Mengelberg, the conductor of Amsterdam's Concertgebouw Orchestra, must have

165

deeply regretted that during the occupation he was no longer in a position to programme works by Mahler whose music at that time had few champions apart from himself and Bruno Walter.

In the late 1920s and early 1930s Mengelberg and his orchestra had been on Columbia's roster but by 1937 he had moved to Telefunken. John Hunt's Mengelberg discography lists an intensive session begun on 9th April, 1940, just over a month before the invasion, at which works by the Dutch composers Hendrik Andriessen and Cornelis Dopper together with Tchaikovsky's *1812* Overture and the Second Symphony of Brahms were recorded. One wonders whether Telefunken had some inside information and used the session to maximum effect in case the volatile political situation should induce the conductor to leave Holland suddenly.

However, Mengelberg stayed with the Concertgebouw Orchestra throughout the occupation and went on recording for Telefunken until November, 1942. These sessions concentrated almost entirely on standard popular works which could be relied on to attract good sales. Wartime conditions naturally limited the distribution of these discs and it was not until well after the end of hostilities that interested collectors generally were able to hear and evaluate the performances of Beethoven's *Eroica*, Dvořák's *New World*, Tchaikovsky's *Pathétique* and Schubert's *Unfinished* and Ninth symphonies. Mengelberg's special feeling for the music of Richard Strauss was well demonstrated in sets of *Tod und Verklärung* (Death and Transfiguration) and *Ein Heldenleben* (A Hero's Life); and, to show that Dutch composers were not being totally neglected, Johan Wagenaar's overture *Cyrano de Bergerac*, a substantial piece requiring four sides, was given its first commercial recording. Serious collectors have been doubly fortunate in that further documentation of Mengelberg's music making in Holland during the war has survived thanks to Dutch radio and other archival recordings which have since appeared on specialist historical labels in LP and CD formats.

Significantly, on a visit to Germany in early July, 1940 Mengelberg recorded Tchaikovsky's Fifth Symphony and First Piano Concerto (soloist Conrad Hansen) with the Berlin Philharmonic, an action which would undoubtedly have told against him heavily when, after the liberation, he was accused of collaborating with the Nazis and was banned from conducting in the Netherlands for six years - a punishment now widely thought to have been unduly severe. This brilliant though frequently controversial conductor spent his exile in Switzerland where he withdrew completely from the international music scene and died there in 1951 shortly before his sentence was due to expire.

Even though from 1938 to 1945 Eduard van Beinum shared the conductorship of the Concertgebouw Orchestra with Mengelberg he was little known outside Holland until after the war. His talent, however, was recognised by Polydor and Telefunken and it was for the latter company that in November, 1941 he recorded Berlioz's *Symphonie Fantastique*.[10] This set was destined to become famous for its great rarity since it was only on sale between December, 1943 and May, 1944 and the masters back in Germany were destroyed during Allied air raids.

The war was an exceptionally dangerous period for Philips, the giant Dutch electrical goods concern, and the autobiography of Frederik Philips, its then head, reads as much like a tense novel as a factual account of the difficulties faced by a major international corporation with its headquarters in an enemy-occupied homeland. Because of Holland's vulnerability in a Europe increasingly dominated by Nazi Germany Philips had already taken the precaution of transferring the designs and technical data relating to many of their products to branches in America and Britain. As a result of the company's foresight their British subsidiary Mullard was able to supply a newly developed radio valve for the radar systems used in RAF aircraft.

In common with other Dutch manufacturing businesses Philips was forced to produce goods for the Germans and this was done under the supervision of a Nazi administrator. Despite the presence of this unwelcome official ways were found in which to be as unhelpful as possible. These ranged from production delays to supplying equipment which worked perfectly on delivery but had ingenious forms of built-in obsolescence to ensure a much more limited life than would normally be the case.

In December, 1942 and March, 1943 the Eindhoven factory was the target of daring low level attacks by the RAF and, to add to the disruption, the workforce there came out on strike on May Day, 1943, a brave gesture that resulted in Frederik Philips being arrested by the Germans. He was released in September but after the Allied landings in Normandy the following year his future was again highly problematical. To preclude being sent to Germany on account of his specialised knowledge and hostage value he went on the run in Holland moving from one safe house to another, usually by bicycle, and doing his bit as an agricultural worker as he went. When Eindhoven was liberated by the Americans on 18th September, 1944 he returned there travelling, as before, by bicycle through what was still hazardous territory and reassumed control of the family business.

Even while in German hands Philips was discreetly taking steps that would enable it to extend its manufacturing scope when peace returned. The resident Nazi supervisor was completely unaware that certain Dutch businesses were being secretly acquired, amongst them, in 1942, what Frederik Philips with tantalising brevity refers to in his autobiography as "… a small gramophone record plant which eventually became the foundation of our worldwide record industry." This pressing factory in Amsterdam had been operating since 1933 when it was started up by a Dutch record shop proprietor who was also the director of Decca Dutch Supplies. After the liberation of Holland, however, Philips's most urgent task was to make good the damage sustained during the occupation and, in the face of daunting post-war economic conditions, bring the company back to a normal commercial footing. It was not until 1950, therefore, that recordings started to be made for issue on the Philips label but once these discs came on sale their technical and musical quality made it abundantly clear that a major new record producer had entered the market.

While the phoney war pursued its deceptive course the French record companies continued with business much as usual. Nevertheless, even before the Nazis annexed Denmark and Norway, life in France had not been entirely unaffected by German military activities. On 8th and 9th March, 1940 Wanda Landowska visited one of EMI's Pathé-Marconi (French HMV) studios in Paris to continue work on a sequence of harpsichord sonatas by Domenico Scarlatti which she had begun early the previous year. During one of these sessions the Luftwaffe was in the vicinity and the microphone picked up the sound of anti-aircraft gunfire as she was playing the Sonata in D major Kk 490 (L 206); Landowska was unperturbed and completed the sonata without faltering.

Before long this indomitable lady whose Jewish descent put her in a position of high risk would be obliged to leave France hurriedly for the United States; fortunately for future generations of music lovers the Scarlatti masters were safely hidden by Pathé-Marconi and the sonatas (including Kk 490 on which the gunfire can be distinctly heard) eventually appeared on 78s after the war. Landowska had also been engaged on a series of Mozart sonatas for French HMV but sadly, in this case, the masters were discoverd by the Nazis and destroyed.

For a time after the Germans' triumphal entry into Paris on 14th June and the conclusion of the armistice a week later the French in the Occupied Zone were agreeably surprised by the punctilious behaviour of Hitler's forces. This did not come about by accident but was the result of deliberate Nazi policy. The Wehrmacht had been instructed that because France, like Germany, was renowned for its cultural heritage it was important that the representatives of the Third Reich should create as civilised an impression as possible. This conciliatory attitude did not last long for when Churchill announced that Britain would fight on alone France automatically became Germany's front line and the harsh realities of occupation in the north and the rule of a puppet government in the south soon revealed themselves.

Curfews were imposed, food was rationed, travel was restricted and French Jews in both zones were discriminated against in matters great and small. As early as October, 1940 the Vichy government passed a law barring all Jews from posts of public responsibility. Concentration camps were set up in the Occupied Zone and run largely by French staff. The most notorious was at Drancy, a little to the north-east of Paris, where a special rail head was built and from here on 27th March, 1942 the first consignment of French Jews was sent off to Germany and the death camps in the east. Such was the zeal with which the Nazis and their French helpers carried out the ethnic cleansing that trainloads of human freight were still being dispatched up until 17th August, 1944, only a week before the Allies liberated Paris; by then some 76,000 French Jews had passed through Drancy on their way to almost certain death.

When the Axis powers took control of the Vichy-governed south in November, 1942 after the Allied landings in French North Africa an ambiguous sort of unity returned to France in as much as the entire population was now directly under the invaders' command, a situation with which Paris, the centre of the country's musical, artistic, literary and intellectual life, was all too familiar.

One of the methods by which the Nazis hoped to ingratiate themselves with the Parisian cultural community was to arrange concert dates in the French capital for leading German musicians. As Wilhelm Furtwängler refused to conduct in France after the invasion (though his conscience permitted him to do so in Copenhagen) the young Herbert von Karajan gained the opportunity to make himself more widely known. His career with Polydor was in its early days when the war began but by the time he first appeared in Paris he had, in addition to a number of short works, already made recordings with the Berlin Philharmonic of Tchaikovsky's *Pathétique* and Dvořák's *New World* symphonies.

At his first Paris concerts on 17th and 18th December, 1940 Karajan, together with his soloists and the chorus and orchestra of the Aachen Stadttheater, performed Bach's B minor Mass. French music lovers were no doubt highly disconcerted to find that the German language programmes bore the heading "Kriegsweihnachten 1940" (Wartime Christmas 1940) beneath which was depicted a stacked tripod of assault rifles surrounded by a ring of flames - an insensitive if not to say barbaric way of presenting one of the most sublime works in the whole field of religious music.

The pianist Wilhelm Kempff and the conductors Eugen Jochum and Clemens Krauss were also brought to Paris by the Nazis; the propaganda value of such eminent artists was considerable and Krauss was even drawn into conducting concerts for the workers at some of the capital's heavy industrial plants. As well as the German and Austrian musicians Willem Mengelberg was another visitor; he gave Beethoven concerts and in so doing committed an act which in Holland could be interpreted as further evidence of his pro-German attitude.

In 1941 Karajan was back again, this time bringing with him the company of the Berlin State Opera and on 22nd May, to commemorate Wagner's birthday, *Tristan und Isolde* was staged with Max Lorenz and the French soprano Germaine Lubin singing the title roles. Lubin began recording much earlier than Karajan for she was eighteen years his senior and had acquired a considerable reputation as a Wagner singer with a pre-war discography that included excerpts from Acts I and 3 of *Die Walküre* on Odeon and French HMV. She had been well regarded by the German musical establishment for a number of years and her portrayal of Kundry in *Parsifal* at the 1938 Bayreuth Festival had won the commendation of Hitler himself; but her unashamedly close association with the highest ranking German military administrators in Paris brought about her disgrace when, after the liberation, she suffered five years "indignité nationale" which involved the confiscation of her property and passport and a three year prison sentence.

Another classical recording artist who unwisely failed to keep a due distance between himself and the occupiers was the renowned pianist Alfred Cortot whose discs of music from the romantic repertoire had long graced HMV's catalogue. Unfortunately the deep interpretative insights he brought to the music of Chopin, Schumann, Liszt and César Franck were not matched by his political instincts. The war, in fact, strengthened his already well developed pro-German tendencies: he accepted an official post proffered by the Nazis; he played at Franco-German cultural gatherings in Paris; and he continued to undertake engagements in Germany. In addition to all this he took to writing articles in support of the Pétain regime for which voluntary service he received various emblematic awards. Like Lubin he too was subsesequently charged as a collaborator but was lucky enough to escape imprisonment, although he was banned for a time from playing in France.

In the world of light entertainment question marks were to hang over other famous names. The singers Maurice Chevalier who recorded for French HMV and Charles Trenet, a French Columbia artist, were seen by many as collaborators, Chevalier for singing on the quasi-autonomous but ultimately German-controlled Radio Paris and Trenet for entertaining German officers at the capital's leading night spots and including at least one Vichyite song in his act. Edith Piaf's unique vocal style had to wait until after the war before the gramophone introduced her to an international audience but during the occupation she also came under suspicion when she agreed to travel to Germany to sing for French prisoners of war. However, when the Wehrmacht withdrew from Paris common sense prevailed and Piaf was cleared of any collusion with the enemy.

Jean Bérard, who was variously a director, joint manager and artistic director of Pathé-Marconi, became a source of embarrassment to the company on account of his right wing views. He made frequent trips to Germany and, to quote David Pryce-Jones's *Paris in the Third Reich*, "... was an advocate of collaboration, [and] a strong anti-Semite" who was bold enough to state publicly in 1941 that "Fascist and Hitlerian doctrines are today championing civilization." Pathé-Marconi's workforce deplored his conduct and, when the Allies had liberated Paris, successfully called for his dismissal. He was later denounced anonymously as a collaborator but the French government's subsequent investigation ended with his acquittal.

In December, 1949 EMI's J. N. Macleod was in Paris looking into the complicated matter of how best Bérard should be financially compensated following the loss of his job. During the Spanish Civil War when Macleod was the side-lined manager of HMV's branch in Barcelona he had experienced at first hand the problems besetting an international record company caught up in the crossfire of a major armed conflict. Since Bérard by now had been legally exonerated Macleod, in a letter to L. J. Brown at Hayes, urged EMI to be generous towards its former employee not least because he, Macleod, was "... convinced that Bérard was of the greatest service to P. M. [Pathé-Marconi] during the war. The fact that the French Company was recovered in such good shape was I think due to him more than to anyone else." In the face of this generous tribute to Bérard's wartime stewardship of French HMV it seems quite certain that, however questionable his politics may have been, his commercial judgment, at least, remained sound.

It is something of a relief to turn from collaborators (whether actual, alleged or merely imagined) to musicians whose attitude to the occupation was distinctly more robust. Showing remarkable solidarity numerous members of the Radio France Symphony Orchestra took themselves off to Algiers rather than stay on in Paris and play for the enemy. By a strange coincidence, two famous flute players, one well advanced in his career, the other an unknown student, also translated their deep-seated anti-German feelings into action. Marcel Moyse was France's foremost flautist of the day and

172

had recorded prolifically throughout the 1930s with a repertoire ranging from Mozart's G major Concerto, K 313 and other standard classics to gramophone premières of modern works such as Manuel de Falla's Harpsichord Concerto and Stravinsky's Octet for Wind Instruments, in each of which the composer participated. British record buyers had been familiar with Moyse's output through his HMV discs of Mozart's D major Concerto, K 314, the Concerto for Flute and Harp in C major, K 299 with Lily Laskine (both in the Connoisseur Records category) and as the sparkling soloist in Bach's orchestral Suite No. 2 in B minor with the Busch Chamber Players. The German presence in Paris was more than Moyse could bear and he and his family moved to the Jura in what was then still unoccupied Vichy France where for the rest of the war their living was reduced to what little they could earn from farming and a few broadcasts and concerts.

The younger man was only seventeen years old when Hitler invaded Poland. Jean-Pierre Rampal's earliest student days were spent at medical school in his home city, Marseilles, but finding it difficult to adapt to life in the Southern Zone he went on the run. As a child he had been taught the flute by his father and a musical rather than a medical career now became his objective. He changed his name, obtained forged papers and made his way to Paris where he enrolled at the Conservatoire which in addition to its academic activities lent encouragement to the Resistance movement. In 1945 Rampal's first public recital was enough to convince the French music world that a brilliant new talent had emerged and by the time the vinyl LP had displaced the shellac 78 his recordings of Baroque and modern French works were appearing on the Argo, Ducretet-Thomson, Felsted and Oiseau-Lyre labels.

As one would expect, the occupying forces indulged themselves to the full in both the intellectual and worldly pleasures that France (and particularly Paris) had to offer. For the young German officer Dietrich Schulz-Köhn being in France meant that he was able to pursue as never before his obsessive passion for jazz.

It cannot be emphasised too often how ambivalent the official attitude to jazz was in the Third Reich. The Party's hard-line ideologists, the Reichsmusikkammer and many provincial authorities would have been glad to see this jungle music totally suppressed but, at the heart of national government, Josef Goebbels well knew that such an action would alienate many Party members (particularly those from the middle class) with whom jazz was highly popular. Instead of resorting to an all-out ban he chose to follow a policy of compromise and expediency; this deliberately cautious approach lent a tinge of authenticity to the persistent but unproven rumours that Goebbels himself had a large, secret collection of jazz records. The overlapping ideological areas of jazz, swing, dance music and race soon generated a maze-like situation the complexities of which are tellingly illustrated by Michael Kater's account of Sigmund Petruschka's band which was

> "... moderately influenced by swing but stressed elements of Jewish folk music as well [and] produced a dance record with Hebrew lyrics ... sold only to Jews through Jewish outlets on the exclusively Jewish record label Lukraphon."

Schulz-Köhn, an otherwise orthodox Nazi, skilfully negotiated the obstacles which stood in the way of the dedicated jazz enthusiast in the Third Reich, buoyed up by his firm belief that the ideologists would eventually acknowledge the superiority of the American or American-inspired product to the tolerated but sanitised German form. He had been in the German record industry since the early 1930s following a letter he had written to Deutsche Grammophon suggesting that the marketing of jazz issues by their German Brunswick subsidiary would benefit from more specialist knowledge than could be provided by the classical musicologist then engaged in this work. DG liked the idea and, after a trial period, took Schulz-Köhn on to their permanent staff as a jazz record production adviser.

He soon became well known as a critic and reviewer and in 1940 published a book on the economics of the international record industry. In Berlin and other major German cities he gave public lectures on jazz which, according to Michael Kater, were "overly scholarly, if not to say bookish affairs." Though his lectures may have been academic in tone, Schulz-Köhn was no mere theorist for his research was based on the large personal library he had built up as a customer of such renowned record stores as Alberti's in Berlin, a Mecca for jazz collectors on account of its stocks of American imports. Alberti's, however, was Jewish-owned and, in due course, became yet another victim of Nazi oppression.

With the coming of the war Schulz-Köhn was drafted into the Artillery as a lieutenant and continued to acquire records during his service in the German-occupied countries. Whilst in France he would have been aware of and, because of their musical tastes, may even have felt some faint kinship with the *zazous*, a youth cult that had sprung up towards the end of 1940. Ian Ousby in his *Occupation: the ordeal of France 1940-1944* relates how

"The boys wore long hair greased with oil, long jackets, high collars and drainpipe trousers; the girls wore jackets with padded shoulders, short pleated skirts and striped stockings; both affected dark glasses, chunky and unpolished shoes and umbrellas kept furled even when it was raining. They listened to jazz - *le swing*, Django Reinhardt and the Hot Club de France ..."

Unlikely as it may seem, these French teen-age rebels were to have their counterparts in Hitler's Germany.

By June, 1943 Schulz-Köhn was in the now occupied south of France busily engaged in congenial, non-military duties. Kater describes how, emulating the *zazous*, this Nazi officer

"... gave a radio lecture at Nîmes, in fluent French, in which he extolled the virtues and played the records of Django Reinhardt. In the Hot Club de Marseille[s] ... the lieutenant span the latest American discs that he had just received from Stockholm, in return for his collaboration as a correspondent for the Swedish tabloid *Orkester Journalen*."

Here we have a first class example of how, often in unlikely circumstances, jazz and Nazi ideology managed to co-exist, for the guitarist Reinhardt, who headed the Quintet of the Hot Club of France after the escape to England of his musical colleague the violinist Stéphane Grappelli, was also a gipsy, a member of an ethnic group the Nazis were intent on exterminating.

Schulz-Köhn's war ended with him still on active service in France with the German troops who had been trapped in the St. Nazaire region since the Allies' invasion of Normandy in June, 1944. This determined pocket of resistance held out for almost a year until May, 1945 when Germany surrendered. Kater tells how this hopeless situation turned briefly into comedy when in early 1945 Schulz-Köhn was responsible for transferring the French prisoners held by the besieged Germans to the United States Army. Once the military formalities were settled the American officer offered Schulz-Köhn cigarettes in exchange for his Rolleiflex camera. Single-minded as ever, Schulz-Köhn countered by asking for jazz records instead but there was no deal as the only discs the American had available for trading were Stokowski and Budapest String Quartet issues. Their disappointment was eased to some extent, however, when the two officers found they shared common ground in their admiration for the French jazz pundits Hugues Panassié and Charles Delaunay.

Using information supplied by continental readers *The Gramophone* was able to publish in 1945 several lists of the most interesting wartime classical recordings by the leading French companies. One immediately notes the number of discs given over to early and Baroque music not only by specialist labels like Les Discophiles Français, Anthologie Sonore and Lumen but also by French HMV and Columbia. The war years in France generated the conditions which, with the arrival of the LP, would result in a positive flood of recorded music from these periods. *The International Record Review* in its obituary of Jean-Pierre Rampal (1922-2000) quoted him as saying that after the Second World War "People were very hungry for music. They needed something quiet, something well-constructed - some kind of order after all the anxieties of the war." Baroque music had by no means been neglected by the French companies before the war but the industry was particularly astute in detecting the early signs of an expanding demand for works from this period.

The post-Baroque age was plentifully represented with new versions of familiar fare; as well as many shorter pieces, sonatas and concertos by Mozart, Beethoven, Liszt, Brahms and Tchaikovsky were recorded by artists ranging from the internationally famous such as Marguerite Long, Yves Nat, Jacques Thibaud and Alfred Cortot (who made new sets of Chopin's Preludes, Studies and Waltzes) to those whose names are now scarcely remembered even by the most diligent scanners of catalogues and discographies. One of these now shadowy performers was the pianist Lucienne Delforge who recorded music by César Franck and Ravel for French HMV and was always ready to air her views on the benefits of collaboration since she believed the Germans were bringing a new impetus to the moribund cultural life of Paris.

Amongst the most significant classical recordings of the war years were five large scale works in terms of the forces needed; apart from one they were also of exceptional length and all were gramophone premières. With these prestige productions the companies concerned signalled their determination to uphold their commitment to the highest musical standards even during the difficult times of the occupation.

The contemporary relevance of Berlioz's Requiem, the *Grande Messe des Morts* (High Mass for the Dead) was obvious. With France under German control the recording (on twenty two sides) would almost certainly be interpreted as a commemoration of all the French who fell not just in 1940 but in the Great War of 1914-18 and the Franco-Prussian War of 1870-71 as well. Though for the most part the music is restrained and meditative there are some great dramatic outbursts and Berlioz's score calls for a very large orchestra and chorus, a tenor soloist and four separate brass bands, ideally stationed at some distance from the main body of musicians. When they took up this challenging project in 1942 French Columbia spared no effort. At a venue endowed with the necessary spacious acoustic the tenor Georges Jouatte, the Emile Passani Choir and the Radio Paris symphony orchestra conducted by Jean Fournet together with their producer and sound engineers achieved a recording that was highly successful both musically and technically.

Arthur Honegger's oratorios *La Danse des Morts* (The Dance of Death) of 1939 and *Jeanne d'Arc au Bûcher* (Joan of Arc at the Stake) of the previous year were both settings of texts by the deeply religious French poet and dramatist Paul Claudel. The inspiration for *La Danse des Morts* stemmed from Hans Holbein the Younger's mediaevalist images in which Death stalks the land culling his victims as he goes. In 1941 French HMV brought together the actor Jean-Louis Barrault, three soloists including the distinguished baritone Charles Panzéra, the Gouvernet Choir and the Paris Conservatoire Orchestra under Charles Münch to record the six sides containing this relatively brief work. Like Berlioz's Requiem, *La Danse des Morts* could also be taken as another potent reminder of the sacrifices made by Frenchmen over the last seventy years in the defence of their country against Germany. The oratorio makes an immediate, though not always favourable impression on the first-time listener. Reviewing the set in the 1948 edition of *The Record Book* the American critic David Hall described the work as "lurid" but at the same time a memorable listening experience; when the 1950 edition of his *Records* came out it had been relegated to a group of Honegger's works he considered unworthy of serious attention. In his stern, academic verdict Hall seems, rather unjustly, to have completely ignored the special resonance this piece would have had for French concert-goers and record buyers during the occupation. Today critical opinion is more kindly disposed to *La Danse des Morts* but, even so, new recordings have been few and far between since Münch's pioneering 78s.

Jeanne d'Arc au Bûcher was first performed at Basle in 1938 and is another of Honegger's compositions in which the words are partly spoken and partly sung. The crucial roles of Joan and Brother Dominic are both spoken ones and French HMV were fortunate in securing Marthe Dugard and Roger Gérome for their recording which would run to eighteen sides. In addition to casting various other speech parts the company had to recruit two sopranos, a contralto, two tenors and a bass; the two choruses were provided by the Cureghem Children's Choir and the Cecilia Choir of Antwerp. All these participants together with the Belgian National Orchestra were conducted by Lodewijk de Vocht, also a Belgian, whose close affinity with the oratorio greatly impressed Parisian concert audiences in 1940.

For a country striving to maintain its national identity Joan of Arc powerfully embodied the spirit of resistance against foreign oppressors. During the Hundred Years War, while still in her teens, she had taken up arms, rallied her fellow countrymen and led them against the English, so showing that where patriotism was concerned the young had as much to offer as their elders. Her martyrdom at the stake in 1431 ensured her iconic status remained unspoiled and in 1920 she was formally canonised by the Roman Catholic church. Coming when it did, French HMV's wartime recording was without doubt a shrewdly calculated appeal to national pride, the coded overtones of which would be picked up by all who longed for France to regain her freedom.

Despite its predominantly vocal content, Berlioz's music drama *La Damnation de Faust*, based on Goethe's masterpiece, is most often called to mind by its three familiar orchestral extracts: the rousing Hungarian March and the enchantingly delicate Dance of the Sylphs and Minuet of the Will-o'-the Wisps. In 1931 French HMV had issued an abridged ten-disc set conducted by their in-house music director Piero Coppola but the first complete version had to wait until, in wartime conditions, French Columbia made good the deficiency with its thirty-sided recording. Because of its diversity *La Damnation de Faust* is a difficult work to sustain convincingly throughout its entire length; the conductor has to be attuned to such contrasts as the merrymaking of boisterous students, the love music for Faust and Marguerite, Mephisto's sardonic Song of the Flea, the headlong Ride to the Abyss and the redemption of Marguerite. Georges Jouatte (Faust), Mona Laurena (Marguerite) and Paul Cabanel (Mephisto), together with the Emile Passani Choir and the symphony orchestra of Radio Paris conducted by Jean Fournet brought to French Columbia's catalogue an eminently satisfying performance that had the field to itself until Charles Münch's Boston set appeared on Victor in the early years of LP.

The fifth of these notable wartime gramophone premières was Debussy's opera *Pelléas et Mélisande*, recorded for the first time in full on forty sides by French HMV in April and May, 1941. To this day on LP and CD transfers it has retained its position as a benchmark interpretation. The baritone Jacques Jansen and the soprano Irène Joachim who sang the title parts had, like Roger Desormière, the conductor of the unnamed orchestra, been associated with this enigmatic work for many years. The neutral conditions of the recording studio, often an inhibiting influence on musicians, in this case contributed to the company's success in capturing the elusive spirit of the opera for the cast could conconcentrate exclusively on bringing out every subtle shade of meaning in the words (the vital importance of which Debussy constantly stressed) without being distracted by the theatrical requirements of a staged production.

The French record industry was justifiably proud of its wartime achievements. Discs by popular entertainers helped to enliven the everyday life of a conquered country but, far more significantly, on the classical side the companies broke new ground by venturing into musical territory that at best had been only partially explored up until then. Pathé-Marconi (the Axis-inclined Jean Bérard notwithstanding) and Columbia acted patriotically in giving such wide coverage to French music including that of Honegger who, though Swiss by nationality, lived and worked mainly in France and was accepted as a member of the French school of composers. The recordings of the Berlioz Requiem and Honegger's *La Danse des Morts* and *Jeanne d'Arc au Bûcher* by inference honoured the fallen in the struggles against Germany and offered hope for the way ahead through the inspiriting example of the martyred Joan. When *Pelléas et Mélisande*, arguably the greatest of all French operas, is added to the tally it is clear that by any standards these issues were immensely heartening symbolic responses to France's plight under the occupation.

To bring out these multi-disc sets at such a time entailed a high level of risk and many difficult decisions had to be made by the companies. Was the heavy financial outlay on the artists' side possible without wrecking their budgets? Would it be right to allocate scarce shellac resources to such lengthy works rather than to shorter and more widely popular pieces? Could they rely on a sufficient return from the average record buyer who, however desirable the music, might think twice when faced with the prospect of finding the money for up to twenty premium-price discs? Luckily, their answers to these searching questions were favourable and the subsequent releases showed that where these two major companies were concerned the future of France's recorded musical heritage could not have been in safer hands.

⋆   ⋆   ⋆

1941 was the year the Second World War became truly global. The North African desert campaign began in earnest in February when the Italians were joined by the Germans under the command of Field Marshal Erwin Rommel at which point the recurrent pattern of advances, retreats and counter-attacks started to show itself. At the same time, however, the first significant British success in the land war was achieved in the Horn of Africa when forces operating from the Anglo-Egyptian Sudan and Kenya drove the Italians out of Abyssinia (now Ethiopia) and restored Haile Selassie to his throne. BBC reporters were with the troops and a few days afterwards listeners back in Britain were able to hear a recorded description of the Emperor's entry into Addis Ababa on 5th May. Considering the fierceness of the fighting in a vast area of inhospitable terrain that posed great logistical problems this phase of the war has received less attention than it deserves, mainly because the welcome victory against the Axis was so soon overshadowed by world-shaking events elsewhere.

On 22nd June Hitler launched Operation Barbarossa, the invasion of Russia, in which the Wehrmacht advanced at such speed that by late November German tanks were within twenty miles of Moscow; but with the Russian winter exercising its iron grip the attack on the capital was halted on 5th December.

Two days later the war was dramatically extended to the Far East when, without warning, Japan bombed the American naval base at Pearl Harbor, Hawaii, following which the Emperor Hirohito's fanatical armed services immediately spread out into the countries of East and South-East Asia and the Pacific. Three days after Pearl Harbor the Royal Navy's most powerful vessels in this theatre of war, the battleships *Prince of Wales* and *Repulse*, were sunk in the Gulf of Siam and on Christmas Day, Hong Kong, Britain's strategically vital crown colony, was forced to surrender to the Japanese. The year in which the spring had brought a brief sign of hope thus ended for the Allies in the bleakest uncertainty.

1941 produced a bountiful supply of raw material for adaptation and use in the propaganda broadcasts by William Joyce that were transmitted from Germany on short wave radio. Always better known by his nickname "Lord Haw-Haw", Joyce, the son of an Irish-American father was born in New York but was brought up and educated in the United Kingdom where he became an active member of Sir Oswald Mosley's black-shirted British Union of Fascists. Shortly before the outbreak of war Joyce, who then held a British passport, travelled to Germany where he loyally served Hitler's cause until the collapse of the Third Reich. He was chosen by the Nazis to take over the English language news broadcasts previously read by Norman Baillie-Stewart, the philandering British ex-army officer who in 1933 had been court martialled and imprisoned for some years in the Tower of London for passing military secrets to the Germans. Joyce was not short of like-minded company from the British Isles and was soon working with the Irish poet, novelist and IRA supporter Francis Stuart who wrote many of Joyce's radio scripts as well as making his own propaganda broadcasts to Ireland.

Joyce's news commentaries were a cunning mixture of the truth, the feasible and the downright implausible, all delivered in the sneering, painstakingly honed upper-class accent that inspired his nickname. He gained a cult following among British listeners to the extent that even schoolboys would mockingly imitate his regular opening words: "Germany calling, Germany calling". The government and press were understandably concerned over Joyce's popularity but, however disheartening his genuine news may often have been, his British audience was unaffected by his less than subtle propaganda and continued to regard him as a mere buffoon.

Although numerous acetates probably still survive in radio archives, few of Joyce's broadcasts have found their way on to commercial recordings. However, some snippets of his microphone style were issued in the late 1980s by the independent company Harlequin to accompany LP transfers of *German Propaganda Swing 1940-1943* as played by Charlie and his Orchestra, a group that furnished the music for Joyce's "news" programmes.

The acetates to which Harlequin had access reveal Joyce gloating over the severe damage done to the British cruiser *Exeter* in the South Atlantic by the pocket battleship *Graf Spee*, though he says nothing about the condition of the terminally crippled German vessel. He excelled at taking the moral high ground in his commentaries; after the destroyer *Cossack* had rescued the British merchant seamen from the German prison ship *Altmark* he described Churchill's congratulations to *Cossack's* captain as the height of cynicism since the incident involved the shooting of unarmed men and the flagrant violation of Norwegian neutrality. On yet another occasion he can be heard in tones of heavy sarcasm berating the Ministry of Misinformation [sic] for frightening British women by suggesting that as protection against bomb splinters they have their milliners make their spring and summer hats from very thin tin plate covered with silk or velvet. Although these examples come from 1939 and early 1940 they are nevertheless typical of the propaganda Joyce broadcast for the Nazis throughout the rest of the war.

The accomplished personnel of Charlie's orchestra changed from time to time when German members were drafted into military service, usually to be replaced by equally skilled musicians from Italy, Belgium or Holland. The band's actual leader for most of its lifetime was Lutz Templin who played the tenor saxophone but its name derived from the vocalist and co-leader Karl "Charlie" Schwedler. Not all of Charlie's men realised that their live radio performances were frequently recorded or that the resulting pressings were broadcast by the German forces' radio stations in the occupied countries. These discs were also handed out to prisoner of war camps where they tended to have a short life once the inmates heard the hard-line propaganda lyrics that had been substituted for the normal well known words. Records by Charlie and his Orchestra were never available commercially, a factor which contributed greatly to their present day rarity.

As an instrumental ensemble Charlie and his Orchestra could be listened to with a good deal of pleasure but, disadvantaged by ideological constraints, the musicians were unable to match the verve and rhythmic bite which the best American and British bands brought to their dance music, especially the swing numbers. Charlie's presentation usually followed a set formula: first Schwedler, whose vocalising veered between singing and speaking, would sing a verse with the authentic words and then continue with a crude propaganda parody which, whenever possible, contained insults to Churchill, Roosevelt and the Jews.

A favourite dance tune given this treatment was *When Day is Done* in which the first lines "When day is done and shadows fall I dream of you/ When day is done I think of all the joys we knew" are transformed with a tortured rhyme into "When day is done and shadows fall we dream of peace/ we can't go on believing in Churchill's victories". This particular arrangement which refers to the war as "Churchill's war" was directed at Londoners enduring the incessant bombing by the Luftwaffe. The tune's original sentimental words were further changed to "Day and night we have alarms,/ Big fires all over town./ London life has lost its charm,/ These air raids get us down" and the song ends with the depressing assurance that "This charming war has just begun."

One of the most bizarre episodes of the war occurred in 1941 and it generated a typically British piece of propaganda. The man at the centre of the incident was Rudolf Hess, Hitler's official deputy who, on 10th May, took it upon himself to fly from Augsburg in southern Germany to Scotland where he planned to enlist the help of the Duke of Hamilton in negotiating an Anglo-German peace settlement. Hess's reputation in Germany was in decline and his journey was as much an attempt to revive his own political fortunes as a purely altruistic bid to bring the war to an end. Hess was an experienced pilot but the flight to Scotland took his plane to the limit of its range and he was obliged to bale out and make a parachute landing. He was captured before he could make contact with the Duke (to whom he was virtually unknown) and his behaviour raised immediate doubts over both his authority to undertake this diplomatic mission and his mental soundness. Hitler was quick to denounce Hess as a pacifist; the British treated him as a prisoner of war in need of psychiatric assessment. After the defeat of Germany the Nuremburg Tribunal sentenced him to life imprisonment at Spandau gaol, Berlin, where he died in 1987.

Hess's arrival in Britain was a nine days' wonder to which the entertainment industry's rapid response was a comedy piece punningly entitled *Thanks for dropping in, Mr. Hess* which the irrepressible Arthur Askey recorded for HMV's bargain price BD label in time for it to appear with the company's July releases. Lighthearted ridicule of this sort (not just in the case of Hess but also in the many songs invoking Hitler by name) served as a highly effective riposte to the pomposity and heavy humour that characterised Lord Haw-Haw's broadcasts.

As well as the Lend-Lease assistance that Britain was receiving before the United States entered the war the Americans had indicated their support in other morale-boosting ways. The journalist Quentin Reynolds who was stationed in London described the terrors of the Blitz for American readers and in June and August he contributed to the BBC's *Postscript* series. These broadcasts for which he was congratulated by Churchill were recorded and subsequently issued by HMV; they took the form of scornful open letters, one to Goebbels, one to Hitler and carried the unambiguous message that Germany could never hope to succeed in bombing or otherwise battering the British into submission. In October HMV brought out Victor's three record set of Alice Duer Miller's *The White Cliffs of Dover* starring the actress Lynn Fontanne who was as greatly admired in Britain as she was in the States. This was a suitable theatrical complement to the recordings of six of Churchill's broadcast speeches which HMV issued in two groups in April and October as part of the company's on-going documentation of the war as described by the Prime Minister in his own words.

The lists of monthly releases for 1941 in HMV's BD series are an excellent guide to the most favoured forms of British light entertainment at this stage of the war. In the country's larger picture houses the cinema organist's interval music had for years been a recognised part of the filmgoers' evening out. The BBC and the record companies made ample provision for listeners who particularly enjoyed hearing old and new popular tunes plus the occasional undemanding classic performed on a theatre or similar organ. HMV's Reginald Foort can be found playing medleys with titles such as *Keep Smiling* and *Tunes of the Times* or, for those so inclined, selections from Gounod's *Faust* and Gilbert and Sullivan's *Yeomen of the Guard*.

These last two discs serve as a reminder that operatic compilations had been a feature of the gramophone companies' output since before the First World War when, because of the limitations of the acoustic horn process, they were usually allocated to military or brass bands. The coming of electrical recording in the late 1920s meant that more appropriate ensembles could be used, sometimes with, sometimes without singers. By 1941 the growth of a new but as yet uncritical classical music audience appears to have raised doubts at HMV whether its own British back catalogue had enough material of the right type to satisfy the requirements of those people who might prefer to take their enjoyment in short, easily absorbed helpings. Thanks to Victor, the Boston Promenade Orchestra was an admirable source of works that on one or two sides were complete in themselves but HMV clearly felt the need for more twelve-inch records that, in a purely orchestral format, gave an overview of a popular opera or a particular composer's best known pieces.

Ironically, the company solved the problem to some extent by marketing pressings on its domestic plum label C series of records from its German (Electrola) catalogue. Thus in November and December, 1941 we find the vaguely named Grand Opera Orchestra performing abbreviated accounts of the best known melodies from Puccini's *Madam Butterfly* and *La Bohème*. The choice for February, 1942 was Verdi's *Il Trovatore* and in September, 1943 came Flotow's *Martha*, familiar not only through its overture and the tenor aria "M'appari" (for which WERM has nearly a full column of entries) but also for the presence of Thomas Moore's

185

"The Last Rose of Summer" that Flotow had smuggled into his score for the soprano soloist. On the non-operatic side a disc was issued in August, 1942 of an anonymous Symphony Orchestra playing gems from Tchaikovsky. HMV's labels discreetly offered no information about the conductor of these selections but definitely some (indeed, probably all) were made by Electrola's tireless music director Bruno Seidler-Winkler with the company's pick-up house orchestra.

Comedians, naturally, were a great asset to the gramophone companies and, reverting to the BD series, HMV was fortunate to have Arthur Askey on its roster for this sector of its catalogue. Askey's voice was always brim-full of laughter and in songs and monologues he had few equals when it came to exploiting the comical aspects of wartime life; so successful were his morale-boosting efforts that scarcely a month went by without one or more of his discs appearing.

Although Decca's Vera Lynn was the leading exponent of the overtly sentimental songs so popular with wartime audiences, HMV had an artist who provided strong competition, but in a totally different style. Leslie Hutchinson (Hutch to all his fans) was accorded no less than eighteen discs in the BD series in 1941. The son of a black father and white mother, Hutch came from Grenada in the West Indies; in his late teens he went to America where in New York he set off on his musical career by playing the piano accompaniments for singers in Harlem clubs. In due course he moved on to Paris and eventually London. There, in revue, variety and as a cabaret artist at exclusive night spots his reputation blossomed and in 1940 the first fruit of his partnership with HMV was a sultry performance of Cole Porter's *Begin the Beguine.*

Hutch possessed a baritone voice of exceptional smoothness well suited to the romantic repertoire in which he specialised. To her admirers Dame Vera's songs provided the comfort and encouragement that might come from a wife, sweetheart or the nice girl next door. Hutch, on the other hand, appealed to a more sophisticated audience and was a special favourite amongst what then was loosely known as high society with various members of which he was on the most intimate terms. HMV had found the ideal contrast: whereas Vera Lynn soothed and consoled her listeners, Hutch raised the emotional temperature of his.

By no means all of Hutch's songs were destined to become ever-greens but in 1941 alone that creamy, seductive voice with its passionate vibrato was featured by HMV in such still enduring numbers as *Just one of those Things, Room Five-Hundred-and-Four, Something to remember you by* and *I don't want to set the World on Fire.*

Russian orchestral music with its colourful textures, memorable tunes and thrilling climaxes was a regular source of pleasure to British concert audiences, many of whose members were possibly encountering Tchaikovsky, Borodin, Rimsky-Korsakov or Rachmaninov for the first time; in addition, two piano concertos, Tchaikovsky's First and Rachmaninov's Second, enjoyed tremendous popularity. The current catalogues of HMV and Columbia were well stocked in this sector but throughout the war new recordings continued to be added in order to replace veteran discs, to offer cheaper alternatives to the latest generation of record buyers or to introduce fresh repertoire.

Tchaikovsky's dramatic Fantasy-overture *Romeo and Juliet*, for instance, could be had at full price on Columbia conducted by Mengelberg or on HMV in the incomparable set by Koussevitzky and the Boston Symphony Orchestra. The latter company, aiming at new collectors, recorded another version in February, 1941 for issue in April at mid-price. Constant Lambert was chosen to conduct the City of Birmingham Orchestra which, for contractual reasons, appeared on the labels just as Symphony Orchestra. Provincial venues frequently raised problems that simply did not occur at EMI's specially designed Abbey Road studios in London. Birmingham's Corinthian Town Hall in winter severely tested the stamina of conductor and orchestra (who had to repeat some sides several times) and the ingenuity of Walter Legge, the producer, and his sound engineers. Special measures had to be taken to muffle the traffic noise of the city centre but even more intrusive was the shrieking of the large flocks of local starlings which treated Birmingham's concert hall as part of an avian Grand Prix circuit. Legge's solution was to station a man outside who would scare away the birds by giving a series of blasts on a loud hooter immediately before the recording of each side was due to start. The making of Lambert's *Romeo and Juliet* is perhaps one of the best examples of the locational difficulties faced by an English record company doggedly pursuing its share of the wartime market.[11]

For Britain, Hitler's invasion of the USSR in June, 1941 had the disconcerting effect of transforming Russia overnight from a signatory of the Russo-German non-aggression pact to an ally fighting a common enemy. The great question now was: given the speed at which the Wehrmacht was storming eastwards, would Russia also soon be part of the Third Reich? British feelings of sympathy for the Russian people at large were quickly roused but it was hard to forget or forgive the eagerness with which Stalin, their leader, had joined in the dismemberment of Poland in September, 1939. The British companies sensibly adopted a policy of wait and see before marking the unlooked-for alliance with any major recordings of Russian music. It was not until October, 1941 that Decca, restricted by its limited orchestral resources, led the way by bringing out the first record in an integral set of Rachmaninov's twenty four Preludes, Op. 23 and Op. 32 for solo piano. Moura Lympany was the artist engaged to undertake this ambitious venture which took almost two years to reach its successful conclusion with the release of the ninth disc in August, 1943.

December, 1941 saw Columbia testing the water. The well known Polonaise and Waltz from Tchaikovsky's opera *Eugene Onegin* on a single disc with Sir Malcolm Sargent conducting the Hallé Orchestra was a certain seller; but, more adventurously, on a three disc set the same orchestra under Leslie Heward with Eileen Joyce and the Hallé's Arthur Lockwood as the soloists gave record buyers the chance to try some contemporary Russian music, Shostakovich's Concerto for Piano and Trumpet, Op. 35 which was not yet ten years old. Up until now practically all the Shostakovich recordings available in Britain had originated in the United States and were of serious symphonic music. English Columbia's perceptive choice helped to create a wider interest in this composer's output and contrived to do so in a painless fashion for, as the editors of *The Record Guide* wrote when reviewing a later version, "... the concerto contains a lot of fun for both performers and the audience... The outlying movements ... are entirely frivolous but brilliantly written and very entertaining."

The coming together of Britain and Russia in the fight against Nazism was a topic treated in a variety of ways by the BBC and on 6th December, the eve of Japan's attack on Pearl Harbor, there was a notable, hour-long broadcast from the Corporation's wartime home at Bedford. It took the form of a play based by the poet Louis MacNeice on the film *Alexander Nevsky* made in 1938 by the Soviet director Sergei Eisenstein and for which Prokofiev had written the score. It was introduced by the Russian Ambassador and as well as the players from the BBC's own drama repertory company the cast included the famous stage and screen star Robert Donat as the heroic Nevsky (who in the thirteenth century led the struggle against the invading Teutonic Knights) and the distinguished actress Peggy Ashcroft as Maria who personifies the patriotic virtues of Russian womanhood. To add yet more weight to this important production, Sir Adrian Boult conducted the BBC Symphony Orchestra and two combined choruses in Prokofiev's music.

Because of its declamatory nature, MacNeice's play may sound stilted and old fashioned to present day ears but it was a significant forerunner of the classic radio dramas which, after the war, were to be such highly praised features of the BBC's new arts channel, the Third Programme. *Alexander Nevsky* was recorded at the time of the broadcast but over the ensuing years was largely forgotten until in 1999 this archival landmark re-emerged in the unexpected format of a sampler disc circulated by the specialist CD transfer company, Dutton Laboratories.

The gramophone industries of the Axis countries were equally hard at work during 1941 and in Germany the companies were under government pressure to keep pace with the heavy demand for records intended for troop entertainment and broadcasting; what is more, special dispensations were granted in order to help the export trade. It was typical of the anomalies littering Germany's music world that although Telefunken was forbidden to sell its celebrated recording by Georg Kulenkampff of Mendelssohn's Violin Concerto in the Third Reich because the composer was Jewish the company was allowed to promote the sale of this profitable set in any foreign markets still available.

Japan had long been a major customer for German classical records and this year the Nazis demonstrated their apparently unassailable power by sending to that country on board a U-boat matrices of Polydor's recent abridged recording of Bach's *St. Matthew Passion* conducted by Bruno Kittel, a sound musician who ostentatiously paraded his allegiance to Hitler at every opportunity; Japanese music lovers showed their appreciation of Germany's grand cultural gesture by buying some 17,000 sets. Perhaps in an effort to impress upon the world the spiritual depths of the German soul another wartime partial recording of the *St. Matthew Passion* appeared on Electrola; amongst the renowned soloists were Tiana Lemnitz, Karl Erb and Gerhard Hüsch who, with Günter Ramin conducting the choir of Leipzig's St. Thomas's Church and the Gewandhaus Orchestra, sang (as did their counterparts on Polydor) a text purged of all references to the Jews.

Not even the war could put a stop to the bewildering succession of changing commercial alliances which had characterised the gramophone industry's history since its earliest days. In 1937 Telefunken had taken over Deutsche Grammophon and moved from Berlin to Hanover but, as Stephan Bultmann relates:

> "Four years later, however, a contract between Siemens and AEG [Allgemeine Elektrische Gesellschaft] resulted in DG going to Siemens & Halske AG, while Siemens' shares in Telefunken went to AEG."

Ernst von Siemens is described by Curt Riess as a "music fanatic" who made use of his Munich-based firm's advanced technical expertise to launch the Siemens Spezial label which he reserved solely for classical music, though the same recording processes were also employed for lighter repertoire on Polydor.

The invasion of Russia again brought into play the Nazi policy of banning all music of an enemy state and the companies could no longer make new recordings or sell existing ones of such favourite works as Tchaikovsky's Fifth and Sixth Symphonies and the First Piano Concerto. Party ideology continued to affect the smooth running of everyday business as in an incident involving Edwin Hein, a senior executive in Deutsche Grammophon's sales section. Hein told Riess how in Berlin

> "One day I was summoned by phone to our main shop in the Friedrichstrasse. I hurried there and found it had been locked by the Gestapo. I had great trouble in getting in and only managed to do so after explaining to several of these men that I was the manager. Inside the confusion was indescribable... They were looking, so they said, for forbidden records but they found none and withdrew several hours later, disappointed.

At the door one of them turned back, came up to me and made a request. He wanted [a particular] song ... from the American musical *Rose Marie* by Rudolf Friml.

I pretended to be horrified: 'But this musical is by Jews!' The man went off looking very sheepish."

[Author's translation]

In Austria, the Vienna Philharmonic's commercial recording schedules for 1941 could almost have been designed to create the impression that the war had in no way curbed the capital's traditionally carefree life style. Telefunken had the orchestra to itself this year and the bulk of the subsequent issues comprised marches, waltzes and polkas by the Strauss family plus Richard Strauss's high-spirited tone poem *Till Eulenspiegel* and the erotically charged "Dance of the Seven Veils" from his opera *Salome*, all conducted by a master of this type of repertoire, Clemens Krauss. The only surprise in this batch of 78s is to find Krauss forsaking the Strausses in favour of Manuel de Falla's concert suite of three dances from his ballet score *The Three-Cornered Hat*, the comic plot of which would, however, have been known to a good many Austrian music lovers since it was the same as that of Hugo Wolf's opera *Der Corregidor*.

Italy brought out a number of extremely ambitious wartime recordings as when in 1940 Italian HMV celebrated the fiftieth anniversary of the première of Mascagni's *Cavalleria Rusticana*. The composer, then in his late seventies, had been invited to conduct the Chorus and Orchestra of La Scala, Milan and a cast headed by the leading tenor of the day, Beniamino Gigli. Side 1 of the set contained a vigorous speech in which Mascagni proudly announced himself and lavished praise on all the fine musicians taking part in the project. Despite the composer's evident satisfaction with the outcome, when the opera eventually reached Britain on HMV's Special List and was reviewed in the January, 1949 issue of *The Gramophone* that discerning critic the late Lionel Salter was so offended by the crudity of the performance in general that he never once mentioned Gigli by name.

1941 marked the fiftieth anniversary of Mascagni's next opera, *L'Amico Fritz*, and he was again asked, this time by Cetra, to put his personal stamp on a commemorative recording. On this occasion the excesses prompted by the *verismo* of *Cavalleria Rusticana* were avoided and the gentle story was allowed to unfold naturally with the soprano Pia Tassinari (Suzel) and the tenor Ferruccio Tagliavini (Fritz) in particular making amends for the stylistic shortcomings of the previous year's misguided effort.

The 150th anniversary of Mozart's death fell on 5th December, 1941. With Britain under siege the record companies were in no position to commemorate this historic day on the scale it deserved and amongst the month's releases the only relevant disc came from Columbia with Leslie Heward conducting the strings of the Hallé Orchestra in the solemn Adagio and Fugue in C minor, K 546. There was, however, no need for self-reproach at EMI for in the previous seven years Mozart's genius had found expression in masterly sets of *The Marriage of Figaro, Così fan tutte* and *Don Giovanni* by the Glyndebourne ensembles under Fritz Busch and the classic account of *The Magic Flute* by Sir Thomas Beecham who had also recorded all the major symphonies from No. 29 onwards with his London Philharmonic Orchestra.

Well in advance of the anniversary, Mozart's Requiem in D minor (which he did not live to complete) was recorded at sessions in Berlin by Bruno Kittel for Polydor in 1939 but it was the Italians who rose most impressively to the challenge of honouring Mozart's death. On 5th December Cetra, a branch of the Parlophone group, was on hand at the church of Santa Maria degli Angeli in Rome to capture a performance of the Requiem which involved some four hundred musicians. Departing from normal practice Cetra documented this very special occasion by printing details of the recording's date and venue on the labels of the original 78s. EIAR [Italian Radio] provided the chorus and orchestra who together with the four outstanding soloists, Pia Tassinari, Ferruccio Tagliavini, Ebe Stignani and Italo Tajo were under the direction of the internationally famous Victor De Sabata. Cetra's recording was widely admired and in 1950, when post-war conditions eventually permitted, HMV added it under licence to the Special List. A little earlier it had also been issued in the United States but while British collectors were still restricted to 78s American record buyers were by then able to acquire the Requiem in the more compact and convenient format of two ten-inch Cetra LPs.

III – 1942 to D-Day

BETWEEN JANUARY, 1942 and D-Day on 6th June, 1944 the war began steadily to turn in the Allies' favour. At first Germany and Japan could glory in their triumphs but by 1943 when both aggressors had seriously over-extended themselves there were portents (which they arrogantly chose to discount) that the outcome of their joint drive towards world domination was no longer a foregone conclusion.

Within four months of Pearl Harbor Japan controlled virtually all South East Asia and Burma as well as vast numbers of island territories in the Pacific. When in early May, 1942 the Battle of the Coral Sea was fought by Japanese and American aircraft carriers the US Navy's *Lexington* was sunk and the *Yorktown* severely damaged but the action halted the Japanese plan to press on into Papua where the capital, Port Moresby, would have provided the base from which to invade northern Australia.

A month later the Americans scored a crucial victory at the Battle of Midway when the Japanese lost four carriers and three hundred aircraft. Despite setbacks, American sea power in the Pacific continued to grow and, in their turn, US submarines inflicted heavy losses on Japanese merchant and naval shipping. The necessary conditions were now in place for setting out on the laborious, island-hopping reconquest of the Japanese-occupied Pacific territories, a task which would continue throughout the rest of the war. In August, 1942 the Australians in eastern Papua and the Americans at Guadalcanal in the Solomon Islands were fighting bloody jungle campaigns against a fanatical enemy for whom surrender was unthinkable; the extent of the difficulties faced by the Allies can be measured by the fact that it took a year to overcome the Japanese resistance in New Guinea and the Solomon Islands.

On the Asian mainland Japan had already gathered in much of China and French Indo-China (Vietnam) before their attack on Pearl Harbor after which they kept up the momentum by adding Siam (Thailand), Malaya and Burma to their enormous empire. India was the next target and they advanced into the north-east of the sub-continent. This, however, was one invasion too many and further progress was prevented by the British and Indian Armies' heroic stands at Imphal and Kohima between March and June, 1944.

Having watched the events in Europe from the side-lines since September, 1939 the American people barely had time to realise their country was at war with Japan than on 11th December, 1941 Germany and Italy declared war on the United States; what had initially seemed an involvement centred on Asia and the Pacific was now a global commitment.

The American military authorities saw that with a worldwide dispersal of their fighting forces it would be vital to sustain their morale by keeping them in constant touch with life back home. One way of doing this was through the programmes provided by the Armed Forces Radio Service (AFRS) from its static and mobile transmitters. Live broadcasts brought news of national and local interest as well as performances or interviews given by visiting entertainers. Recorded material naturally formed a considerable part of AFRS's output and included the Service's own 16-inch vinyl transcription discs of the radio shows of such popular comedians as Bob Hope and Jack Benny as well as dance music programmes by leading bands which were often presented as if coming live from the notable hotels or night-clubs at which they were resident.

Commercial gramophone records accounted for a good deal of airtime in AFRS's schedules but only six months after America's enforced entry into the war a major problem arose over this important source of ready-made entertainment. During the 1930s a formidably complex argument had been rumbling on between the record companies, radio networks, professional associations representing composers and music publishers and the American Federation of Musicians (AFM) led by the militant James Caesar Petrillo. At the heart of the matter was the broadcasters' nonchalant use of commercial discs the labels of which clearly stated they were unlicensed for broadcasting. An exasperated RCA took its

194

grievance to law but a surprising decision by a Supreme Court judge in 1940 went against the record company. Petrillo contended that not only did his union members fail to receive any financial benefit from their recordings going out over the air but they were also being deprived of the chance to earn more money through live performances, a thesis with which by no means all the musicians concerned agreed. Ignoring expert advice Petrillo brought his members out on strike in August, 1942, banning them from any further recording work until such time as the gramophone companies prevented their discs being illicitly broadcast and used for public entertainment on that prime component of American youth culture, the jukebox.

Petrillo may have thought that wartime pressures would work in his favour in the prompt settlement of what, to a large extent, had become a personal vendetta; if so, he miscalculated badly. For any major industry to give in at such a time to a union boss's ill-conceived threats would not be in the national interest and the Army's Morale Branch rapidly devised a scheme that would safeguard the forces' musical needs. As part of the war effort musicians would be asked to record without payment and no royalties would be paid to composers or music publishers. Furthermore, when the war was over all matrices would be destroyed as well as all surviving pressings. Petrillo could not object to the proposal without appearing unpatriotic and thus the V Disc came into being.

These records were twelve-inch discs cut with a narrower than usual groove that allowed up to six minutes playing time per side though this had the built-in penalty of some loss of quality towards the end of sides. When it came to choice of repertoire the guiding principle was admirably clear: the troops were to be given what the troops wanted to hear. Monthly batches of recordings were sent out to the AFRS and also to individual military bases, camps and units which, as part of the plan, had been provided with the necessary record playing equipment. Forms on which requests and preferences could be fed back to V Disc's headquarters were included with the shipments and, not surprisingly, the leading jazz, swing and dance bands came top of the list. These, of course, could not possibly supply all the recorded material required but by resorting to the countless groups of lesser renown that catered for the whole spectrum of American popular taste there was music aplenty (though not always of particularly high quality) available on V Discs with which to create a familiar background atmosphere.

Deferring to the forces' preferences meant that V Discs contained relatively little classical music; likewise, recordings of overt propaganda or exaggeratedly patriotic sentiments were also given a decided thumbs down.[12] The occasional touch of triumphalism, however, did not come amiss as demonstrated by the hit tune *Johnny Zero* which celebrated an American pilot's victory over a Japanese Zero fighter plane. V Disc's substantial contribution to the morale-boosting process brought not only music to the American forces; many of the recordings also had a distinctive characteristic, not to be found on commercial discs, in the form of a short, cheery message spoken by one of the featured artists before the music began. With the solidly home-linked entertainment provided for them by AFRS and the V Disc service US troops in the Pacific theatre of war could count themselves fortunate and, to the relief of the military authorities, were therefore unlikely to be swayed by the propaganda broadcasts of Tokyo Rose, an American woman of Japanese parentage, who was the Far Eastern equivalent of Germany's Lord Haw-Haw.

The record companies' stocks of new discs awaiting release soon ran out and were partly replaced by reissues of previous successes which had dropped out of the catalogues. Odd as it may seem, the AFM was open only to instrumentalists so the singers who had worked with top bands were still free to record commercially. This anomaly arose because, according to Petrillo's doctrine, it took years for instrumentalists to learn and perfect their art which had to be protected against exploitation. Vocalists, on the other hand, served no such lengthy apprenticeship and, in Petrillo's view, were on a lower musical plane since, to anybody with a half-decent voice, singing just came naturally.

The major companies were happy to record these soloists (many of whom were stars in their own right) in partnership with small, non-unionised backing groups or purely vocal ensembles. Recording costs were correspondingly reduced and the companies, by chance, were paving the way for the change in public taste which, by the end of the war, was beginning to shift away from the big bands towards the more intimate style of singers like Frank Sinatra whose musical personality was all the more expressive when not having to share the limelight with a group of famous instrumentalists.

The best examples of the new popular music format were also issued in Great Britain and in November, 1943 *The Gramophone's* reviewer was much taken with the backing by the Song Spinners for two romantic numbers sung by Dick Haymes on a Brunswick disc. He was even more impressed by the Song Spinners on their own in a coupling of *Johnny Zero* and *Comin' in on a Wing and a Pray'r* and praised the way "Four men and three girls blend their voices into harmony and produce sounds that are almost orchestral ...". Yet a third Brunswick recording, the Mills Brothers' *Paper Doll* paired with *I'll be around* was given a similarly warm welcome together with the information that "... 200,000 copies of this disc have been sold in the States, and 200,000 Americans can't be wrong!".

Without the staple fare formerly supplied by their big bands the record companies soon found that Petrillo's ban was having damaging effects on their production and sales, even taking into account the shortages of shellac and vinylite. Since RCA's legal action against the broadcasters had come to nothing there was little point in going down that road again and eventually the companies were obliged to make their own financial deals with the AFM in order to bring the bands back into their studios. Amongst the first to do so in October, 1943 was Capitol, the new West Coast label which had been set up in the same year that the Petrillo ban came into force. From the outset, Capitol had been an enterprising company, a point well illustrated by Donald Clarke in his book *The Rise and Fall of Popular Music* where he relates how it "... signed a young and not very good bandleader because his father owned a warehouse full of shellac.". Being of such recent origin Capitol more than most of its rivals was badly in need of an early settlement because it had no back catalogue to help sustain it during the strike, whereas the long-established RCA and Columbia were able to hang on until November, 1944 before making their reluctant peace with Petrillo.

It was ironic that when swing was at the height of its popularity its leading exponents should be recording exclusively on V Discs which, come the end of the war, were pledged to be destroyed. This impending loss, however, was to some extent offset when normal conditions returned to the gramophone industry and many artists

197

who had had major hits on V Discs went on to rerecord them commercially. With classical music so thinly represented there was minimum risk of any especially valuable performances being lost even though the artists' roster included conductors as celebrated as Arturo Toscanini. When all V Disc metal masters were systematically smashed in 1949 it was in the nature of things that numerous pressings should somehow escape the same fate and find their way into private collections there to become unofficial archives of a unique episode in American gramophone history.

* * *

Australia and India which Japan was intent on adding to its list of victims each had a thriving gramophone industry dating back to the beginning of the twentieth century when the Gramophone Company set up offices in Sydney and Calcutta. During the First World War Australians were well supplied with patriotic recordings from mainly home-based sources; the same can be said with regard to World War II when, judging solely by their titles, some numbers such as *They buttoned Uncle Alfie into Khaki, Fall in, Brother* and *Who put the I in the AIF?* still had a touch of 1914-1918 about them. *Digger* and *Just a Brown Slouch Hat* were two more songs with specifically Australian associations but it is interesting to note that British hits like *The White Cliffs of Dover, Bless 'em all, There'll always be an England, The King is still in London* and *We're gonna hang out the Washing on the Siegfried Line* were also being recorded by Australian artists.

Attack from the air was a fact of everyday life for the British but two recordings, *Our Air Raid Shelter* sung by Jack Davey and *I'm such a blooming Nuisance in a Blackout* sung by Bebe Scott, are sharp reminders that, with the apparently unstoppable advance of the Japanese whose carrier forces roamed the Pacific, Australia was also a potential target for enemy bombers.

Of all the fine Australian-born singers undoubtedly the most prolific as a recording artist was the baritone Peter Dawson who for the greater part of his career worked exclusively for HMV. Because he was fifty seven when the Second World War broke out he was no longer eligible for military service and decided the most useful thing he could do was to help with the running of the family's metal industry plant in Australia where, true to form, he still found time to record the stirring patriotic songs *The AIF is marching, Swinging along the Road to Victory* and *V for Victory*.

An Australian vocalist and comedian as yet scarcely known to British audiences was Dick Bentley who after the war joined Jimmy Edwards and June Whitfield in BBC radio's immensely popular comedy series *Take it from here* in which he played the dim-witted Ron. During the early 1940s, however, he was in the Australian studios recording standard numbers such as *The Army, the Navy and the Air Force* and *Praise the Lord and pass the Ammunition* as well as the short-lived *Der Fuehrer's Face*.

It was only right and proper that the linked military roles of Australian and American forces in the Pacific war should have been celebrated in music and 1942, the year when the fight-back in New Guinea and the Solomon Islands began, was a particularly appropriate time for the recording of a song with the encouraging title *The Aussies and the Yanks are here*.

★   ★   ★

In India, as elsewhere throughout the world, the cylinder recording pioneered by Edison soon went out of favour once the Gramophone Company entered the market with Emile Berliner's flat disc. The subsequent events in the sub-continent are described in broad outline in Santosh Kumar De's monograph *Gramophone in India* which helps us to appreciate the distinctive nature of his country's record industry and to understand its commercial structure at the time of the Second World War.

The Gramophone Company, set up in London in 1897 to establish Emile Berliner's presence in Europe, saw India as an exciting business prospect and in 1901 J. Watson Hawd was sent out to investigate the possibilities. He reported favourably, with the proviso that any Indian catalogue would need to be solidly based on recordings of ethnic music. Hawd's recommendations were accepted and the Gramophone Company (or, more correctly, the Gramophone and Typewriter Company as it was named at this stage) opened an office in Calcutta in November, 1901.

Hawd's views on repertoire were shared by Fred Gaisberg who, on his first recording expedition to India in the following year, saw the great opportunities offered to the gramophone by a land with such a diversity of languages and cultures, though he was dismayed by the lack of interest shown in Indian music by the Company's British factors and agents. However, the perceptive repertoire policy that was drawn up for India assured the Gramophone Company's future there and the first recordings, pressed in Hanover on ten-inch single-sided discs, were soon on sale.[13] The long lines of communication ceased to be a problem when in 1908 the Company set up its own recording studio and pressing plant on the spot in Calcutta. The Indian record industry as a whole grew vigorously and the Gramophone Company's original factory was vacated in 1929 when all manufacturing processes were transferred to larger premises in the Dum Dum district of the city.

The wide range of the discs available during the industry's formative years is also described by Santosh Kumar De. Instrumental music was very popular and vocal recordings could be bought in Burmese and a dozen Indian languages and dialects. Light entertainment was provided by ventriloquists or bird and animal imitators and folk music naturally exerted a strong attraction; nor was the serious side of life neglected for devotional songs and readings from religious and classic literary works were also well represented.

An important and enduring extension to the repertoire came in November, 1932 when HMV brought out its first recordings of Indian film music. Then as now, the majority of Indian popular films contained a song or two by stars who were as much adored by their multitude of fans as were Hollywood's Fred Astaire and Ginger Rogers in the West. At first the recordings were studio remakes, often produced in alternative language versions, until more advanced technology enabled the music to be taken directly from the original film's sound track.

Numerous recording companies started up and failed to last the course but other domestic independent firms managed to co-exist with the Gramophone Company. Serious competition came from abroad at the end of the 1920s when HMV's main English adversary, Columbia, arrived and was swiftly followed by Lindström's Odeon, though neither had the advantage of its own pressing facilities in India. The ensuing contest between HMV and Columbia grew so intense that there came a point when each was prompted to bring out lower priced series on the Twin and Regal labels respectively.

The HMV and Columbia film music discs generated a new marketing strategy. As a general rule they were issued in the upper price bracket and then, after the initial demand had slackened, were re-released on Twin or Regal, thus giving a new lease of life to the recordings and another chance for less affluent buyers to obtain a copy. Outside the Indian trade this sales tactic seems to have been little used until it became a standard practice in the LP era.

The Second World War brought important changes to the major companies at the heart of the Indian record industry. The damage sustained by EMI as European affiliates successively fell into the Nazis' hands was partially countered in India when Columbia turned the tables and took over Odeon. There was further consolidation in 1943 when the Ruby Record Company's rights to the Columbia and Odeon catalogues were bought by HMV which thus gained overall control of the Indian record industry's international sector in which it was agreed that the two great British rivals, HMV and Columbia, should continue to trade separately.

Because of the substantial and widespread British population the Dum Dum plant had always pressed western as well as Indian HMV recordings so that off duty gramophone enthusiasts amongst the forces stationed in or near any of India's large cities could enjoy the thrill of the chase at the metropolitan record stores. Up-country it was a different matter but, as a correspondent using the pen name Viator told readers of the Christmas, 1943 issue of *The Gramophone*, consolation might still be found in the most unlikely places.

Viator's route to India had been a long and roundabout one taking in Abyssinia (where he reached Gondar the day after the capture of the city in spring, 1941) and adjacent Eritrea, the former Italian colony on the Red Sea. In the castle at Gondar his unerring nose for gramophone records led him to several hundred discs which disappointingly turned out to be speeches by Mussolini, just one of many such collections found in the ex-colonies and mainland Italy as the war went on and which apparently did little but gather dust from the day they were distributed. Fortunately the record outlets he visited in Eritrea still had excellent stocks of Italian operatic discs which he bought in quantity but when the time came to move on to India his collection, as on past occasions, had regretfully to be left behind.

Luck was certainly on Viator's side when he was posted to

"... a *very* out-of-the-way part of India. One evening I was taken by one of my senior officers 'to hear some music' ... I think my host had every chamber music, instrumental or orchestral record one could ask for, *but* not one vocal record sullied his cabinets ... That was the first of some perfect evenings when the war seemed very far away ..."

For a devoted music lover thousands of miles from home there could hardly have been a more Arcadian interlude but Viator, accustomed as he was to the upheavals of wartime service life, knew only too well how abruptly the idyll might be shattered.

Gramophone memories of a different kind were recalled some forty years after the war by David Atkins. Still in his early twenties he was in command of an Indian motor transport company which in 1942 was engaged in moving men, munitions, petrol and other supplies from the malaria-ridden base at Dimapur along the makeshift single-track mountain road (often subject to landslips) to the garrisons at those vital strategic points on the Burma front, Kohima and Imphal. Fortunately at this time there was a lull in the fighting for the Japanese, too, were seriously stricken by malaria and other tropical sicknesses, a situation that forced them to defer their assault on India until 1944.

In the course of his exhausting convoy duties Atkins frequently encountered the gramophone, virtually the only (and therefore much prized) form of entertainment in those remote parts. Interestingly, he confirms that the British soldiers there were no fonder than their comrades in other theatres of war of brashly patriotic ditties; sentimental songs like Jerome Kern's *Smoke gets in your Eyes* were by far the most often played items in the fragile collections of shellac 78s.

Atkins was at pains not to neglect the leisure needs of his Indian troops and from company funds he bought

"... six gramophones and a large number of Indian gramophone records. Up till now they had not been used much but they were to be a great source of pleasure during the three years we were on the frontier. Every month each platoon changed their records with one another. One of their favourite records was 'Master Jawani' which translates as 'Little Mister Soldier'."

When the chance presented itself other members of the forces were glad to use recordings not for listening pleasure but as a means of keeping in touch with their far away kith and kin. Since 1936 at main railway stations and similar public places in Britain one could go into a small booth housing a coin-in-the-slot machine and make a recording of a brief message on a five-inch aluminium disc. These or similar gadgets might, with luck, be found in India and perhaps even in Burma prior to the British withdrawal. Most recordings of this type, however, would have been made by a team from the War Office's Broadcasting Section which toured widely in India providing a much appreciated service, for the compact, light and relatively strong discs could confidently be entrusted to the post. For the loved ones of soldiers who made such recordings but did not survive the war the little discs would commemorate the man whose voice could now only be heard speaking the same few words to them through their gramophones.

★ ★ ★

North Africa in late October and early November, 1942 was the scene of one of the great turning points of the Second World War. In the desert the opposing armies had fought intensively for two years during which first one side and then the other held the advantage, but by this time Rommel had driven the British so far eastwards that the fall of Alexandria, Port Said, Cairo and the Suez Canal seemed imminent. General Bernard Montgomery had arrived in August to take command of the 8th Army and in October the BBC recorded a broadcast[14] he made declaring that the British would hold on to their positions at El Alamein and Alam Halfa or perish: further retreat was not a permissible option. The battle of El Alamein began on 23rd October and lasted until 4th November when the Axis forces, unable to stem the powerful British onslaught any longer, were ordered by Rommel to withdraw. The morale of the retreating troops would not have been improved when a few days later news was released of the successful Allied landings in French North Africa; the Germans and Italians who so recently had been on the verge of taking Egypt now found themselves between the proverbial rock and a hard place. Many fierce battles ensued on both the eastern and western flanks of this theatre of war but eventually, on 12th May, 1943, all the Axis armies in North Africa acknowledged defeat and surrendered.

The BBC's war reporters together with their recording equipment followed this pivotal desert campaign closely throughout and kept listeners at home well informed of the latest developments. The pulverising artillery bombardment of the Axis positions at the start of the Battle of El Alamein was impressive to hear as was Godfrey Talbot's description of British tanks moving forward by moonlight through a "fog of sand" towards the enemy lines. On 15th November, only eleven days after the 8th Army achieved its breakthrough, the bells of Tobruk were recorded ringing out in celebration of the Axis troops' departure from the seaport that had changed hands so many times. A week before Christmas, 1942 on the borders of Tripolitania Talbot met a group of soldiers enjoying a singsong in which they were led by a corporal playing the clarinet. With some difficulty they were persuaded to perform the seasonal *First Noel* for the benefit of the BBC's radio audience, though on the recording Talbot had to admit this carol was somewhat outside the men's normal army repertoire.

It fell to Frank Gillard to recount the last action in the North African war when Allied bombers and artillery pounded the German 90th Light Division which was holding out in the Tunisian mountains behind the Cape Bon peninsula. The respect the opposing desert armies had for each other is reflected in Gillard's forthright summing up of the 90th Light Division as "some of the finest fighters that ever came out of Germany." Whether by design or not, this report, by openly paying credit to the enemy, would undoubtedly have boosted morale at home through its emphasis on the exceptional toughness of the resistance the Allies had overcome.

The harsh, unforgiving desert could, paradoxically, also display a serene beauty. Early in the campaign John (later Sir John) Verney, the painter and illustrator, was an officer in the Royal Armoured Corps when the British were being steadily pushed back by Rommel. The few occasions they were able to rest up came as balm in Gilead and during one of them he wrote to his wife telling her of the magic he once experienced as he listened to some favourite classical music.

"I still carry my gramophone around, but I seldom get time to play a tune on it. One lovely night, though, I shall always remember. A full moon, a clear sky and the desert air cool and thyme-scented, I perched the machine on a tin of petrol and played the Mozart clarionet concerto until all the anger and worrying of the day had sunk to the bottom."[15]

More bizarre uses were found for both gramophones and gramophone records in a variety of strange circumstances during the war. One innovation was introduced by James Riddell, the vice-captain of the British ski team that competed in the 1936 Winter Olympics attended by Hitler at Garmisch. While serving in Syria in 1942 Riddell heard that the Australian forces wished to set up a mountain warfare school in a specially suitable area behind Tripoli once it had been cleared of the enemy. Riddell volunteered his expert knowledge and was placed in command of a unit which trained large numbers of Allied servicemen in the art of high altitude skiing. The school needed to be as self-sufficient as possible and even made its own wooden skis which on reaching the waxing stage were treated with melted down gramophone records.

A few months after the fighting in North Africa was over a significant event occurred in Algiers. Saturday's child, so the nursery rhyme tells us, works hard for a living and the accuracy of this adage would certainly be borne out for those who on Saturday, 1st January, 1944 were present when the British Forces Experimental Station (BFES) Algiers went on the air for the first time. The Nazis had an inadvertent hand in the success of this venture for the first broadcasts were made using a German transmitter that had been "liberated" in Tunisia. No doubt the enemy was even more vexed to discover the new radio service had also appropriated *Lilli Marlene*[16] for its signature tune though, at the suggestion of higher authority, this was soon replaced by *Rule Britannia*.

Lilli Marlene, in a manner of speaking, was the international theme music of the desert war for it had appealed to the fighting men of the Axis and Allied powers alike. The original Electrola recording made by Lale Andersen attracted little attention at first but when it was used as the regular signing-off tune of a German forces broadcasting station in Belgrade its popularity rocketed. Transmissions intended for Rommel's Afrika Korps could of course, also be picked up by men of the 8th Army on their own radios with the result that *Lilli Marlene* became as well loved as any British sentimental song. Andersen's recording went on to be the first German disc to sell a million copies, a commercial landmark also reached by Anne Shelton's excellent English language version issued by Decca in 1943.

The broadcasters at BFES Algiers would have needed all their ingenuity to avoid undue repetition in their earliest programmes since they relied on recorded material for a good deal of their output; but, as Alan Grace discloses in his book *This is the British Forces Network*, their record library to begin with consisted of a mere fifty five discs. In March, though, the special focus of interest at BFES Algiers was the arrival of the vehicles and equipment that would form two mobile broadcasting units, record libraries included, which by the end of the month were ready to set off and join the British troops on the ground in Italy.

*   *   *

The Allies' decision to use Italy as the southern gateway through which the Mediterranean war would be carried into Europe called first for the capture of Sicily, the necessary springboard for the attack on the mainland. The invasion of Sicily was an Anglo-American operation that began with a night time drop of parachute troops ahead of the seaborne landings on 10th July,1943 by Montgomery's and Patton's forces. After a month of heavy fighting the Germans began to withdraw and on 17th August the Allies were in Messina from where, across the Strait, lay Italy itself.

When Mussolini resigned on 25th July Marshal Pietro Badoglio, an anti-Fascist, took control of the country and an armistice was agreed with the Allies in early September. Predictably, the Germans opted to fight on and the British 8th Army, the Desert Rats as they were now universally known, moved across the Strait of Messina and pushed into the mainland where the important naval base of Reggio di Calabria was soon in their hands. Further north more Allied landings took place on 9th September at Taranto on the heel of Italy's geographic foot and at Salerno, south of Naples.

The following day the Nazis, showing the utmost contempt for their former Axis partners, took over Rome. Mussolini was now being held prisoner in a remote area of the Abruzzi but, in another display of German strength, was rescued in a daring commando raid led by Otto Skorzeny and, with Hitler's approval, installed as the head of a new puppet Fascist government in northern Italy.

The Allied landings at Anzio in January, 1944 were planned to support the drive north towards Rome but their element of surprise was cancelled out by the failure to move inland quickly enough. This miscalculation resulted in the bridgehead coming under intense day and night attack for a month; the situation was desperate but eventually Allied air superiority in conjunction with massive land and sea bombardments forced the Germans to give up their efforts to contain the invasion.

As the Allies slowly edged northwards the Germans fell back from one strong defensive line to another in central Italy. The tenacity with which the Wehrmacht clung to its strategic fortresses is perhaps best recalled by the battle for the historic Benedictine monastery of Monte Cassino which was largely laid waste by bombing and artillery attacks in February, 1944. The Germans held on there for another three months against a series of gallant assaults by, amongst others, New Zealand and Indian troops. Fittingly, when the ruins were finally captured, the honour went to Polish, predominantly Catholic, soldiers. It was no less auspicious that the American 5th Army entered Rome only a matter of hours before the Allies' successful D-Day landings of 6th June on the Normandy beaches.

The preparations for the invasion of Sicily bring John Verney back into the picture. German air bases in Sardinia were a serious threat since the aircraft stationed there might be used to back up the Wehrmacht in Sicily and Verney was chosen to be one of a small raiding party whose task would be to destroy as many German planes on the ground as possible. The original plan was for a submarine to land the men secretly but the vessel developed engine trouble and had to return to Algiers. Tantalisingly, one of the submarine's officers possessed "... a passion for music and he had on board a good collection of classical records which, for fear of detection, could not be played at sea." With tongue in cheek, Verney goes on to remark that "Enemy asdic apparatus was said to be particularly sensitive to the sound of Beethoven." After this initial delay the commando group parachuted into Sardinia where, at the end of the mission, Verney had the misfortune to be taken prisoner of war.

The BBC reporters' recorded dispatches covered every aspect of the war that came their way. At the end of the Sicilian campaign, for instance, Garry Marsh spoke to General Patton shortly before he entered Messina, so enabling the Commander in Chief of the American 7th Army to pay tribute to "the magnificent fighting qualities and superhuman endurance of the soldiers of the 3rd Division" who had taken the city. In complete contrast, a few days later Frank Gillard was in Lentini listening to the town band playing music by Bellini and Verdi; the programme was rounded off with spontaneous and very creditable performances of the British and American national anthems which Gillard recorded for the BBC's listeners. The sound archives of this period also contain General Montgomery (a great believer in keeping the troops under his command as well informed as possible) breaking the news of the first Allied landings on the Italian mainland. "Forward to victory", he urged, "let us knock Italy out of the war." But the Germans had different ideas and continued to resist the Allies in Italy until the death of Hitler and the fall of Berlin signalled the end of the war in Europe.

The dangers and hardships faced by the Allied forces were shared by the radio reporters and their recording engineers who, within the limits imposed on them by the military authorities, worked on the straightforward principle: the nearer the front, the hotter the news. Wynford Vaughan-Thomas, the ebullient Welshman, described the action at the Anzio beachhead a day or two after the landing. Flares illuminated the scene as what had already become the "usual" German night attack got under way; artillery and small arms fire was unrelenting and so close that he could see the "recording truck rocking on its springs."

Three months later, after the hard-won Allied breakout from the beachhead, Anzio had been transformed into a rest area and Vaughan-Thomas was again on hand to give a vivid account of time out of war. Where once men had to take advantage of every scrap of cover in order to stay alive troops could now relax and enjoy themselves. Those coming out of the front line could indulge in the luxury of a hot shower and eat fresh bread from the bakery that had been set up. The sound of massed pipes filled the air and rugger was played; for one day only there was a Brigade point-to-point and a donkey Derby. War or no war, the Americans could not do without their doughnuts; they had a factory, no less, operating at Anzio and there was even a machine within two miles of the front line turning out this essential fare. ENSA was there to provide live entertainment, the troops had their own concert party called The Waggoners and Vaughan-Thomas was full of admiration for a sergeant of the Army Kinematograph Unit who screened films in a small dug-out for capacity audiences of thirty five men.

At a Polish command post Godfrey Talbot recorded his account of the terrible conditions endured by the men who that day had at last dislodged the Germans from Monte Cassino. For the attackers the only approach to the monastery ruins had been by "appalling mountain tracks" under constant enemy fire and the only way to transport supplies had been by mule and finally by men on foot. In many areas "you could by day remain alive only in a hole in the ground. To show yourself and move in daylight was death." Before he left the base a small piece of paper was passed to him. It had come by carrier pigeon from the remains of the abbey to let headquarters know that the battle was over; the message consisted simply of a pencilled letter V and the signature of a Polish Lieutenant of Signals.

Another historic event at which Talbot was present was the Allies' entry into Rome. In a recording he made standing in the thronged Piazza Venezia he described how everyone was gazing up at the balcony of the Palazzo where so often Mussolini had strutted and addressed the multitudes. Looking down at the square now, however, were three Allied soldiers, steel-helmeted and carrying their rifles, accompanied by two Roman citizens, all proudly waving their national flags.

From the examples referred to it is instantly clear that the BBC's recorded war reports were notable for their immediacy and diversity. Although they lacked the visual impact of newsreel films, the gung ho and embarrassingly facetious commentaries heard by cinema audiences were not imitated. Each of the BBC's team of clearly spoken, articulate radio journalists could effortlessly paint verbal pictures that brought the heroism, tragedy and occasional humorous moments of the land, sea and air wars vividly alive for home front listeners. The playing of these reports on the wireless during regular news programmes provided first hand coverage of the conflict for the British civilian population but without the formal structure and vocabulary of official communiqués. Not only did they help discourage the growth of overly parochial attitudes at home towards the war but they also lent encouragement to the fighting men by conveying the actuality of their dangers and hardships to a wider world.

Prosaically identified as B3 and B4, the two Army mobile broadcasting units that were shipped from Algiers went their separate ways on arriving in Italy. They followed closely in the tracks of the 8th Army and at times were only three miles behind the front line. Like Wynford Vaughan-Thomas's recording truck at Anzio, the broadcasters' vehicles were no strangers to artillery and bombing attacks but even so, thanks largely to the discs they carried, it rarely happened that the troops within transmitting range were deprived of their welcome, lighthearted entertainment.

In addition to their commercial recordings, B3 and B4 (or GLADYS as the latter was later affectionately known) would also have been in line for material produced by the London-based Army Radio Unit and the Overseas Recorded Broadcasting Service (ORBS). At EMI's Abbey Road studios (which remained open throughout the war) and at a couple of West End theatres ORBS, using acetate discs, recorded programmes by such well known artists as Paul Fenhoulet and the Skyrockets Dance Band of No.1 Balloon Centre (who recorded commercially for Parlophone), George Melachrino and his fifty piece orchestra of service musicians, Sidney Torch the cinema organist, the tenor David Lloyd and the comedians Terry Thomas and Charlie Chester. The importance of the role played by ORBS is made clear by Doreen Taylor in her book *A Microphone and a Frequency* where she tells how "In the third year of the war, ORBS discs were helping to fill 125 hours of airtime which the Army had managed to find on 22 broadcasting stations all around the world ..."

Despite the hard conditions and limited resources a lighter side to field broadcasting often asserted itself as when B3 was quartered for a time with the religious community at Campobasso in the Appenines and, in Alan Grace's words, "... could claim to be the only station in the world to have broadcast 'In a Monastery Garden' from a monastery garden."

There were both amusing and serious aspects to a radio joust between B4 and the German station nicknamed Axis Sally which pumped out propaganda at the Allied forces. Just how the Germans came by them is uncertain but at one stage Axis Sally

210

Third Reich. Hitler's Inferno, *released in America in 1959 by Dauntless International.*

French gramophone publicity. A 1930s advert for French HMV's jazz recordings.

Third Reich. Nazi anti-Semitic propaganda. H.S. Ziegler expounds the ideology of his Entartete Musik (Degenerate Music) exhibition, Düsseldorf, May 1938.

DECCA

Has the honour of presenting

THE MOST THRILLING RECORD EVER ISSUED

AIR BATTLE OVER THE ENGLISH CHANNEL

SP.35. 12-inch. 2/6.

**An eye-witness account by CHARLES GARDNER.
As broadcast by the B.B.C. on Sunday, 14th July, 1940.**

Most people who heard this dramatic and thrilling broadcast will want to hear it over again, and those who did not, now have an opportunity of listening to a recording of a broadcast—which may never occur again—of an actual Air Battle with all its accompanying thrills.

This record will be of historical interest for years to come.   You **MUST** add it to your collection.

Profits from the sale of this Record will be given to the Royal Air Force Comforts Fund.

Also issued under the SP. series

SP.34.   **How to deal with Incendiary Bombs**
12-inch. **2/6**   Side I—Preparation
                      Side 2—Action

Exclusive to

DECCA

THE ★ ALL STAR ★ RECORD

---

*World War II. Decca leaflet for Charles Gardner's on the spot description
of a Battle of Britain dogfight.*
(PERMISSION COURTESY OF DECCA MUSIC GROUP LIMITED)

World War II. Recording stars of the day donate unwanted records for recycling in response to the Royal British Legion's 1942 appeal.

music

from

the USSR

Music is part of the daily life of the people of the U.S.S.R. Their young composers are becoming well-known throughout the world. Now for the first time an important work by a Russian composer played by a Russian symphony orchestra can be heard in this country.

A sound track of this work was made in the U.S.S.R. to be played in the remote towns and villages throughout the vast country. A recording from the sound track now brings the same original performance to the people of this country.

Aran Khachaturian was born in Tbilisi in Armenia in 1904. In his compositions, he aims to combine the folk songs of his country with the principles of classical music, a striking illustration of this is the violin concerto for which he was awarded the "2nd. Stalin Premium" of 50,000 roubles in 1941.

Aran Khachaturian

David Oistrakh (*Violin*)
With the **U.S.S.R. State Symphony Orchestra**
conducted by A. V. Hauk

K1082 — K1086.   Concerto for Violin *by* **Khachaturian**

1st movement. Allegro con fermezza. *2nd movement.* Andante Sostenuto. *3rd movement.* Allegro Vivace

presented on

Decca records

Issued by The Decca Record Co. Ltd., 1-3, Brixton Road, London, S.W.9

World War II. Decca's advert in The Gramophone, *February 1943, for the first release in a series of Russian-made recordings.*

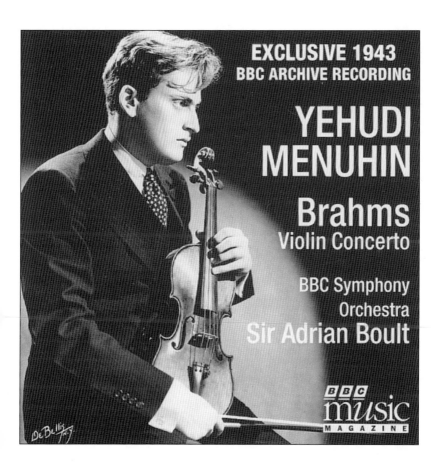

*World War II. In April, 1943 when Yehudi Menuhin was in Britain
entertaining the American Forces the BBC recorded this broadcast
of Brahms's Violin Concerto.*

(PHOTO BY DE BELLIS, NEW YORK)

World War II. British Forces mobile broadcasters prepare a programme in their record library.

began broadcasting new recordings of swing and dance music by leading American bands. The frustrating thing was that the British mobile units did not have these discs so B4 enterprisingly recorded them from Axis Sally's transmissions and, after some judicious editing, played them on their own wavelength to highly appreciative listeners. The Germans made indignant noises and, when their protests about radio piracy went unheeded, sent in a small force of bombers to destroy B4 but the pilots, fortunately, failed to locate their target.

In due course, Rome was the host city to the British station B5 which pioneered the phone-in record request programme in which studio and library staff combined to have the asked-for discs on the turntable with minimum delay. B5 also had the considerable advantage of being able to supplement its own collection with recordings held in the Vatican Radio's extensive library from which by kind permission of the Cardinal-Engineer it was privileged to borrow.

By an odd coincidence, Albert Ketelby's *In a Monastery Garden* had been a childhood favourite of a young Grenadier Guards officer, Viscount Lascelles, who was serving in Italy in 1944. He was the son and heir of the 6th Earl of Harewood and in his autobiography *The Tongs and the Bones* he tells how gramophones had been an integral part of his life since his early days. In the nursery at Harewood House, the family residence in the West Riding of Yorkshire, he had listened, entranced, to a single-sided disc of Chaliapin singing Mussorgsky's *Song of the Flea* played on an ordinary wind-up machine. Downstairs in the Music Room there was a strikingly handsome instrument in a splendid mahogany case adorned with the royal crest of King Amanullah of Afghanistan who had given it as a present to his mother, Her Royal Highness Princess Mary, the Princess Royal. Understandably, this could be played by him only on special occasions and under strict supervision.

Amongst other places, the war took him to North Africa and on his travels he was able from time to time to send details of new European recordings he had come across to *The Gramophone* which published occasional lists to whet the appetites of its readers for discs which, when peace returned, they might wish to add to their collections.

Whenever on leave, like so many other enthusiasts in the forces, he could not resist the lure of the record shops and in Tunis in 1943 he acquired a large amount of vocal music on Polydor, Odeon and French HMV, the last named providing the greatest prize, Roger Désormière's historic wartime recording of Debussy's *Pelléas et Mélisande*. He also equipped himself with a portable gramophone which went with him to Italy where in Naples in 1944 he trawled every second hand shop he could find and to his delight netted a gratifying number of golden age vocal discs. However, the pleasures of serendipity were soon to become nostalgic memories.

On 18th June, barely a fortnight after the Allies liberated Rome, he was on what in theory should have been a fairly routine patrol but he and his men were intercepted and in a sharp encounter he was badly wounded and taken captive. The Germans soon discovered they had a rather special prisoner for Viscount Lascelles not only stood to succeed to his father's earldom but, even more importantly, through his mother he was a nephew of the British monarch, King George VI. He was accordingly classified by the Germans as a *Prominenter* - a VIP - and in due course joined a group of other British officers whose links to the establishment and the aristocracy made them valuable hostages whose lives could be used as bargaining counters in Germany's hour of need. So it was that Viscount Lascelles arrived at the ultimate high security prisoner of war fortress, Colditz Castle.

* * *

At the beginning of 1942 it was clear that barring miracles there was no hope of an early end to the war in Europe. Although the Germans did not succeed in taking either Moscow or the besieged Leningrad they nevertheless controlled vast areas of Russia and Stalin pressed insistently for a second front to ease the relentless pressure on the Red Army. The Allies' resources were not yet sufficient for the full scale invasion of France that Stalin would have wished and the landings in Italy were something of an interim measure. Unfortunately, what Churchill believed would be the soft underbelly of Europe turned out in the terse words of General Mark Clark, the Commander of the US 5th Army, to be "a tough old gut" and after D-Day the Italian campaign took second place to the liberation of France.

Even before the Normandy landings the USSR's enormous reserves of manpower, its manufacturing bases safely located behind the Ural Mountains and the Army's ability to turn the ferocious winters to its own best advantage enabled the Russians to stem the German advances and start driving the invaders back. Indeed, by Christmas, 1943 about two thirds of the territory taken by Hitler's forces had been recovered and in early January, 1944 Soviet troops were pushing westwards into Poland.

Stalingrad, standing on the west bank of the Volga, was of special significance to the USSR not only as a key manufacturing and communications centre but also because of its close historic links with Stalin himself in the days of the civil war which followed on the Revolution of 1917. When in August, 1942 General von Paulus ordered the German 6th Army to take the city there ensued what has been described as "the most titanic and terrible battle of the Second World War." The savage fighting lasted until the end of January, 1943 when, encircled by the Russians, von Paulus was forced to surrender. The price the Germans and their Axis allies paid at Stalingrad is terrible to contemplate; exact figures can never be known but it has been calculated that in the region of a million and a half men were killed, wounded, missing or taken prisoner. The tenth anniversary of Hitler's becoming Chancellor fell on 30th January, 1943 and Goebbels and Goering made speeches to mark the occasion. It was not until 3rd February that the news of their country's defeat was announced to the German people and, such was the scale of the disaster, three days of national mourning were proclaimed.

The sea war in the North Atlantic in 1942 and 1943 was dominated by the battle with the U-boat wolf-packs preying on the Allied convoys. The Germans did not know that the British were intercepting and reading masses of their military signals traffic encoded under the Enigma system which the Nazis believed was uncrackable. The wolf-packs' reliance on radio contacts yielded much valuable information and, with improvements in anti-submarine detection equipment coinciding with the extension of air cover, the balance gradually swung in the Allies' favour.

The convoys sailing from British ports to carry war materials to Russia faced yet more hazards as they steamed to North Cape and into the Barents Sea *en route* for Murmansk or Archangel. The

213

long summer hours of daylight in those latitudes increased the risk of being spotted by German reconnaissance planes which could then alert the battleships and cruisers based in northern Norway. The winter months brought shorter days but also the appalling Arctic weather which tested to the limit the powers of endurance of the crews aboard the merchant vessels and their naval escorts alike.

On the British and German home fronts at this time the war was being experienced mainly through the medium of the aerial bombing campaigns. The RAF targeted the ancient Hanseatic port of Lübeck on 28th March, 1942 to which the Germans responded with the so-called Baedeker raids on historic British cathedral cities. The Allied raids on Germany steadily intensified with the Americans attacking in the daytime and the British at night; ever larger numbers of aircraft took part and ever more powerful bombs were dropped. After a lapse of a year night raids were again mounted against Berlin and it was probably no coincidence that on 30th March, when von Paulus was about to surrender at Stalingrad, the RAF made its first daylight raid on the German capital. The celebrated attack on the Möhne and Eder dams came in mid-May and at the end of that month the RAF carried out its first 1,000 bomber raid on Cologne.

It was the turn of Hamburg in July and early August, 1943 when the RAF destroyed and burnt the greater part of the city in a terrifying fire storm. American casualties were particularly heavy in the August and October attacks on the major ball bearing production plant at Schweinfurt in Bavaria which was far beyond the range of fighter escorts; on these two operations one hundred and twenty Flying Fortresses were lost and US daylight bombing was temporarily halted.

After its Baedeker raids of 1942 the Luftwaffe was so heavily involved in the fighting on the Russian front that attacks on Britain slackened off until 1944 when for a week in February London was subjected to the most concentrated bombardment for nearly three years.

Between the evacuation of Dunkirk and D-Day many special operations by commando-type forces were carried out in Norway and France. In February, 1942 important new German radar equipment in use at Bruneval was captured and brought safely back to England; a month later the dock gates at the entrance to the German submarine base at St. Nazaire were blown up and in December the same year a party of Royal Marines went under cover of darkness up the Garonne river to attack the U-boat base at Bordeaux.

These were operations requiring only a relatively small number of men; sadly, the largest attempt at a landing on the French coast prior to D-Day was a disaster. Some 3,600 of the 6,000 British, Canadian, American and Free French soldiers who went ashore at Dieppe on 19th August, 1942 were killed or taken prisoner while commensurate losses were suffered offshore by the Navy (one destroyer) and the RAF (106 aircraft). The object of the raid was to test the German coastal defences in France and the unfortunate outcome was a serious shock to the Allied military planners. Failure though it was, important lessons were learned from the operation and the knowledge gained was of critical value in ensuring the success of the Normandy landings on D-Day, 6th June, 1944.

There were marked contrasts between the standards of living in Britain and Germany in 1942. With the resources of the occupied countries to draw on, the German people had as yet experienced little in the way of serious shortages. The British, on the other hand, were becoming more and more familiar with the problems posed by the rationing of such basic items as food and clothing. From April onwards even white bread, that staple of the family diet, was no longer allowed to be baked and consumers had to make do with the far from popular coarse wholemeal loaves. For the more affluent, the pleasure of dining out also lost some of its attraction when the top price of meals in hotels and restaurants was pegged at five shillings (25p) in the interests of social fair play and as a means of cracking down on profiteering and black market trading. Although food and drink were in short supply there were still plenty of ways in which to enjoy precious leisure hours. Theatres, cinemas and concert venues continued playing to full and enthusiastic audiences and dance halls everywhere were particularly popular with American servicemen.

Artists from the United States regularly came to Britain during tours on which they gave shows for the American forces. Not all these visitors were from the worlds of popular music or comedy for amongst them was the violinist Yehudi Menuhin. He was briefly in the country in October, 1942 and returned in April the following year when he was the soloist in a memorable broadcast of Brahms's Violin Concerto. Sir Adrian Boult and the BBC Symphony Orchestra, normally based at Bedford during the war, returned to the Maida Vale studio in London for the occasion which was recorded on film soundtrack, a medium with which the BBC was experimenting at that time.

The existence of this recording was little known until, about fifty years after it was made, the Corporation began to run a series of programmes devoted to outstanding performances preserved in its archives. The recording was rebroadcast and, in very acceptable sound, it was possible to hear once again Menuhin's enthralling reading accompanied by an orchestra and conductor renowned for their affinity with the music of Brahms. Record collectors were eventually given the chance to acquire the concerto when the BBC brought out a CD transfer which was distributed with the September, 1997 issue of its *Music Magazine*.

Recordings document many aspects of the air war in Europe waged by Allied flyers operating from British bases during the period from 1942 to D-Day. When the BBC set up its equipment at a rural location on 19th May, 1942 it was hoping to record the nocturnal song of the neighbourhood's nightingales. On this particular date, however, there were noises off for the chosen site turned out to be under the flight path of a large force of bombers whose target that night was the industrial city of Mannheim. Luckily the nightingales were not alarmed as the planes drew near, passed overhead and gradually faded from earshot. The sound of bird song and the heavy drone of bombers on the resulting recording might fancifully be said to symbolise the contesting voices of peace and war with the nightingales as the victors. Leaving aside such niceties of interpretation, the BBC had by chance produced a most unusual sound sketch which deserved to be widely available and permission was given to HMV to issue it commercially in the BD series the following September.

One of the most action-packed of the BBC's war reports was made on 3rd September, 1943 when Wynford Vaughan-Thomas and his recording engineer Reg Pidsley took part in a night raid on Berlin. This eventful mission was described by Pidsley especially for John Snagge and Michael Barsley's book *Those Vintage Years of*

Radio from which we learn that the Lancaster aircraft's payload included a Big Cookie, a bomb weighing four thousand pounds. The journey to Berlin and back lasted over eight hours, for more than six of which the bomber was open to attack from anti-aircraft fire or enemy fighter planes. It is not surprising that in these conditions Vaughan-Thomas was on a high, so much so that he was advised by a crew member to hold some adjectives in reserve for when they arrived over Berlin. Pidsley kept his recording blanks warm by tucking them inside his battledress top and was ready to record whenever required.

Because he had been breathing oxygen Vaughan-Thomas's voice was unluckily not as clear as usual but, with his equipment connected to the Lancaster's intercom, Pidsley achieved a highly atmospheric recording of the approach to the target, the release of the bombs and the attack by an enemy night fighter. Once freed from the deadweight of Big Cookie the Lancaster suddenly soared upwards, a movement which took it out of the path of the pursuing German plane and at the same time caused the recording head to dig deeply into the acetate disc. However, with great skill Pidsley kept everything under control and continued to record.

The BBC's audio cassette compilation of reports from the Second World War includes an extract from this sound document in which the listener hears the reaction of the Lancaster's crew when their own gunners send the night fighter down in flames. During the hubbub one jubilant voice shouts "Bloody good show", a verdict which might equally well apply to the remarkable recording Vaughan-Thomas and Pidsley brought back home with them.

Not all recorded reports (this one amongst them) were broadcast immediately. Delays imposed for security reasons by the military authorities could sometimes have disappointing consequences as when a report on a January, 1943 raid on Berlin was pre-empted by the German radio's prompt account of the Luftwaffe's reprisal raid on London.

The air war occasionally figured in the output of popular song writers. *Comin' in on a Wing and a Pray'r* which had been such a hit for the Song Spinners in the USA also did well in Britain where, in addition to Brunswick's original recording, excellent cover versions were added to the Decca and Parlophone catalogues in 1943 by Ambrose with Anne Shelton and Billy Thorburn's The Organ, the Dance Band and Me with Helen Clare. The song's scenario was simple. An overdue aircraft at last makes radio contact with its base where hope for its return had been fading. One engine is out of action but "With our full crew on board/And our trust in the Lord/We're comin' in on a wing and a pray'r." This unaffected statement of faith risked (but avoided) sounding merely sentimental and the listener is left to conclude that the damaged plane made a safe homecoming. Flyers, ground staff and civilians living near military aerodromes were well aware of what might result if an emergency landing went badly wrong but the lyric of a popular song was not the place to enlarge on the grim realities of war.

Like *Comin' in on a Wing and a Pray'r*, *The Bombardier Song* by the famous team of Rodgers and Hart was not set in any specific theatre of war. It does not appear to have had much attraction for non-American audiences and in the United Kingdom it made so little impact that there is not a single entry for it in Rust and Forbes's *Discography of British Dance Bands on Record, 1911-1945*. The song's brief account of a successful bombing mission is overshadowed by the patriotic chorus which progresses from the twee ("The weather's fine for flying,/The fog has gone to bed") to the overblown ("Let's fill the air with eagles,/Let's fill the clouds with men"). The words were certainly not one of Lorenz Hart's best efforts and in the 1942 recording by Bing Crosby the male vocal group does not improve matters by singing in a style uncomfortably reminiscent of German servicemen belting out a Nazi marching song.

The BBC's Dance Music Policy Committee, the watchdog which ensured that broadcast popular music was free of slush, had no problem with *Comin' in on a Wing and a Pray'r* but in 1943 *Silver Wings in the Moonlight* was briefly banned from the air although at least five British commercial recordings were made between the end of June and mid-August. Probably the tune was enjoyed more than the words for two of the five discs were by strict tempo dance orchestras without a vocalist whilst the other three were made by well-known bands whose singers, though, were not amongst the foremost of the day.

Keeping pace with the constantly growing public interest in classical music the BBC introduced the record programmes *Marching and Waltzing* and *Let Us Be Gay* (then an unambiguous term) to the breakfast time schedules. The selections played were

218

designed, as the programme titles indicate, to give listeners a lively start to their day and came mainly from commercial discs currently available in the shops; the individual items of music did not usually exceed two twelve-inch sides, roughly seven to eight minutes. The British catalogues contained an ample store of pieces suited to the bright and breezy, short and sweet radio format for which the choices could be either complete in themselves or extracted from larger works amongst which suites of ballet music offered good pickings.

During the late 1930s Antal Dorati, who was then conducting for the Ballets Russes de Monte Carlo, recorded for HMV and Columbia dances from the scores of the company's productions of *Le Beau Danube* (Johann Strauss), *Les Cents Baisers* (by banker/composer Frédéric d'Erlanger), *Cotillon* (Chabrier) and *Scuola di Ballo* (Boccherini), all of which contained titbits ideal for morning broadcasts. Another prolific provider was Sir Thomas Beecham with his London Philharmonic Orchestra whose discs of the overtures to Rossini's *The Silken Ladder* and *The Thieving Magpie* and Mozart's *Marriage of Figaro* together with Chabrier's *España* and the Arrival of the Queen of Sheba from Handel's *Solomon* were particular favourites. In an age that is often unduly sensitive to such harmless nuances it is heartening to recall that in the midst of the Second World War listeners to *Marching and Waltzing* were still capable of enjoying the mock solemnity of Gounod's *Funeral March of a Marionette* in Sir Henry Wood's recording without any feelings of guilt.

A joint project set up by the British Council and HMV enabled the company to embark on a series of première recordings of large-scale modern British works. The first of these, E. J. Moeran's Symphony in G minor with Leslie Heward conducting the Hallé Orchestra, appeared in January,1943 and to the present day it remains a benchmark account of a powerful but unjustly neglected composition. Heward was closely connected with the Symphony for it was he who gave its first performance in London in 1938; sadly, by the time of the recording sessions in the composer's presence at the Houldsworth Hall, Manchester in November, 1942 Heward was already in the last stages of tuberculosis from which he died not long after the set was issued. Heward's commitment is obvious throughout; the Hallé responded with playing to match;

and Walter Legge and his engineers captured what the American critic David Hall was later moved to describe as "... one of the most thrilling listening experiences in the entire disc literature." The untimely death of Leslie Heward while still in his forties deprived the British musical world of an exceptional talent but there could be no finer memorial to his artistry than his recording of the Moeran symphony.

There followed in quick succession Sir William Walton's brilliantly scored oratorio *Belshazzar's Feast* conducted by the composer (issued March, 1943), Sir Arthur Bliss's Piano Concerto with Solomon and Sir Adrian Boult who had premièred the work at the 1939 New York World Fair (issued July, 1943), Bax's Symphony No. 3 and Vaughan Williams's Symphony No. 5 both conducted by Sir John Barbirolli (issued February and May, 1944 respectively) and Gustav Holst's *The Hymn of Jesus* conducted by Sir Malcolm Sargent (issued July, 1944).

This wartime enterprise not only produced much excellent but relatively unfamiliar British music for record collectors at home but also furnished valuable material for the Council's representatives in neutral countries overseas where they were busily promoting Britain's cultural achievements. The Foreign Office was also involved in this activity and whenever possible allowed the use of the diplomatic bag for sending sets of records abroad.

The musical and technical quality of these discs is vouched for by the fact that they held their place in the HMV catalogue until 1954 or 1955, well into the LP era,[17] before the deletions axe fell. Last of all to be both recorded and issued before the end of the war was Elgar's *The Dream of Gerontius* conducted by Sir Malcolm Sargent, but the intriguing history of this great performance falls chronologically in the following chapter.

Between 1942 and the beginning of 1944 Columbia saluted the USSR's part in the war with a sequence of recordings by their specialist conductor of Russian music, Constant Lambert. These discs, made with the Hallé and Liverpool Philharmonic orchestras, consisted not of *bonnes bouches* but of serious, dramatic works. The list was headed by Tchaikovsky's Fourth Symphony, *Hamlet* overture and Tatiana's Letter Scene from *Eugene Onegin*, intensely characterised by the Australian soprano Joan Hammond. Borodin's Second Symphony and Rimsky-Korsakov's overture to his opera

Ivan the Terrible added further weight to an impressive collection. What is more, Glazunov's symphonic poem *Stenka Razin* which was issued appropriately in early 1943 had a strong wartime significance for its story linked the recording historically with the battle of Stalingrad.

In 1670 Razin, the Cossack leader of a peasant revolt against the land-owning aristocracy, seized the city of Tsaritsin but was subsequently captured and taken to Moscow where he was publicly executed as a warning to all other would-be revolutionaries. Almost two hundred and fifty years afterwards Stalin himself fought in the defence of Tsaritsin against the White Russian forces in 1918. In due course this event was celebrated by changing the name of the city; Tsaritsin, redolent of an imperial past, vanished from the map to make way for Stalingrad.

It tends to be forgotten that before the arrival of the LP sleeve note collectors were seldom given much information about the music they were purchasing except in the case of album sets of four discs or more. *Stenka Razin*, complete on two discs, was sold in envelopes which in pre-war days would have carried advertisements for the record company's products but had now, for economic reasons, degenerated into flimsy, plain brown paper covers.

The relevance of Glazunov's symphonic poem was likely to have been appreciated by only a small number of musicians and record buyers but the British public at large was kept in daily touch by the press and radio with the progress of the battle for modern Stalingrad. On 9th February, 1943, a week after the fighting ceased, the BBC's correspondent Paul Winterton reported on the scene of desolation that had formerly been a vast industrial centre. In sober, measured tones he told how the Russians, women as well as men, had held out against the enemy. Now, wherever he went, there was the detritus of war: helmets and discarded weapons strewn on the ground, rubbish blowing about the ruins and "... any number of smashed corpses lying where they fell or stacked up in great frozen heaps for later burial ...". Although the city where the dead of both sides were awaiting disposal was destroyed it would bear the distinction of being the point at which Germany's drive eastward was finally halted.

Decca had always been skilful at keeping pace with its EMI rivals and a number of recordings issued between 1943 and 1945 competed against Constant Lambert's Columbia discs for the attention of record buyers with a special interest in Russian music. The on-going set of Rachmaninov's Preludes by the pianist Moura Lympany was providing a small supply of instrumental pieces, but except for certain works by Dvořák and Smetana Slavonic chamber music was not often played by the groups of artists on Decca's roster. A further major difficulty was that the company had no symphony orchestra on which it could call as the main London and provincial ensembles were fully occupied with their public concerts and recording sessions for HMV and Columbia. Decca's solution to the problem of how to create a new, attractive Russian repertoire was, in essence, very simple: it would turn to recordings made in Russia by leading Soviet artists.

The company's full page advert in the February, 1943 number of *The Gramophone* proudly announced the arrival of 'music from the USSR''. The work was Khachaturian's Violin Concerto of 1940 in which the USSR State Orchestra under Alexander Gauk accompanied David Oistrakh, a name then virtually unknown to British collectors. The advertising copy included the information that in order to bring the concerto most effectively to the widest audiences, particularly in the most remote areas of Russia, it had been recorded on film soundtrack from which Decca made its own 78 r.p.m matrices. Prudently bearing in mind EMI's wartime practice of publishing its new British classical recordings on mid-price labels Decca encouraged potential buyers to investigate the five-disc set by marketing the Khachaturian concerto in its comparable K series.

Together with the same orchestra and conductor Oistrakh was also the soloist in Nikolay Miaskovsky's Violin Concerto, Op. 44 which was followed by this composer's Symphony No. 21 performed by the USSR State Orchestra conducted this time by Nathan Rakhlin. The critical view that, in general, Miaskovsky's music lacks substance and individual character is hard to deny, but in the context of Decca's efforts to build up its own distinctive Russian catalogue the two chosen works served a useful purpose since they posed few listening problems for record buyers keen to investigate territory so far unexplored by Columbia or HMV.

In more familiar repertoire Danya Shafran was the cellist in Tchaikovsky's *Variations on a Rococo Theme* with Gauk conducting the Leningrad State Philharmonic Orchestra whilst the field of opera was covered by arias from Tchaikovsky's *Eugene Onegin,* Glinka's *Ruslan and Ludmilla* and a generous four-disc selection from Borodin's *Prince Igor.*

What promised to be one of the most interesting sets fell short of collectors' expectations for Prokofiev's recording with the Moscow State Philharmonic Orchestra of the Suite No. 2 from his *Romeo and Juliet* ballet music was both dim in sound (even for Russian discs of this vintage) and run-of-the-mill in performance. Even so, Decca released it on five full price ten-inch discs. There should have been a sixth depicting Juliet the little girl, but as Michael Smith notes in his Decca discography the stampers for these two missing sides were "possibly damaged in wartime transit from Russia".

If any British enthusiasts were hoping to be offered Shostakovich's new Seventh Symphony, the *Leningrad,* they were unlucky for conditions in Russia were not conducive to such a long work being recorded there, even for prestige purposes. Inspired by the composer's experiences in the besieged city during 1941, the *Leningrad* had its Russian première in Kuibyshev the following year. The score was also sent to Britain and America where the symphony was as warmly welcomed as it had been in the USSR. The likelihood was that one of the USA's major orchestras would be the first to record it commercially but, in the event, it was the lesser known Buffalo Philharmonic under William Steinberg which took the lead with an eight-disc set for the independent Musicraft company.

Decca's list did not consist solely of Russian nineteenth and twentieth century classical works. Other recordings were drawn from the store of morale-boosting patriotic music and discs to go on sale in British shops included the Red Army Dance and Song Ensemble in *Oh, Ye Steeds of Steel;* the Choir and Orchestra of the Bolshoi Theatre performing the *Soviet Airmen Song;* and the bass Mark Reizen, an outstanding interpreter of the title role in Mussorgsky's *Boris Godunov,* in the *Soviet Fatherland Song.* On yet another cultural level, two discs of military music featured the Band of the People's Commissariat of Defence playing such pieces as the march *At the Call of Lenin* and the *Anti-Nazi March.*

The retail prices of these Russian-derived recordings seem mainly to have been governed by the type of music involved. The

Khachaturian Violin Concerto and Venriks's *Song of Triumph* (which also came from film soundtrack) were enticingly released on the mid-price K label but from then onwards classical music was almost always sold at premium price.[18] Pieces with folkish titles were spread between the ten-inch mid-price M series and the ten-inch bargain-price F series; the latter, normally given over to dance music and similar light entertainment, was also where the most overtly patriotic Soviet music would be found. Two discs in the F series by the tenor Sergei Lemeshev are distinct oddities, however. Lenski's aria from *Eugene Onegin* was a natural enough choice, even though it might have been expected to appear on a dearer label; but a much bigger surprise was furnished by the other three sides which for some obscure reason were filled by well known excerpts from Verdi's *Rigoletto* and Flotow's *Martha*.

Decca's wartime Russian connection has attracted remarkably little attention in the literature of the gramophone. It would be interesting to know who originally had the idea that Decca might profitably distribute Russian recordings most of which had been made for the USSR label of the State Music Trust. The two organisations were separated from each other by the breadth of Nazi-occupied Europe and direct communication, even if permitted by their respective political masters, would have been difficult to say the least. Almost certainly the Russian Embassy in London was the prime intermediary once the relevant government departments of both countries had given their blessings to the scheme.

Fascinating questions spring to mind. How were the necessary matrices or stampers conveyed to England and by what route did they travel? What did Decca provide in return for being given access to Russian recordings? Did the project have any significant propaganda value for either Britain or Russia? Finally, how well did British collectors respond to the availability of this Russian music?

For a commercial record company this, of course, was the crux of the matter. Memory, admittedly an unreliable guide, has it that enthusiasm for the classical issues was somewhat guarded, perhaps because buyers were used to the higher technical standard of British and American recordings. The table of deletion dates in Michael Smith's discography shows that the bulk of the Russian classical items departed from the Decca catalogue on 1st April, 1950 after a life span of seven years at most. The first to go, though, was the dubbing of David Oistrakh's film soundtrack recording of Khachaturian's Violin Concerto which was marketed in February, 1943 and lasted only until the following July, an unusually brief existence which possibly is accounted for by production problems rather than lack of interest. As for the others, the fact of deletion is not conclusive evidence of low sales for during the first four months of 1950 Decca was in the early stages of clearing classical 78s from its shelves prior to introducing the first British long-playing records in June that year. Whether or not this wartime venture turned out as successfully as had been hoped is a matter on which it is therefore probably best to return an open verdict.

★   ★   ★

For at least two years before D-Day the German gramophone companies, like the rest of the country's industries, were at risk from bombing raids by the British and American air forces. At the same time, territories formerly controlled by the Nazis began falling to the Allies; the Axis powers were driven from North Africa in 1943, by mid-1944 the Germans were no longer a presence in Italy south of Rome and the Red Army was advancing westwards into Poland and Romania. Safe havens for industrial relocation were soon to be restricted to what could be found within the boundaries of Greater Germany. Curt Riess tellingly likens the German record industry at this stage of the war to a travelling circus, constantly on the move from one place to the next not only in order to carry on recording and turning out a modicum of pressings for the disrupted retail trade but also to find secure storage places for its precious matrices. As well as destroying their buildings air raids further undermined the struggling companies by interrupting carefully planned studio sessions and demolishing long-established recording venues such as the Berliner Singakademie which had been regularly used by Telefunken. This company sent some of its matrices to Prague where they were put to good use at its Czech pressing plant; unfortunately, however, they failed to survive the war. Others zigzagged around Germany from Berlin to Königsberg, the capital of East Prussia, from there south to Silesia and finally northwest to Saxony and a location near Dresden.

The Wehrmacht's insatiable demands for manpower resulted in the record companies losing many of their most skilled staff and the gaps were filled by women or men unfit for military service but, inevitably, few of these had any previous experience in the industry. As one would expect, record output fell sharply; Telefunken produced some three million discs in 1939 but by 1943 the number had dropped to 1.6 million, though this is by no means a negligible figure when one considers that the company had ceased making dance music discs. Deutsche Grammophon's Hanover factory was severely damaged in a bombing raid in September, 1943 and in January the following year its administrative headquarters in Berlin were completely destroyed in another air attack. It was a very different world from that of 1941 when Richard Strauss, Germany's most illustrious living composer, re-recorded his *Ein Heldenleben* and *Don Quixote* with the Bavarian State Orchestra for DG's Polydor label. Ironically, these patriotic sets of music by the Aryan Strauss did not deter the Gestapo from reminding Deutsche Grammophon officially in May, 1942 that it was forbidden to record Jewish artists and that all matrices and pressings featuring them must be destroyed.

On the other hand, ideological restrictions were lifted for some companies and, just as Telefunken had been allowed to export Kulenkampff's recording of the Mendelssohn Violin Concerto as a means of bringing in foreign currency during the war, so Lindström was granted a dispensation under which it could market records from its Swing Series catalogue in any of the German-occupied European countries.

Quite early in the war Telefunken discovered the benefits to be had from recording outside Germany and during the period 1940-1943 the company was busily engaged in Italy making operatic excerpts from Verdi's *Otello* and *Falstaff* with the orchestra of La Scala, Milan and such renowned singers as the tenor Aureliano Pertile, the soprano Gina Cigna and the baritone Mariano Stabile. With the same orchestra the Italian conductors Antonio Guarnieri and Gino Marinuzzi recorded overtures and other orchestral pieces from a wide range of Italian operas, but undoubtedly Telefunken's most significant achievement came when it introduced the brilliant young pianist Arturo Benedetti Michelangeli to record buyers in performances, again with La Scala's fine orchestra, of the Grieg and Schumann concertos. After the war Michelangeli went on to become a pianistic legend and his recordings were lovingly collected by his admirers not least because, as his career progressed,

226

his public appearances were increasingly liable to last minute cancellation.

Worsening conditions in Berlin drove Telefunken to move its recording division to the comparative safety of Vienna but the administrative offices remained in the German capital until the end of the war. Vienna had much to offer record companies which could afford to undertake sessions with the Philharmonic and the singers and orchestra of the State Opera, but after its 1941 recordings with Clemens Krauss and Rudolf Moralt Telefunken did not resume operations with the great Viennese ensembles until what were to be its final wartime sessions in July and the autumn of 1944.[19]

Electrola was particularly active in Vienna in 1942; the company had Hans Knappertsbusch, Karl Böhm and Rudolf Moralt amongst its conductors and John Hunt's discography of the Vienna Philharmonic shows that a considerable number of that year's Electrola recordings were not subsequently published indicating, perhaps, that the matrices were later either lost or damaged. It seems that in the Vienna of 1943 Telefunken was unable or unwilling to emulate Electrola's ambitious programme of the previous year but by now all the major German companies were fast nearing the point when they would have no option but to pull down the shutters. For administrative offices, studios, factories, show rooms and retail outlets there was no escape from the effects of the Allied bombing offensive; with matrices dispersed around the country and raw materials in desperately short supply the industry was on the verge of total collapse.

While the regular German record buyer watched the source of his entertainment drying up certain high-ranking Nazis were having more than their fill of the gramophone. Albert Speer, a trained architect, came under Hitler's spell in 1930 and such was the rapport between the two men that Speer was appointed the Führer's personal architect, a position he held throughout Hitler's lifetime. In addition to designing the setting for the Party's 1934 Nuremberg rally he was also commissioned by Hitler to draw up plans for a complete rebuilding of Berlin, a project on which they collaborated closely; the war, however, prevented any of Speer's neoclassical designs from gracing the streets of the capital. Other even more important work lay ahead for Speer when in 1942 he became the minister for armaments and munitions; with the sweeping powers given to him and direct access to the unlimited slave labour on hand in the concentration camps the Wehrmacht was kept thoroughly equipped until late on in the war.

It was Hitler's custom to summon generals, ministers and senior Party officials to his Austrian mountain retreat near Berchtesgaden to take part in meetings and discussions on the current military situation and policy for the future. In the early days his guests were entertained in the evenings with film shows but these were later dropped as a mark of sympathy for the soldiers of the Reich who were enduring extreme hardships for the sake of their Fatherland. Films were replaced by gramophone records of which there was an excellent collection and in his memoirs Speer described those bizarre gatherings.

"Hitler always preferred the same music. Neither baroque nor classical music, neither chamber music nor symphonies interested him. Before long the order of the records became virtually fixed. First he wanted a few bravura selections from Wagnerian operas, to be followed promptly with operettas. That remained the pattern. Hitler made a point of trying to guess the names of the sopranos and was pleased when he guessed right, as he frequently did.

To animate these rather barren evenings, sparkling wine was handed around... From one o'clock on some members of the company, in spite of all their efforts to control themselves, could no longer repress their yawns. But the social occasion dragged on in monotonous, wearying emptiness for another hour or more, until at last Eva Braun had a few words with Hitler and was permitted to go upstairs. Hitler would stand up about a quarter of an hour later, to bid his company goodnight. Those who remained, liberated, often followed those numbing hours with a gay party over champagne and cognac."

Elsewhere in Germany, prisoners of a different kind were deeply indebted to the gramophone. Captured Allied flying officers held at Stalag Luft III near Sagan in Silesia had, thanks largely to the International Red Cross, a record library of about 3,500 discs which included most of the great classical symphonies, concertos, chamber music and instrumental works then available on 78s.

On 24th March, 1944 Stalag Luft III was the scene of the mass breakout which came to be known as the Great Escape. At one time, no less than three tunnels, code-named Tom, Dick and Harry, were being excavated; circumstances forced the abandonment of two, leaving only Harry as a feasible escape route. Seventy six prisoners eventually inched their way along the tunnel, beneath the camp's perimeter wire defences and emerged into the outside world on the edge of a wooded area that provided some cover for them once they were above ground. Only three succeeded in making their way back to England and the rest were soon recaptured. The scale of the escape so outraged the Nazis that they selected and shot fifty of these men as an example of what any other Allied prisoners of war in Germany who might be planning escapes could expect.

The record library played an important part in the escape preparations when, at crucial times, particularly loud music was played on a gramophone in the camp theatre to distract the guards' attention and to help muffle the sound of tunnelling going on below. Even damaged records had their uses and any oddments of shellac were collected, heated and moulded into non-magnetic cases for escapers' compasses. The dedicated tunneller led a physically exhausting and dangerous life as much of his day was typically spent in the claustrophobic confines of a tunnel the roof of which might cave in at any time. Men temperamentally unsuited to this sort of work were often able to bring unsuspected talents to other aspects of the escape projects; some tailored civilian or military clothing, others forged identity papers and travel documents, all of which, with luck, would pass muster if not too closely scrutinised. Captivity often brought with it deep psychological problems and for many thus troubled the music in the camp's record collection was a lifeline to normality which, in a mysterious way, helped to give them an inner strength with which to bear the loss of their accustomed pre-war existences.

In Germany from the mid-1930s onwards there began to emerge a lively youth subculture, members of which were linked by their love of jazz and swing, especially the admired American varieties. Berlin and major cities like Düsseldorf, Leipzig and Münster had their own jazz clubs, described by Michael Kater in his *Different Drummers* as "decidedly adolescent in nature" where, as well as demonstrating their own amateur instrumental talents, they played records and enthused over the music of their choice. The social background of these teenagers was almost entirely middle class and Jews were not excluded from their gatherings. Kater tells how members of the Berlin club "would frequent the Wannsee beaches to meet confrères, all with portable gramophones, and six out of ten of them were Jewish." The coming of the war did little to subdue the activities of these young individualists. In Frankfurt am Main, like their *zazou* counterparts in France, the boys went in for long hair and the girls dressed provocatively. Having well-to-do parents meant that money was not a problem and they could afford to have any favourite discs that were in short supply copied for them by a private recording studio in the city. Kater goes on to relate how the Gestapo hunted "rebellious youths who would listen to the BBC and seditiously play swing records on portable players ... in small vessels on the Main river, where the secret police would then chase them with speed boats."

The most extrovert of all these groups was centred in Hamburg. Its "members" were particularly keen on dancing to swing music, a form of recreation eventually banned by the Nazis; they referred to themselves as Swing-Boys and Swing-Babies and after the war became known collectively as Hamburg Swings. In common with their contemporaries elsewhere in Germany the Swings' dress also closely mirrored that of the Parisian *zazous*, even down to the boys' furled umbrellas, personal ornaments which were seldom opened, whatever the weather. They paraded the streets of Hamburg to show off their nonconformity; if at all possible they evaded joining the ranks of the Hitler Youth, the ethos of which was totally alien to their own "cool" life-style. They put little value on discretion and some of the most daring played their discs on portable gramophones in public air raid shelters. Sooner or later they were bound to come into conflict with the city police or the Gestapo and their efforts to avoid being conscripted into the Forces landed a number of them in prison or punishment camps. However, when the Nazis could no longer tolerate their anti-German behaviour the Swings retreated to the safety of their parents' expensive homes in the leafy outer suburbs where they continued, more or less unchallenged, to indulge themselves with their records, dancing, drinking and casual sex.

★　　★　　★

Planning for the Allies' eventual return to the western European countries from which they were driven at the time of Dunkirk might almost be said to have begun as soon as the evacuation had been completed. Another eighteen months, though, would elapse before the USA entered the war and, with its contributory manpower and military resources, at last brought an invasion within the realms of possibility. Anglo-American discussions were under way in early 1942 but with the war against Japan then still his prime concern it was not until December, 1943 that the Supreme Allied Commander, General Dwight D. Eisenhower, was ready to assign the formidable task of drawing up the detailed plan of action to Britain's General Bernard Montgomery.

The months of preparation were due to culminate in Operation Overlord on 4th June, 1944, the original D-Day. Unfortunately, at the last minute bad weather forced the cancellation of Overlord which was rescheduled for 6th June when, despite less than perfect conditions, the invasion armada set off for the beaches of Normandy. The opening phase of the assault was to be undertaken by airborne forces who, under cover of darkness, would parachute directly into enemy-held France or cross the Channel in troop-carrying gliders. Once landed, their mission was to secure vital strategic points to enable the speediest possible thrust inland by the troops who would be coming in by sea.

On the eve of D-Day southern England was swarming with media representatives who, in their various ways and subject to the delaying powers of censorship, were building the foundations of a massive historical archive. For the BBC Frank Gillard recorded his account of the sights he had seen on a hundred mile journey through a countryside transformed (to quote his own memorable phrase) into "one enormous ordnance dump and field park." Robin Duff, another BBC reporter, described what it was like to be on board ship where everybody was keyed up waiting for the hour of departure. One of the few moments of light relief came when the sounds of jazz played on a minesweeper's gramophone wafted across from the other side of the harbour.

Save in one respect, the scenes witnessed by a special correspondent writing for *The Times* were typical of what was happening as parachute units prepared to spearhead Operation Overlord. He was particularly impressed by the great quantity of heavy battle gear the Paras carried strapped to their bodies. As the time drew near senior officers spoke cheerful words of encouragement and a

Padre led all present in a short prayer, after which "... in the gathering darkness they drove off to the aerodromes with the men in the first lorry singing, incredible as it seems, the notes of the Horst Wessel song at the tops of their voices."

Richard Dimbleby, founding father of the radio and television dynasty, was even closer to the starting line. Speaking from a southern airfield, his recorded voice only just audible over the roar of the plane's engines, he had the privilege of telling radio listeners: "There she goes now, the first British aircraft leading the attack on Europe."

IV – D-Day to VJ Day

D-DAY SAW the BBC's team of war correspondents sharing all the dangers faced by the Allied forces at sea, on land and in the air. They made their reports in a variety of ways: some were recorded on the spot or at the earliest possible opportunity after the event by the reporters themselves, others were recorded by the BBC from broadcasts made from mobile transmitters in or near the war zone and even, in some cases, live from the scene of the action.

Descriptions of what took place throughout the twenty-four hours of 6th June, 1944 can be heard on the BBC's compilation of *D-Day Despatches* and again one is struck by the professionalism of these radio journalists working in the most difficult conditions imaginable. The details of what they witnessed were conveyed with admirable clarity, scarcely any verbal hesitation and in an objective style that virtually precluded sentimentality or jarring heroics. One of the earliest, perhaps the very first, of the BBC's reporters to set foot in German-occupied France was Guy Byam who crossed the Channel in a troop-carrying aircraft and, with all his non-combatant gear strapped to his person, jumped with the pathfinder paratroopers who would secure and illuminate the designated landing zones for the glider-borne troops soon to be approaching the French coast.

With the latter was the American, Chester Wilmot who in a recorded report and later in his authoritative book *The Struggle for Europe* gave a vivid account of the cross-Channel trip in less than ideal weather conditions and the crucial moment when the gliders touched down. These aircraft were big and strong enough to carry a Jeep and its trailer or an anti-tank gun as well as its quota of soldiers. Wilmot's glider landed and came to rest at 3.32 a.m. (two minutes late), suffering little damage in the process. Others were less lucky and ended up with their noses stuck in French soil; two in Wilmot's group crashed into each other and in such cases the men inside had to hack their way out through the robust wooden fuselage.

Between midnight and the early hours of the morning the Canadian, Stanley Maxted was on board one of the Motor Torpedo Boats ordered to ensure at all costs that no high speed German surface vessels penetrated the great invasion armada as it crossed the Channel. Maxted's reporting style was somewhat more colourful than that of his British colleagues and he described with gusto the dashing skipper of the MTB and the Scottish machine gunner whose fine marksmanship caused a German E-Boat to burst into flames.

Colin Wills watched the great naval bombardment of the French coastline from a landing craft approaching the shore and continued recording his impressions until the command "All hands to beaching stations" was given, whereupon he had to shoulder his equipment and prepare to wade ashore.

That well known pre-war BBC sports commentator Howard Marshall was in the first assault wave of landing craft on a barge which was badly damaged when it struck a German in-shore mine. Many other barges were also in trouble but their tanks and troops landed successfully, meeting surprisingly little resistance.

Richard Dimbleby seems to have been in a state of almost perpetual motion throughout D-Day. The term "friendly fire" had not yet been coined when he saw a British aircraft disintegrate in the sky above Normandy; there was no enemy anti-aircraft fire or Luftwaffe activity at the time and the only explanation was that the RAF plane had taken a direct hit from a shell fired in the naval bombardment. The BBC also recorded a transmission which Dimbleby sent live from the observer's seat of an RAF Mosquito that was following a fighter formation of Spitfires; on one sweep over the beachhead they were flying so low that Dimbleby could distinctly glimpse a red-capped British military policeman directing the advancing traffic.

On shore, Frank Gillard drove along a road newly created by bulldozers, then through farmland to the front line where, lying full length on the ground, he recorded the sound of battle.

As soon as they were cleared by the military censors these recordings were broadcast to British listeners by the BBC. There was no doubting the enormous difficulties yet to be overcome by the Allies but these eyewitness reports on the successful initial stages of the invasion of western Europe were a source of tremendous encouragement to all at home who heard them.

The BBC reporters frequently remarked as they followed the Allied troops from the beaches into the Normandy countryside how little notice the French livestock took of the conflict going on around them. The same applied to the peasant farmers who were often observed stolidly carrying on as normal tending their beasts and working their land dangerously close to the front line. The further inland the Allies drove the greater were the problems posed by the landscape itself. The *bocage* consisted of narrow, sunken roads running between high banks and hedges beyond which lay a patchwork of small, enclosed fields and orchards - ideal ground for the delaying tactics of defending forces but totally inhospitable to the attackers whose forward momentum was severely limited.

Although Cherbourg fell to the Americans on 27th June the Allies, even with their Mulberry harbours, were for the time being, short of port facilities. However, they had the inestimable advantage of air supremacy and gradually the Germans were prised out of strongly held positions at Caen, St. Lô, Mortain, Argentan and Falaise. The Wehrmacht came under even more pressure when they were faced with the need to defend a second front in France following the Allied landings in the south on 15th August. In the north they could no longer hold out against the Allied advances and on 25th August French forces headed by General Leclerc marched into Paris.

Amongst the important new objectives now were Brussels and Antwerp, then Europe's largest port, which was to be a vital logistical base for further operations in Belgium and Holland once the Germans had been cleared from their commanding positions on the Scheldt estuary.

Operation Market Garden, Montgomery's plan to capture five strategically vital river and canal bridges in Holland in order to assist the Allies' drive into Germany, began on 17th September, 1944. At first all went well with the Americans taking two bridges north of Eindhoven and two more near Nijmegen; the fifth, crossing the Lower Rhine at Arnhem, was allotted to the British First

Airborne Division which encountered much stronger German resistance in the area than had been expected.

Two of the BBC's war reporters, Stanley Maxted and Guy Byam, witnessed the tragedy of Arnhem. Maxted was a man of many talents who had worked as an administrator for the Canadian Broadcasting Corporation and had also pursued a parallel career on the radio as a popular singer with a pleasing tenor voice. He was, moreover, no stranger to the commercial recording studio for in the 1930s he had put songs taken from A.A. Milne's Christopher Robin verses on disc for Canadian Brunswick. Maxted was in a glider that crash-landed at Arnhem on the first day of Operation Market Garden. He had with him a typewriter and his portable recorder and his first action was to dig a slit trench for his own safety; this was to be his home and work base for the next nine days.

Some news reports after scrutiny by the field censors were sent *en clair* in Morse code by Army signallers. For the rest of the time Maxted had to rely on his BBC portable recorder to which he dictated his impressions and fed in the sounds of battle; unfortunately, most of the discs he had cut and the recorder itself were badly damaged by a German mortar bomb which landed uncomfortably close to his slit trench. Byam's recorder also suffered the same fate. When the order came to withdraw Maxted made sure that the BBC's latest recording technology was of no use to the Germans and the now long defunct *Daily Herald* newspaper quoted him as saying: "The only infantile piece of fun I had was taking a pickaxe to the thing and beating it up." Three or four of Maxted's recordings were unharmed and these he tucked safely inside his battle dress top before embarking on one of the small craft that carried out the rescue operation under cover of darkness. Courageously, Guy Byam decided to swim across the river, so releasing a place in one of the boats for another British survivor.

A year after the battle an official British documentary film, *Theirs is the Glory*, reconstructed the bitter struggle on the actual ground where it had been fought. It was made in black and white and needed no famous screen stars for it had all the actors it required in men of the Allied forces and the gallant people of Arnhem. Amongst those in the cast was Stanley Maxted who recreated his experiences as a war correspondent striving to make and preserve a sound picture of those nine desperate days.

★   ★   ★

For more than a year before the Normandy landings two under-cover British radio stations had been treating the German armed forces in western and northern Europe to a carefully devised mixture of propaganda, disinformation and highly enjoyable jazz, swing and similar music frowned on by the Nazis. The powerful short wave Atlantik transmitter and the deceptively named Soldatensender Calais both operated from southern England under the direction of Sefton Delmer who from the early 1930s until the fall of France had been a European political and war correspondent for the *Daily Express* newspaper. The broadcasts from Soldatensender Calais were so subtly organised that many German soldiers were deceived into thinking it was one of their own radio services. As well as using commercial records on their programmes the two stations also had access to specially made propaganda discs by well known bands of the day. Pre-eminent amongst these was the Glenn Miller orchestra that in late 1944 was at EMI's Abbey Road studios in London. Here, in their instantly recognisable style, they recorded popular music of the day for an American propaganda radio station. Following the lead of Charlie and his orchestra in Germany, subversive messages were sometimes substituted for the original lyrics though it must be admitted that the laboured German of Miller's vocalist was no more verbally convincing than Charlie's ultra-precise English. It seemed at one time that these non-commercial Miller recordings were lost for ever but they came to light again some fifty years later and were issued on two CDs by the Happy Days company. This compilation reveals the band at the peak of its form playing what the critic Martin Gayford has called "some of the most potently nostalgic music in existence".

The success of mobile broadcasting in Italy had impressed the military planners and in early December, 1944 four Field Broadcasting Units set off from England for mainland Europe to follow in the wake of the British forces. In addition to giving the troops the sort of programmes they wanted to hear these Units also acted as a valuable counterbalance to German propaganda stations such as Radio Arnheim which was picking up the Allied Expeditionary Forces Programme and relaying it laced with its own slanted news items and unsettling commentaries. Since the early Italian days resources for field broadcasting had improved considerably and each of the new Units had a library of around four hundred records to draw on for its daily needs when not relaying BBC programmes. Such riches, however, had to be treated with discretion and shortly before Christmas, 1944 the first list of banned recordings was issued; amongst the undesirable numbers were Ronald Frankau's saucy and provocative *Oh, You Ladies in the Forces* and for a time, to much dismay, the universally loved *Lilli Marlene* on account of its German origin.

★   ★   ★

Generally speaking, the forces stationed in Britain were well catered for by the programmes of recorded music devised by Walter Legge which were circulated from one military unit to another by ENSA. The music by and large would be wartime classical pops and a typical programme would probably comprise an overture, an operatic aria or two, a concerto and a symphony or other orchestral work.

Such fare was agreeable enough to the majority but it served only to whet the musical appetites of the late Geoffrey Miller, the well known sports writer, and a group of kindred spirits on the RAF base at Sullom Voe in the remote Shetland Islands. They proposed setting up their own music club with records bought from RAF funds, a scheme approved by their Squadron Leader provided that the organisation and handling of the club's affairs was their responsibility alone. The challenge was gladly accepted and, having acquired some suitable playing equipment, the twice weekly meetings attracted large and enthusiastic audiences, the harsh acoustics of a Nissen hut notwithstanding. Geoffrey and his colleagues did their record buying either in their local shops whenever they went on leave or in London at that discophile's Mecca, the Gramophone Exchange in Shaftesbury Avenue, where they could purchase new issues and possibly pick up some welcome desiderata from the second hand department presided over by the proprietor, the formidable Mr. Russell.

In early 1945 Geoffrey returned to Sullom Voe where the station was being prepared for closure and all unwanted stores were being burnt or otherwise disposed of. In a letter to the author Geoffrey described what a nostalgic time this was for

"The records were all still there, in the same old Nissen hut. My old companions were gone, but I found two new fellow-enthusiasts, and we had musical meetings of three listeners only.

238

When we finally left ... we helped ourselves to what records we wanted and saved them from destruction."

It is a measure of the old music club's wide-ranging collection that Geoffrey chose, amongst other items, to rescue a true connoisseur's piece, Decca's three disc set of the Sonata for Viola and Harp by Sir Arnold Bax.

*　　*　　*

For many of the RAF personnel a spell at the northern outpost of Sullom Voe must have felt rather like a prison sentence. They were isolated on the bleak, storm-lashed Shetlands which themselves were separated from the Scottish mainland by the more southerly Orkney Islands. Some, like Geoffrey Miller and his friends, sustained themselves with fine music whilst others went in for courses of study or programmes of more general reading.

It is interesting to compare their activities with those of a group of real prisoners of war, the Italian captives at Camp 60 on Lambholm in the Orkneys where they were engaged in constructing the new sea defences guarding the Royal Navy's base at Scapa Flow. Unlike British or German POWs in this sort of situation, escape did not figure prominently in their thoughts. Instead, to provide an outlet for their creative talents, they set about transforming the two Nissen huts which acted as their place of worship into a chapel more expressive of the glory of God. Amongst the prisoners were a number of master craftsmen, adepts at using to full advantage whatever scrap or otherwise discarded items they could come by. Biblical figures or small tableaux were sculpted in concrete and with the help of paint and other decorative materials they produced a remarkable spiritual retreat which is visited to this day. There was no Vatican representative at the inaugural service but the Holy Father's approval was ingeniously conveyed by playing in the vestry gramophone records of the bells and choir of St. Peter's, Rome.

Colditz Castle in central Germany was seen as the supreme test by the dyed-in-the-wool escapers who, together with the VIPs, formed the bulk of the inmates. Men who had outwitted German prison camp guards regularly in the past tended to land up at Colditz on the assumption that they would be less trouble in a camp where security was tight to the point of paranoia. Whereas Beethoven's late string quartets in recordings by the Busch and Lener Quartets became a source of intellectual stimulation for such as Viscount Lascelles, other Colditz prisoners, professional escapers, sometimes had hopes of non-musical benefits from the discs supplied under the auspices of the International Red Cross. On at least one occasion MI9, the military intelligence department in charge of getting escape materials to British prisoners of war, arranged with HMV for a special disc of *The British Grenadiers* to be made. To all appearances it was a perfectly ordinary 78 but the upper and lower playing surfaces were, in fact, two distinct rounds of shellac between which were sandwiched a detailed escaper's map of Germany. Notice of the arrival of this disc was to be signalled by a prearranged message and access to the map was simple - all that needed to be done was to break the disc. This method of smuggling in maps had an unfortunate side effect for many records in the Colditz collection were smashed by would-be escapers in the vain hope of finding more such aids.

Another unusual consequence was that with fewer records available for playing the strong main spring of a wind-up gramophone was cleverly converted into a handsaw which was used in the construction of a two-seater glider that was being built in the castle's spacious roof area. It was feared that with the fall of the Third Reich now imminent many of Colditz's VIPs would be killed in retaliation; the glider makers determined that there would be two prisoners who, with luck, might reach the advancing Allies and warn them of the Nazis' probable intentions. Just how the glider would be launched from inside the castle's roof is still uncertain but there was, presumably, a feasible plan in readiness for this if the glider itself is anything to go by. In the 1990s a small, independent British firm built a copy of the plane using the designers' original specifications; to the delight of the Colditz survivors who had been involved in the project the replica of their glider took to the air like a bird and performed perfectly.

⋆　　⋆　　⋆

In Britain the gramophone industry's contribution to the war effort went far beyond just providing new records for a music-hungry domestic market. Decca's sound engineers headed by the resourceful Arthur Haddy were enlisted by the government to apply their specialised knowledge to problems facing the RAF and the Navy. The RAF wished to record and analyse the radio traffic generated by German night fighter pilots whilst the Navy urgently needed sensitive recordings for use in training men operating underwater detection systems in order that they should be able to distinguish between the sounds of German and British submarines. The requirements of both Services were met by Haddy and his team who, without going into technical details, successfully extended the range of frequencies that could be handled by their current recording equipment.

The experience gained was later brought to bear on the production of Decca's commercial discs and on 8th June, 1944 the National Symphony Orchestra directed by its founder Sidney Beer recorded Tchaikovsky's Fifth Symphony in which the youthful Dennis Brain played the horn solo in the second movement. When it was released in the following December *The Gramophone* referred to it as "Technically, a very satisfactory recording." Likewise, in the February, 1945 issue of the magazine Eric Coates conducting his *The Three Elizabeths* Suite was judged to be "Capitally recorded ..."

Decca, however, waited until the war in Europe was over before telling the general public about these new developments. When the news was broken there was no false modesty in the full page advert in *The Gramophone* for July, 1945.

"ffrr Decca full frequency range recording announced by Decca on June the 8th, has been in daily use in the Decca recording studios for the past twelve months. Decca Red Label records, made the ffrr way, demonstrate the unquestionable superiority of Decca full frequency range recording: the outcome of extensive pioneer research by Decca engineers making possible for the first time the recording of the full range of musical frequencies with all their overtones."

Amidst all the company's well received classical discs of this time there was one war-related ten-inch record which *The Gramophone's* Alec Robertson found totally lacking in any praiseworthy qualities. It had been made under the auspices of the Society for the Promotion of New Music and consisted of two short works. Benjamin Frankel's *Toulon* was inspired by the scuttling of the French fleet on 27th November, 1942 to prevent the ships falling into German hands; this was coupled with Geoffrey Corbett's *Raiders*, a piece depicting a commando action. Robertson doubted whether either subject was suited to musical treatment and dismissed the piano accompaniments as quite inadequate for the purpose. Moreover, it seemed that even Decca's ffrr system could

241

do nothing to clarify the deplorable diction of the fellow-travelling Choir of the Workers' Music Association.

★   ★   ★

The last desperate German counter attack in Western Europe came in December, 1944/January, 1945 when von Rundstedt's army in what became known as the Battle of the Bulge attempted in the forests of the Ardennes to drive a wedge between the British and American forces and strike westwards to retake the port of Antwerp. The Germans advanced some seventy miles but their success was short-lived and by mid-January the Allies were once again in possession of the territory they had briefly forfeited. The losses on both sides were heavy with the Germans suffering 100,000 and the Allies 76,000 casualties; additionally, the fast-vanishing stocks of German military equipment were further depleted by the loss of 600 tanks and 1,600 aircraft.

On 8th March, 1945 the capture of the Rhine bridge at Remagen before it could be destroyed by the Wehrmacht enabled the Allies to establish a bridgehead at Wesel and, in the wake of concentrated aerial bombardments, the advance into Germany began to gather pace. As the recordings in the BBC's sound archives show, the Corporation's war reporters were in the thick of the action. Wynford Vaughan-Thomas vividly recounted his night time crossing of the river on 24th March taking what little cover he could on board a Buffalo, a tracked, amphibious troop-carrier which for the whole journey was battling against the fierce current to reach its objective in the inferno on the far shore of the Rhine.

Richard Dimbleby described the scene from one of the large British aircraft towing a glider with its airborne troops to their destination. As at Arnhem, Stanley Maxted again went in by air but as his Hamilcar glider was about to touch down it ran into heavy German machine gun fire and he and one of his associates received head wounds. Maxted made no attempt to spare his listeners' feeling and told how

> "One of the men was on the floor staring fixedly at nothing as one of his legs, rigid in front of him, was quivering in convulsions like a stricken eel. I saw the Bren carrier go inexorably out of the nose of the glider carrying the whole works ahead of it and wiping two signallers off the top of it like flies. Even then

the bullets kept crashing through the wreckage. It didn't seem fair, but then - there's no fair or unfair in airborne fighting."

Their recorded despatches, devoid of sentimentality, once more reveal the self-control with which these radio journalists faced up to the savage realities of front line warfare. What is more, as the Allies pressed on into western Germany the BBC's reporters were also witnesses of the horrific evidence being brought to light of the Nazis' systematic liquidation of the Jews. It was Richard Dimbleby's unhappy duty to describe the liberation of the concentration camp at Bergen-Belsen on 19th April, 1945 and he summed up his feelings in eleven simple words: "This day at Belsen was the most horrible of my life." He was in a place where it was difficult to tell the living from the dead, where, on the ground, the barely alive supported their emaciated frames against the corpses of the deceased. He saw a woman thrust a bundle into the arms of a soldier as she shrieked for milk to be given to her child. When the wrappings were undone it was all too clear that the baby had been dead for days.

One of the most angry pieces of British recorded reporting heard by the author came from Wynford Vaughan-Thomas who was dismayed that a month after the crossing of the Rhine there was still no sign of a surrender. This, he suspected, was due largely to the Nazis' indoctrination of the German people with the belief that it would be an honour to commit mass national suicide in the service of Hitler and the Reich. The time for such sacrifice had come and the Fatherland was now being defended wherever the need arose by the teenage boys and elderly men of the Volkssturm, the equivalent of Britain's Home Guard that had been stood down as no longer required in early December, 1944. Anyone who has seen the German newsreel clip of a frail, glassy-eyed Führer moving slowly along a line of boy soldiers, frequently stopping to pat them in an avuncular way on the cheek as he encourages them to give their all for their country, will realise how efficiently the Hitler Youth Organisation had done its work.

On 24th April, 1945 Vaughan-Thomas was with men of the Desert Rats who had taken possession of the Hall of Honour of the National Socialist Party of the District of East Hanover at Buchholz. In tones of the deepest contempt and disgust he portrayed the unsavoury building that, to him, seemed an obscene parody of a place of Christian worship; as a political meeting hall it had, in fact, functioned as a nursery of fanaticism for all who had aspired to make a name for themselves in the local Party machine.

Vaughan-Thomas went on to relate how "Rummaging about in the basement we found endless piles of National Socialist gramophone records and with a gramophone, slightly dusty from our shelling, all ready to play them on. Heavy, tramping, jackboot music it is." It obviously gave him great pleasure to tell his listeners that when the BBC had finished recording one last job remained to be done at Buchholz; the Desert Rats would carry out the orders they had been given and blow the abominable Hall of Honour to smithereens.

Vaughan-Thomas's longing for peace was soon to be fulfilled for during the last three days of April Mussolini was shot by Italian partisans and Hitler committed suicide. Nor did the partisans spare Mussolini's mistress, Claretta Petacci, who had loyally stood by her lover in good times and bad. Their bodies were taken to Milan where, in a public square, they were hung by their ankles for all to see: the Fascist dictator who had championed serious Italian music and the woman who at the Palazzo Venezia in Rome had spent many solitary hours, to quote Christopher Hibbert, "looking up at the signs of the zodiac painted in gold on the blue vaulted ceiling and listening to gramophone records playing sentimental songs or dance tunes over and over again."

As the end approached, Hitler, contrary to expectations, did not withdraw to his Alpine redoubt but stayed on in Berlin until the time came when he elected to take his own life. The Russians were now scarcely a mile away from the Chancellery and the Führer's bunker to which access was becoming ever more difficult even for the most senior and influential Nazis needing to speak personally with Hitler. Inside his own quarters the boundaries between reality and fantasy had become increasingly blurred but protocol still ensured that the Führer's birthday was officially celebrated on 20th April, 1945. The formal proceedings must have been short and stilted but afterwards Eva Braun, in an attempt to brighten up the party, invited friends to her private room where they played dance music on a gramophone.

Bizarre events followed one upon the other at the bunker. Almost the last official duty of Traudl (Gertraud) Junge, Hitler's personal secretary, was to take down at the Führer's dictation his

244

will and political testament of which she was asked to produce three copies. These were his justification for having reduced Germany to ruins in the fight against Communism and the Jewish menace; former leading Nazis, especially Goering and Himmler, were denounced as traitors and he appointed Admiral Karl Dönitz who had masterminded the German U-Boat war as his heir to the leadership of the Third Reich.

A few hours later Traudl Junge's office was the setting for an extraordinary scene of bourgeois conformity when Hitler and Eva Braun became man and wife in a German wartime civil wedding ceremony conducted by one of Goebbels's executives from the Berlin Gau administration. The reasoning behind this act has been the subject of much speculation but Eva Braun had long wished to change from being the Führer's mistress to being his wedded wife, Frau Hitler. She was relatively little known to the majority of Germans but her unfaltering loyalty to Hitler was now receiving the greatest reward it was still in his power to confer.

Once the brief ceremony was over the bride and groom greeted their privileged guests at the traditional wedding breakfast which had been cobbled together from the sparse food supplies still remaining in the bunker. No wedding, even in the besieged heart of Berlin, would have been complete without music and dancing but, as Traudl Junge related in a filmed interview many years later, gramophone records had become even more difficult to find than at the time of Hitler's birthday a week earlier. A thorough search brought only one suitable disc to light, a popular dance tune called *Rote Rosen* (Red Roses); since these flowers symbolise the deepest love and devotion the record carried an apt message. It may never be known definitely whose recording provided the entertainment on this weird occasion but there is one highly tantalising candidate. Listings show that in the early 1930s, certainly prior to 1936, Electrola issued this tango played by Barnabas von Geczy and his orchestra. This was the band Hitler had enjoyed listening to so much at Berlin's Kaiserhof Hotel in 1933 while he waited to be summoned to high office by President von Hindenburg. If it was von Geczy's version this would surely have been the most ironic coincidence of Hitler's life.

The following day, 30th April, the Third Reich came to its Wagnerian end. Hitler and Eva Braun had already entered into a suicide pact to avoid being captured by the Russians; when the time came she took poison and he shot himself. In accordance with his instructions, their bodies were taken from the bunker into the surrounding grounds where they were soaked in petrol and burnt; a nearby bomb crater served as their grave. The Russians subsequently conveyed the impression that they had little interest in Hitler's fate and Stalin even announced his belief that Hitler had escaped and been granted sanctuary in Spain or Argentina. However, it later transpired that for devious political reasons Hitler's charred corpse was secretly exhumed and taken to Moscow where, no doubt, it was subjected to close forensic study. Its final resting place is still unknown.

As soon as news of Hitler's death reached the outside world via Hamburg radio the broadcasting service went into deepest mourning, interspersing news bulletins with solemn music. The following day further grim events took place in Berlin where, after poisoning their children, Goebbels and his wife also chose death at the bunker before it was taken by the Russians into whose hands the city fell on 2nd May, 1945.

It was inevitable that during Germany's last stricken hours the music of Wagner, the composer so adored by the Nazis, would be broadcast. Of all his works there could have been nothing more appropriate than Siegfried's Funeral March from *Götterdämmerung* played in a recording by Furtwängler and the Berlin Philharmonic Orchestra, though whether this was taken from the conductor's commercial Polydor disc or from a radio tape is unclear.

Wagner's Austrian disciple Anton Bruckner was another source of music with which the radio could express German national feeling at this sombre turning point in the country's history. Under the Nazis Bruckner had become a cult figure for his majestic, sonorous symphonies embodied so many of the qualities they regarded as basic to the Germanic race, character and culture. Whether or not the Party's advocacy was genuine or merely a political posture it is hard to say but Bruckner was officially glorified in June, 1937 when Hitler himself dedicated a bust of the composer at Walhalla, King Ludwig I of Bavaria's German pantheon near Regensburg.

During the 1930s Telefunken with Eugen Jochum and the Hamburg Philharmonic and Electrola with Karl Böhm and the Saxon State Orchestra vied with each other in releasing fine versions of the best known symphonies. Special mention must also be made of Electrola's impressive première recording in 1938 of the dark, brooding Ninth Symphony performed by Siegmund von Hausegger and the Munich Philharmonic, sadly this conductor's only commercial recording. In 1942, despite the shellac shortage, Electrola contrived to issue an excellent eight-disc set of the Seventh Symphony by the same orchestra under its conductor Oswald Kabasta who, after the war, committed suicide, seemingly out of remorse for his close links with the Nazis.

The war gave added impetus to the deification of Bruckner and as late as 1943-44 players were being recruited for the new specialist Reichs Bruckner Orchestra based at Linz. In 1944 radio recordings were made of the standard nine symphonies in which the playing was shared principally by the Linz and Amsterdam Concertgebouw orchestras with the conducting divided between Eugen Jochum and his less well known brother Georg-Ludwig. Over fifty years later these historic documents eventually came into the commercial market place when the French company Tahrah brought out an integral set of transfers on CD.

The death of Hitler did not bring the war to an immediate halt for Dönitz, tucked away in Schleswig-Holstein, pompously declared that he considered it his duty to continue fighting the Russian invaders, an absurdly disingenuous excuse for clinging to his tattered remnants of authority. Surprisingly, a less important but nevertheless renowned figure also chose to stick to his post until almost the bitter end. On 30th May the *Daily Telegraph* reported that in a wood close to Flensburg two British officers had taken captive a civilian they came across gathering firewood. He convincingly passed himself off as a German until he rashly spoke a few words of English when his distinctive, sneering voice gave him away. It was William Joyce, Lord Haw-Haw, who when challenged over his identity made as if to reach for a gun, a rash action for which one of the officers promptly shot him in the thigh. Such was the painful prelude to Joyce's imprisonment, trial and execution for high treason.

Joyce's last broadcast has always generated controversy and even a cursory examination of the subject reveals a bewildering number of contradictions and discrepancies over what happened when and where. It has been questioned whether, in fact, this broadcast ever took place but a news report in the *Daily Telegraph* of 2nd May

247

accurately reflects the recorded evidence which was later discovered. What remains unresolved is whether what the *Daily Telegraph's* informant heard was Joyce live or Joyce pre-recorded for the Germans made at least two Magnetophon tape recordings of the speech.

Alan Grace has related how BFN, the British Forces Network broadcasting service, its mobile days in the field now over, came across one of these tapes soon after taking up residence at its impressive new base in Hamburg's Musikhalle. Before passing the tape over to British Military Intelligence BFN prudently made some 78 r.p.m. acetate dubbings one of which in its turn was copied for the author in 1947 when he was the station's record librarian. The following year another tape of the Joyce broadcast turned up at BFN and was found to run for three minutes longer than the recording that had surfaced earlier, thus adding a further twist to the tangled story.

Whatever one's personal interpretation of the events surrounding the broadcast may be, BFN's acetate dubbings were the means of saving a valuable sound document in which, with Germany in ruins about him, a British traitor continued faithfully to defend the actions of Hitler and the Third Reich. The speech as a whole is relatively unfamiliar and the following extracts transcribed from the author's acetate copy provide a telling illustration of the never-never land into which Germany had degenerated by the end of the war.

At the beginning Joyce speaks condescendingly, more in sorrow than in anger, as he pleads the case for his adopted country:

"This evening I am talking to you about Germany. That is a concept that many of you may have failed to understand. Let me tell you that in Germany there still remains the spirit of unity and the spirit of strength. Let me tell you that here we have a united people who are modest in their wishes. They are not imperialists. They don't want to take what doesn't belong to them. All they want is to live their own simple lives undisturbed by outside influences. That is the Germany we know."

He brushes aside Germany's conduct towards Poland and Czechoslovakia but is deeply concerned over the vast territories Stalin has now acquired in eastern Europe. Somewhat disconcertingly he then harks back to the topic of Danzig:

"I ask you to remember that in 1939 in August the only question was that of bringing Danzig back into the Reich, no more and no less. What a small problem that was in comparison with those that confront us today. Surely if only we had had the common sense to agree that the German people of Danzig should go back to the Reich then we might have had peace. We might have avoided all the terrible sacrifices of the last five and a half years. We might have avoided the hatred which can only be very gradually repaired."

His drunkenness momentarily causes him to lose the thread:

"Now I say to you my English listeners, the trouble is this. Germany, if you like, is not any more the chief matter in Europe. Germany may be, I may be wrong, I will only say that German arms have been in many battlefields defeated."

The longer he goes on the more emotional he becomes, thumping his desk to emphasise each new point, especially when speaking of the battle of Berlin.

"Now in this most serious time of our modern age I beg you to realise the fight is on. You have heard something about the battle of Berlin. Good. I would only say the men who have died in the battle of Berlin have given their lives to show that whatever else happens Germany will live. No coercion, no oppression, no measures of tyranny that any foreign foe can introduce will shatter Germany. Germany will live because the people of Germany have in them the secret of life, endurance, will and purpose."

The valedictory close of Joyce's apologia for Nazi Germany is well known and strikes an unexpectedly moving note which can only be fully appreciated when heard in its deeply emotional spoken form:

"And therefore I say to you in these last words: you may not hear from me again for a few months. I say: Es lebe Deutschland [*Long live Germany*]. Heil Hitler. And farewell."

After the fall of Berlin hostilities in northwest Europe were soon over and Wynford Vaughan-Thomas can be heard describing the scene on 3rd May in Lauenburg, a collecting centre between Lüneburg and Hamburg where, along streets whose buildings were hung with white surrender flags, the Wehrmacht was bringing the remains of its motorised transport and weaponry into the custody of the Allies.

Twenty-four hours later Field Marshal Bernard Montgomery was recorded by the BBC reading out the terms of unconditional surrender the German forces in Holland, northwest Germany, Schleswig-Holstein and Denmark were required to accept. On 7th May, 1945 Thomas Cadett recorded for the BBC his impressions of the actual moment of surrender at General Eisenhower's head-quarters when the Reich's General Alfred Jodl signed the docu-ment of capitulation; after doing so he made the following comment in German: "With this signature the German people and the German Wehrmacht are, for better or for worse, delivered into the victors' hands." The gravity of the occasion was, in Cadett's forth-right view, seriously marred by the frantic activity of the hordes of photographers all trying to get their own unique angle on a defin-ing moment in world history. It was, indeed, highly incongruous that the bitter war in Europe which had lasted nearly six years should officially come to an end in the midst of an undignified media scrum.

⋆   ⋆   ⋆

In London on VE Day itself, 8th May, 1945 the BBC described and recorded what was going on in the capital where such unin-hibited jubilation had not been seen since the relief of Mafeking during the Boer War forty-five years previously. Winston Churchill broadcast the news of Germany's surrender and King George VI came to the microphone to give thanks to God for the great Allied victory and to urge his people to address the problems of the peace in Europe with the same spirit of determination they had brought to the winning of the war. Both these addresses to the nation were recorded by HMV and issued with the June releases.

On their mid-price ten- and twelve-inch labels the major British companies marked the end of the war in a variety of styles. The lion's share of celebratory recordings came from HMV who brought out the music from the Service of Thanksgiving held at St. Paul's Cathedral on 13th May and Churchill's broadcast speech of the same date in which he surveyed the history of the European war and, with the Far East in mind, looked forward to the time when "... the whole task is done and the whole world is safe and clean." The Victory Bells of such great national places of worship as

Westminster Abbey and York Minster rang out stirringly on another disc in company with those of the more modest parish church of St. Mary's at Puddletown in rural Dorset. The religious theme was also taken up by Joseph McLeod who read the Lord's Prayer and the 23rd Psalm, The Lord is my Shepherd.

This was by no means all that HMV had to offer for John Gielgud contributed well known patriotic passages from Shakespeare's *Richard II* and *King John* which were supplemented by Sir Adrian Boult and the BBC Symphony Orchestra playing *Rule Britannia, The British Grenadiers* and *God Save the King*. There could also have been no better time for HMV to delve into its back catalogue and reissue its *England my England: a Pageant of National Songs* which had originally appeared in 1937 at the time of George VI's coronation; the singers, backed by massed symphony orchestras were the contralto Betty Bannerman and the baritone Dennis Noble.

Fittingly, Columbia brought out a set of *National Anthems of the Allies* played by the Band of the Grenadier Guards and on the same mid-price, ten-inch label the company's regular light music ensemble, the Debroy Somers Band, offered a medley of cheerful songs with the conveniently inclusive title *Celebration - for all Occasions*.

Classical music was well represented in the victory record issues. For its ffrr series Decca chose Beethoven's Fifth Symphony (the wartime connotations of which were known to everybody) with Malcolm Sargent conducting the National Symphony Orchestra. Columbia paid an imaginative tribute to a staunch ally when they published a mid-price two-disc set of Grieg's *Four Norwegian Dances*, Op. 35 with George Weldon conducting his City of Birmingham Orchestra.

It was HMV, however, which expressed the inmost feelings of the time with Barbirolli and the Hallé Orchestra in Anthony Collins's completion of an orchestral elegy by the young English composer Michael Heming. This poignant lament, posthumously published under the title *A Threnody for a Soldier killed in Action*, was sketched by Heming while on his way to North Africa where, sadly, he was one of the many who lost their lives at the battle of El Alamein.

Although not specifically intended for issue at the end of the war, June, 1945 was also the month in which one of the finest recordings of Elgar's *The Dream of Gerontius* made its belated appearance. It formed part of HMV's sequence of recordings of modern British works receiving financial sponsorship from the British Council and, as Carl Newton has related, was added to the list of proposed future projects as early as April, 1943. A considerable time then elapsed before the interested parties, the British Council, the BBC and EMI started seriously to think about such matters as the performers to be engaged and the overall cost of what would be the first complete recording of *Gerontius*.

Much discussion went on as to whether Boult, the BBC Symphony orchestra and the Luton Choral Society (favoured by EMI's Walter Legge) or Sargent, the Liverpool Philharmonic and the Huddersfield Choral Society should be the foundations on which the project would stand. Of the singers, Heddle Nash in the title role was the only one on whom there seemed to be any general agreement.[20] In July, 1944 the Council's Music Advisory Committee was still doubtful as to whether *Gerontius* was, at this well established stage of the work's life, a suitable candidate for a British Council subsidy. Arthur Bliss came out strongly against it since he believed that music by Dowland, Byrd and Delius had the greater claim. Opposing Bliss was William Walton who urged that *Gerontius* should be recorded straight away with Sargent, the Liverpool Philharmonic and the Huddersfield Choral Society; in the event, it was Walton's recommendation that was adopted.

Undercurrents of dissent persisted almost until recording began on 8th April, 1945. Paradoxically, from these clumsy negotiations there emerged a classic account of one of Elgar's greatest compositions though at whose prompting it had arrived on the British Council's short list in the first place is a question which even now cannot be answered with any certainty. When the twelve-disc plum label set reached the shops in June, 1945 it was, however, immediately recognised as a landmark in the artistic and technical history of the gramophone and an invaluable addition to the Elgar discography.

★   ★   ★

Burma in the Second World War is not a location one readily associates with recorded music recitals and a revealing light is shed on conditions there in a letter published in the December, 1944 number of *The Gramophone*. Arnold Levy, a Signaller, had been in the Arakan region for almost two years and found that even in the forward areas the presence of gramophones and small, private record collections was not altogether uncommon. In his own unit groups of enthusiasts somehow managed to hold weekly meetings just as gramophone clubs did in less vulnerable parts of this theatre of war. He praises the work of the Army Education Corps which in the rear areas had provided record libraries and gave regular recitals for both classical music lovers and servicemen with less sophisticated tastes. At the time he wrote Levy had been posted to India and he sounds almost regretful to have left behind all those like-minded comrades, honorary members one and all of what he affectionately terms the Arakan Gram. Club.

Rangoon was retaken in early May, 1945 and two months later gramophone concerts began to be one of the recreational options on offer to the troops. Another letter in *The Gramophone* for October, 1945 told how, to begin with, suitable premises were in short supply and the assembled music lovers sat on the floor in cramped rooms or on the stairs while their music contended with the street noises drifting in from outside. Later, the Elite Cinema which had an excellent sound system was the venue for the Sunday afternoon gramophone concerts and, with the help of a twin turntable from another Rangoon cinema, music lovers were treated to record reproduction of excellent quality.

This correspondent, Major F. H. Smith of the 12th Army's headquarters staff, was glad to report that

"We expect to be playing to the full capacity of 650 before long, and, apart from running a 'second house', it does not seem that much more can be done to cater for the considerable demand for music."

The programmes given at the Elite Cinema clearly did not consist entirely of classical pops for one Beethoven recital included the relatively unfamiliar Second Symphony and the seldom played Triple Concerto. Gramophone buffs were obviously thick on the ground at Rangoon and plans were soon being made for extra meetings, designed especially for connoisseurs, to be held at the Welfare Centre where "on the table grand acoustic machine" enthusiasts would be able to listen to "some of the more unusual works and discuss them at length".

By the end of 1944 Japanese resistance had ceased at Leyte in the Philippines where fierce land, sea and air battles had raged since October; but there was still much to be done before the Islands were free of the Japanese occupying forces and it was not until March, 1945 that the capital, Manila, was liberated. By then, with landings on Iwo Jima in February and Okinawa a month later the Americans had brought the war close to the threshold of Japan. Despite the massive incendiary bomb raids on major Japanese cities the Allies' demand at the Potsdam Conference for unconditional surrender was rejected. An American invasion of Japan could now only be avoided by adopting extreme measures and on 6th August the world's first atomic bomb was dropped on Hiroshima; but even the terrifying power of this agent of mass destruction failed to persuade Japan to sue for peace.

Accordingly, on 9th August, another bomb was exploded at Nagasaki and Leonard Cheshire V.C., the experienced leader of many major RAF bombing raids against Germany, was on board the B-29 Superfortress as one of the British observers. A recording of Cheshire's report on the second deployment of America's nuclear weapon is preserved in the BBC's sound archives and to this day makes chilling listening. What Cheshire saw affected him for the rest of his life and was later instrumental in his decision to set up and work for the Cheshire Homes for the incurably sick. With the war still to be won, however, he sounds as dispassionate as a scientist noting the results of a laboratory experiment.

In preparation for the explosion everybody on the B-29 had donned the darkest of polaroid glasses but even so the visual effect was that of night having been turned into day when a vast ball of fire half a mile in diameter rose two thousand feet in the air. We hear how much heat the fire generated (almost ten million degrees) and how fast it sped upwards (about 20,000 feet a minute). The fire gave way to cloud which took less than five minutes to reach a height of 60,000 feet. Cheshire felt that no words would ever be adequate to describe that cloud for

"Unlike any other phenomenon the world has ever seen it was possessed of some diabolical activity as though it were a horrible form of life. Its heat was so great that even at a range of twenty miles we could see dust from the earth being sucked up into the air like a vortex... Throughout the whole time it

254

remained a boiling, turbulent mass and continued expanding until it reached some two miles across."

The plane's crew and the Allied observers had been briefed on the need to stay clear of the sulphur yellow cloud's lethal nuclear fallout and it was from a distance of five or six miles that Cheshire viewed this disquieting spectacle.

The American bombing offensive had a devastating effect on civilian morale in Japan but the hard-line military elite still clung to the belief that martial honour had to be preserved at all costs. An American invasion would have resulted in further enormous loss of life on both sides and the United States threatened to drop a third nuclear bomb; though the Japanese did not know it, this was a calculated bluff for there were then no more atomic weapons ready for immediate use.

Fortunately, the warning alone proved sufficient and Japan's acceptance of the demand for unconditional surrender came on 14th August, 1945. In the Imperial Palace Emperor Hirohito recorded (some say on tape, some say on disc) a message to be broadcast to his people whom he exhorted to brace themselves and prepare "to bear the unbearable." The Imperial household still contained some elements of the do or die officer class and an attempt was made to prevent the recording leaving the palace but an official, disguised as a beggar, managed to smuggle it out to Tokyo's radio station. Even in the studio the broadcasting staff were intimidated by an army officer in a last ditch effort to stop the recording being transmitted. Not until the broadcasting authorities had obtained clearance from the highest military level was the recording allowed to go out over the air, an event which drove a grief-stricken nation into mourning for several days. Hirohito's future status had not yet been resolved by the Allies but, under pressure from the Americans, he relinquished his divine attributes in January, 1946 and took on the unaccustomed duty of introducing democratic, constitutional government to a country that had until recently enslaved the greater part of eastern Asia and the Pacific.

*   *   *

Britain's reaction to the defeat of Japan is, perhaps, best described as a deep collective sigh of relief. People had little appetite for further displays of triumphalism like those of VE Day and were longing to settle back into their peacetime routines. The General

Election of July, 1945 resulted in Churchill's coalition government being replaced by a Labour administration headed by Clement Atlee. It was soon apparent, though, that socialism would bring about no magical changes in the prevailing standard of living and the country embarked on a long spell of the old familiar shortages, rationing and domestic austerity.

When the war began to turn in Britain's favour the toilers in Tin Pan Alley had soon encountered a sharp fall in demand for the patriotic, propagandist and morale-boosting material with which they and the record companies helped to keep up the nation's spirits in less hopeful times. Thousands had discovered the pleasures of classical music and, on a lower level, public taste was harking back to that anodyne mixture of romantic, sentimental and mildly humorous songs that, together with an occasional novelty number, had been the dance bands' standard pre-war fare. The middle ground of ballads and operetta continued to be held by such popular singers as the husband and wife team of Webster Booth and Anne Ziegler whose performances on the stage, radio and disc attracted hosts of fans.

In Britain the gramophone's frugal response to VJ Day reflected these changing conditions. The only truly war-related disc to be issued seems to have been King George VI's *Victory Message to the Empire* which was broadcast by the BBC on 15th August, 1945 but had to wait until October before it was released by HMV. On a Columbia twelve-inch mid-price disc issued in September Clive Richardson's *London Fantasia* for piano and orchestra just scrapes into the reckoning on account of its realistic air raid section. *The Gramophone's* reviewer was much taken by the composition which he considered "one of the finest pieces of descriptive writing" he had heard for a long time.

Although the work was not war-related HMV's September release of a complete set of Verdi's *Requiem Mass* rose imaginatively to the occasion. It had been recorded by the company's Italian branch at the Rome Opera House in 1939 under the masterly direction of Tullio Serafin and the line-up of soloists could hardly have been more imposing, consisting of the tenor Beniamino Gigli, the soprano Maria Caniglia, the mezzo Ebe Stignani and the bass Ezio Pinza. Alec Robertson, one of *The Gramophone's* most respected critics, especially in the field of religious music, was impressed but

256

(unlike the American pundit David Hall) not overwhelmed by the ten red label discs. He found them adequate technically but not in the same class as HMV's recent *Dream of Gerontius*. It was the singing, though, which came in for his sharpest disapproval, particularly Gigli's intrusive aspirates, *portamento* and trademark sobs; Caniglia was also found wanting because of her readiness to ignore Verdi's dynamic markings. Stignani was not seriously faulted but Robertson's highest praise was reserved for Pinza whose vocal artistry he found outstanding in every respect. Coinciding as it did with the successful end of the Second World War Verdi's *Requiem Mass* (despite this set's shortcomings) was a highly discerning choice by HMV for, as Robertson wrote, "It portrays a God of Justice".

Earthly retribution for the captured Nazi leaders was dispensed by the International Military Tribunal which sat at Nuremberg from November, 1945 until October, 1946. Similar trials were held in Tokyo and the world at large learned in detail of the horrors perpetrated in Europe and the Far East during the Third Reich's and Japan's quests for empire. Of the twenty-one men indicted at Nuremberg, some were executed, some escaped the gallows by committing suicide and some, like Rudolf Hess whose sanity was in doubt, were condemned to the enervating patterns of life imprisonment. In a situation where there were no guiding precedents, justice was finally seen to have been done.

*   *   *

During the forty-seven years which separated the beginning of the Spanish American War and the end of the Second World War the gramophone evolved from the acoustic cylinder and the primitive flat disc to the electrically recorded 78 r.p.m. shellac record that could accommodate an often astonishing range of sound.

Entertainment pure and simple was the gramophone's main but not exclusive product. From as early as 1898 it readily took on an archival role in wartime by recording such memorabilia as the trumpet calls used to command Theodore Roosevelt's Rough Riders in action in Cuba, the din of a British gas shell barrage on the Western Front in October, 1918 and an eye witness account of the dropping of the atomic bomb on Nagasaki in August, 1945.

The persuasive power of the gramophone was perceived in Britain during the Boer War when recordings of patriotic songs like

The Soldiers of the Queen were legion. With the outbreak of the Great War of 1914-1918 the Gramophone Company and its rivals quickly spotted the marketing niche that awaited the specially composed recruiting songs which had a legitimate place at recruiting rallies but were also played by self-appointed recruiting officers (usually women) at social gatherings where they aimed to prick the conscience of young men not yet serving in the forces.

The gramophone also provided educational recordings (most often, perhaps, in the form of foreign language courses) and sets of well planned programmes for people who enjoyed their daily session of physical jerks. Charitable giving also featured amongst the activities of the record companies who, especially in wartime, would channel the profits from certain discs to good causes.

Fred Gaisberg pioneered the use of the gramophone as a weapon of war in its own right when he played enticing propaganda messages to enemy front line troops in Italy during World War I but it was in the political arena of the 1930s that the machine's potential for manipulating the minds of a targeted audience came to be more widely employed.

Extreme political parties and governments used the gramophone to promote themselves, though the discovery by Allied forces of many caches of recorded speeches by Mussolini and Nazi military music suggests that more often than not the supply of such discs greatly exceeded demand. In the case of the enormous output of Second World War German marching songs this was hardly surprising since they were constantly to be heard on the radio, newsreel sound tracks and public address systems everywhere.

For all its versatility the gramophone has always been more closely associated with music making than anything else. On cylinder and disc singers of the Golden Age and a number of instrumental virtuosi ensured that the talking machine had to be taken seriously even though its otherwise populist repertoire did not stretch far beyond banjo solos, farmyard impressions and the ubiquitous *Whistling Rufus*. As public acceptance increased, a broader and more serious repertoire emerged, as a study of HMV's World War I listings makes plain. The new spirit of adventure certainly infused Germany's Polydor company when in the early 1920s it brought out an acoustic set of Mahler's lengthy *Resurrection* Symphony conducted by Oskar Fried.

The arrival of the electrical recording process in 1925 resulted in much improved sound reproduction across the whole range of the gramophone's output. Significantly, technical research by the British companies did not come to a halt when the Second World War broke out; indeed, to a certain extent it became part of the war effort and various discoveries made at that time were later profitably adapted to the making of commercial recordings.

When Japan surrendered in August, 1945 the shellac 78 was nearing the end of its days. Long playing coarse-grooved transcription discs used in the broadcasting studio pointed to the way ahead and in 1948 American Columbia unveiled its 33⅓ r.p.m. microgroove LP; not to be outdone, RCA Victor entered the market the following year with its extended play (EP) 45 r.p.m. disc. Without even needing to alter the traditional flat disc format the gramophone industry had at one and the same time transformed and regenerated itself yet again.

Aftermath:
Some Personal Memories
1945-1947

WHEN VE DAY came I was kicking my heels in a holding company at Bruges expecting to be posted as a driver to some very ordinary Royal Army Service Corps transport unit. For an impressionable nineteen-year-old it was a fascinating place and with plenty of spare time available I was able to explore the historic city and enjoy its generous hospitality. Intermittently the peaceful atmosphere was broken by acts of violence as when a paint shop, said to be owned by a collaborator, mysteriously went up in flames; more deeply disturbing because it happened within our midst was the suicide for no clear reason of a young soldier at the holding company.

Such events, though, were the exception and what stands out most clearly in my mind was the occasion I was invited to watch from a first floor window the ancient religious ceremony of the Procession of the Holy Blood (banned during the Nazi occupation) as it moved along the street below.

The days passed pleasantly but when on parade one morning volunteers were called for to join a staff car company I broke with barrack room custom and offered myself. I never regretted doing so for No. 784 Car Company turned out to be attached to Supreme Headquarters, Allied Expeditionary Force (SHAEF) which I joined at Versailles. There I was kept busy ferrying middle rank British and American officers between Louis XIV's palace and the Parisian venues of the conferences and dinners they were constantly attending.

I had only one free evening in Paris and it was curiously quiet as there were few civilian vehicles on the roads and with the food shortages the cafés and bistros had not yet recovered their pre-war liveliness. My parents were both keen music lovers and I could not remember a time when there was not a gramophone in the house. It was therefore a particular pleasure on that evening to renew direct contact with recorded music for the first time since joining the Army in March, 1944. At one of the fine Parisian public buildings either ENSA or NAAFI was giving a record recital at which a large, appreciative audience of British servicemen and women had the pleasure of sitting not on War Department furniture but on elegant, red-upholstered, gilded chairs as they listened to a programme the main items of which were Schubert's *Unfinished* and Beethoven's *Pastoral* symphonies.

The surroundings and the entertainment left one longing for more but 784 Car Company was about to accompany SHAEF on its migration to Frankfurt am Main where it had taken over the headquarters of Germany's industrial giant IG Farben - just deserts for an organisation with so shameful a war history. As far as the gramophone was concerned Frankfurt had little to offer. I was billeted in a commandeered house where there was a small classical record collection which included Wilhelm Kempff's Polydor set of Beethoven's Third Piano Concerto but, frustratingly, there was no longer a gramophone on which to play these discs.

I had been at Frankfurt for only a few weeks when the Car Company was off again, this time to join the Control Commission for Germany's representatives in Berlin, well inside the Soviet Zone into which we travelled via the already notorious Russian checkpoint at Helmstedt where traffic to and from the east was subjected to endless bureaucratic delays. Berlin itself was split into four sectors governed by the British, American, French and Russian occupying powers and here my acquaintance with the gramophone was resumed on a more regular basis.

It was purely coincidental, of course, but it somehow seemed appropriate that I should arrive in Berlin on VJ Day; we celebrated the end of the war in the traditional alcoholic style but I remember little in the way of rowdy boozing. Instead, one was conscious of an enormous feeling of relief that the fighting was over at last, though the awesome power of the two atomic bombs which had forced Japan's capitulation was, as yet, scarcely realised.

Even with so much of Berlin in ruins it was surprisingly easy to travel about thanks, mainly, to the U-Bahn, the underground railway system which reeked of acrid tobacco smoke and cheap scent. Above ground the Berliners, mostly old men, women and children had toiled to clear the streets and footpaths of rubble and wreckage which was then piled as neatly as possible in front of the jagged skeletons of bombed-out buildings. Despite all the efforts to restore a semblance of order, the warmth of the summer sunshine made it sickeningly obvious that in places the ruins still harboured the remains of undiscovered bodies.

It was possible to go through the Brandenburg Gate into the Russian Sector and visit what was once the heartland of German government. As soon as duties permitted I joined the tourist trail being trodden by members of all the occupying forces to see what was left of the Reichstag and Hitler's Chancellery where, to my surprise, I was able to wander more or less at will, though there was no access to the Bunker area beyond. I was determined to have a souvenir of some sort from this former seat of power and on the floor in a corner of a large hall I found two record albums made to hold twelve-inch 78s. The red covers bore the Nazi eagle and swastika insignia and there were stout, hinged sleeves, enough to hold, I suppose, ten or a dozen discs. The albums, alas, were empty and possibly had never even been used or else some efficient German clerk would surely have written details of the records on the contents lists printed inside the front covers. On my next leave I brought them back to England where for many years they held discs I had acquired in Berlin.

The Car Company was situated just off the Kaiserdamm towards the western end of the British Sector and in walking to and from our nearby mess the main road often served as the stage on which many strange and shocking scenes of life in occupied Berlin were played out. The bridge where the road crossed over a busy railway was the haunt of young boys who would plaintively ask any passing soldier who happened to be smoking a cigarette for "Stummel für Vati, bitte" (fag end for Dad, please). If Dad was actually in Berlin he was most likely trying to find a customer for a camera, a pair of Wehrmacht binoculars or a Nazi dagger. Payment for such popular mementos would be in the only meaningful currency of this period, namely cigarettes and chocolate to which the Americans could add the purchasing power of real coffee, a beverage that had long since vanished from the German table. The cigarette ends collected by the boys were almost certainly not destined for Dad anyway and would probably be passed over to some small-time tobacco baron making a living by recycling whatever the youngsters salvaged.

Displaced persons and refugees, including large numbers from the east, poured into Berlin in search of families, relatives, friends and work. Most were undernourished and others, clearly on the verge of starvation, were at a loss to know what to do with themselves. Some simply gave up the unequal struggle and I remember seeing one (it could have been either man or woman in that bundle of rags) deliberately step into the path of a heavy lorry. Death was instantaneous and gruesome.

The Russians took scant notice of the sector boundaries and in the British area were once spotted trying to dispose of some rough wooden coffins and their contents in a tattered little public park. At night they roved the streets of central Berlin in search of unattended transport belonging to the Western Allies; any such car, van or truck they discovered was liable to be hoisted up and towed away to spend the rest of its days in the service of the Red Army.

Sheer determination and a vigorous entrepreneurial spirit helped to keep Berlin alive and small businesses and shops were soon trading again. In the vicinity of the ruined Kaiser-Wilhelm-Gedächtniskirche and the Kurfürstendamm there was a refreshing oasis for gramophone enthusiasts both passive and active. Patrick Wallace had also volunteered at Bruges to join the intriguing Car Company and we soon found we shared a number of interests. In our spare time we wrote one or two sketches which we thought so hilarious that they deserved to be preserved for posterity. When they had been polished and thoroughly rehearsed we took ourselves at Pat's suggestion to the Phono-Vox studio in the Rankestrasse where a phlegmatic German engineer (probably the proprietor) recorded our efforts on flexible plastic 78 r.p.m. discs. My copies survive to this day but I have not plucked up the courage to play them for many, many years; perhaps such memories are best left undisturbed. It was not a question that could be asked, of course, but it would have been interesting to know how this modest, private studio maintained its stock of recording blanks when the German commercial world was in near-total disarray.

Nearby there was a cramped, inconspicuous record shop which I visited now and again; the German gramophone companies were still managing to scrape up a few records for outlets like this but the bottom of the barrel had been reached and choice was extremely limited. I did find one or two treasures such as Toscanini's Beethoven Seventh with the New York Philharmonic on Electrola though it was pressed on such low grade shellac that the ear of faith was needed to separate the music from the surface noise. Less muffled listening was provided by two Odeon sets: Jacqueline Blancard and the Suisse Romande Orchestra under Ernest Ansermet in Falla's *Nights in the Gardens of Spain* and the unaccountably neglected Dutch pianist Cor de Groot with the Brussels Radio Orchestra under Eduard Flipse in Richard Strauss's *Burleske*, both of which provided undiluted pleasure. Over the coming months I also added to my collection two of Victor De Sabata's famous Polydor recordings with the Berlin Philharmonic, the Brahms Fourth (about which critical opinion has always been somewhat divided) and Strauss's *Death and Transfiguration* which in *The Record Book* duly earned David Hall's highest praise both as a performance and a recording.

The Philharmonic was back in action giving public concerts again by the time I reached Berlin and I was naturally eager to hear this great ensemble in the flesh. Furtwängler had been relieved of his post as chief conductor until such time as the investigation into his relations with the Nazis was satisfactorily completed and the little known Leo Borchard was appointed his successor. His tenure, however, was brief in the extreme before, due to a failure in communication, he was shot and killed by a trigger-happy soldier of the occupying forces. Stability returned to the orchestra with the arrival of the Romanian conductor Sergiu Celibidache whose performances thrilled younger members of the audience like myself but were less appreciated by German concert-goers accustomed to the spirituality of Furtwängler's music making. In the mind's ear I can still recall the brilliance of Tchaikovsky's Fourth and Beethoven's Seventh Symphonies as well as the atmospheric textures of Debussy's *La Mer* and Ravel's *Rapsodie Espagnole*. The concerts during the winter of 1945/46 were especially notable for the way in which the orchestra continued to give its all in the unheated Theater des Westens to audiences only too glad to be wearing overcoats and gloves.

Fraternisation with the Germans was officially forbidden and most of the city's surviving bars and places of public entertainment were out of bounds but fortunately the Car Company was conveniently placed for visiting NAAFI's recently opened Services' club. There of an evening one could enjoy a decent meal followed by an hour or so relaxing in a comfortable chair while dipping into a large and well chosen classical record collection. I became particularly fond of Cortot's discs of Schumann's Piano Concerto and César Franck's *Symphonic Variations* both with Sir Landon Ronald directing the London Philharmonic and my lifelong admiration for the music of Sibelius took root thanks to the magnificent readings of the First and Second Symphonies by Robert Kajanus and Koussevitzky respectively.

On my driving trips from Frankfurt and Berlin I saw many of the ravaged cities which constituted post-war Germany. One indelible memory was the sight of Cologne's majestic cathedral standing seemingly undamaged amidst an otherwise flattened townscape. The industrial powerhouse of the Ruhr looked as if it would never recover from the Allied bombing; driving here was a slow and risky procedure for the roads were studded with potholes many of them large and deep enough to wreck a Humber Snipe staff car's springs and axles. Sometimes there was the added hazard of the rails of street tramways sticking up in the air waiting to puncture the unwary driver's tyres or do even worse damage to the underside of his car.

From Berlin one of my expeditions in the winter of 1945/46 took me to Hanover where, from 1898, the Gramophone Company's London branch (soon to achieve worldwide fame as HMV) had pressed its recordings prior to the opening of its own plant at Hayes, Middlesex in 1908. Before listing its manufactures and industries a British gazeteer of the 1930s made special mention of Hanover's "fine parks and suburbs, picture galleries, museums [and] libraries" but most of these were no longer apparent for the city had suffered badly in the bombing war.

Somehow or other I had learnt that Deutsche Grammophon was still operating a warehouse in Hanover and that records could actually be "bought" there. Without too much difficulty I tracked down the address I had been given and introduced myself in my best German to the sole member of staff on the premises. We were a little wary of each other at first for there was well over half a century's age difference between this grey haired old man and myself;

265

however, once I had convinced him of my gramophonic credentials the tension eased and in the icy cold building we got down to the serious business of selecting records.

My attention was caught by a couple of off-the-beaten-track Polydors, some obscure Telemann, the details of which I no longer remember, and Busoni's delightful arrangement for two pianos of the finale of Mozart's Piano Concerto No.19 in F major, K459 played by A. and H. Schmidt-Neuhaus. The old man obviously thought he had something special which no gramophone enthusiast should miss and in a reverent whisper asked me if I had heard any of the records by "der neue Furtwängler". Baffled, I shook my head and he went off to the shelves returning with an armful of discs which he laid out on a table. There was a Polydor set of Dvořák's *New World* Symphony by the Berlin Philharmonic and on Siemens Spezial, a label new to me, Brahms's First Symphony and Richard Strauss's *Don Juan* both by the Concertgebouw Orchestra. And so it was that I first encountered the artistry of Herbert von Karajan.

There came the time when 784 Car Company was disbanded and, after my long sojourn in Berlin, I was posted to a transport unit quartered in a well appointed barracks at Neumünster in northern Germany. Memory is stubbornly unhelpful over what the company's function was or, for that matter, what I myself was doing. After the kaleidoscopic life I had experienced in Berlin, time at Neumünster passed in a haze of boredom. Pat Wallace had fared better and soon after leaving Berlin had joined the staff of the Presentation Department at the British Forces Network (BFN) radio station in Hamburg. We had kept in touch and through Pat I heard that the post of Record Librarian would be falling vacant in the early summer of 1947 when the late Arthur (Roy) Hewartson was due to be demobbed. I approached BFN asking to be considered as Roy's successor and it was agreed that I should go to Hamburg on a provisional posting when his departure was imminent. Pat Wallace kindly dropped a discreet word or two as to my keenness and discographical know-how, after which it was a matter of just waiting and hoping.

In Berlin I had been promoted to the rank of Corporal and this resulted in my being called on with monotonous frequency to act as guard commander at Neumünster. That much, at least, stands out in the memory but the past comes into sharper focus when in the savage winter of 1946/47 I was sent to a company detachment further north still in deepest Schleswig-Holstein where for much of the time we were snowbound in our farmhouse HQ and its adjacent cottages.

When any vehicles ventured out they were fated more often than not to get stuck in snowdrifts from which they had to be retrieved and it was not unknown for the rescue trucks also to come to grief in the same way. Conventional heating fuel was in desperately short supply and was reserved strictly for use by the cookhouse. In the farmyard there was a large compound fenced with barbed wire which held a German stockpile of worn out rubber tyres awaiting retreading or some other profitable form of recycling. Theoretically we were responsible for the safekeeping of this dump which was out of bounds to all unauthorised persons, whether British or German. At night, however, when the darkness hid the black smoke, those who could stomach the horrible smell fed the stoves in the cottages with pieces carved from tyres ingeniously filched from the compound. Here at this remote unit I celebrated my twenty-first birthday with a welcome ration of rum - on guard duty yet again.

It was a pleasure to return eventually to the relative comforts of Neumünster where in due course news came through that it was time for me to be off to Hamburg. I arrived there on 9th June 1947, a beautiful summer's day, and reported for duty at BFN's studios in the imposing Musikhalle which was the city's main concert venue. When the clerical formalities were over Pat introduced me to Roy Hewartson and I was given a guided tour with special attention to the wonderfully airy and spacious Record Library. The windows rose almost from floor to ceiling, there were listening rooms for broadcasters auditioning records and an impressive bank of turntables stood ready for use by the Library staff. On steel shelving row upon row of discs took up most of the floor space:I knew straight away I would be in my element.

Once I had familiarised myself with the building's layout the rest of the day was my own which was a great piece of luck. On entering the Musikhalle I had seen the notices advertising the first post-war Hamburg concert to be given by Wilhelm Furtwängler that very evening. By this late stage every ticket had been snatched up but as I was now officially attached to BFN I was allowed to stand at the back of the hall. A new point in my musical pilgrim's progress was reached when that gaunt figure made his way to the rostrum and launched the Hamburg Philharmonic into a typical Furtwängler programme: Beethoven's Leonore No. 2 Overture, Strauss's *Death and Transfiguration* (both highly symbolic and emotive pieces in the circumstances) and Brahms's Second Symphony. It was a personal triumph for the revered conductor and I had never before heard anything to compare with the hysterical and seemingly endless applause as he was recalled time after time to the platform at the end of the concert. Even from outside the hall Nan Pomeroy and Denis Shaw, two members of BFN's staff on duty that day, could hear the ominous cries of "Sieg Heil, Sieg Heil" from an audience that had still not discarded all the shibboleths of the Hitlerite past.

Roy Hewartson devoted his remaining hours at Hamburg to giving me a crash course in the job of Record Librarian; he must have reported favourably on me as I was soon added to BFN's company strength. When I ran into a problem Pat Wallace, now a seasoned member of staff in the Presentation Department, would usually have the answer for he was involved in one way or another with virtually all aspects of the station's broadcasting activities.

I inherited two German clerks who did most of the office work including cataloguing the new records as soon as they arrived from England, registering and keeping track of the discs needed each day in the studios and then reshelving them on their return to the Library.

More than forty years later I was embarrassed to read in Doreen Taylor's *A Microphone and a Frequency* that at some unspecified time in 1947 records from BFN "... were finding their way on to the black market at Hamburg's Altona station..." Losses would not necessarily have been immediately noticeable since at least two copies of all commercial discs were sent to the Library in order to cover accidental breakages. If this occurred before my arrival I cannot remember being told about it; even now though, so long after the event, it is particularly galling to think this leakage might have been going on during my custodial term of office. However, the black market culture was an integral part of everyday life at this time and Alan Grace has told how in various ways it operated even within the hallowed precincts of the Musikhalle. One wonders what sort of records were being traded and what they yielded in return. Because of Nazi ideological restrictions, American jazz, swing and dance music would, perhaps, have been the most sought after genres and it is a slight consolation to imagine that some such discs may have joined the collections of appreciative Hamburg Swings.

My first tour of the Library's shelves revealed that the British commercial recordings were supplemented by a wide range of other fascinating material. There were V Discs and sixteen-inch AFRS wide-groove transcription discs playing at 33⅓ rpm which had been donated to us by our American colleagues. BBC recordings with Tommy Handley's comic *ITMA* series at one end of the spectrum and the Home Service's Sunday evening classic serial at the other were available to BFN's programme planners. Most unusual of all were the Canadian sixteen-inch transcription discs which reproduced well but had the drawback of being made from an extremely fragile type of glass.

The Record Librarian's contributions to BFN's output went well beyond just supplying discs to the studios. Every now and again I was responsible for compiling the programme for what might be called the Wakey Wakey slot of music designed to kick-start the British services' day. On looking back I wonder whether I was, perhaps, a little too enthusiastic in my choices which may sometimes have been on the frenetic side of lively. On receiving new recordings I informed the broadcasting staff of all the notable discs in their particular fields of interest. These overlapped to a considerable extent so that, for instance, Decca's latest classical issues employing the company's recently developed ffrr (full frequency range recording) system would be eagerly auditioned not just by the Music Department but also by those concerned technically with the sonic advances in the post-war record world.

When I suggested to Music Department that an occasional classical record review might be fitted into their broadcasting schedules I was delighted to have the idea accepted and thrilled, considering I had only a very basic knowledge of music, to be given the chance to write and present the first one. There was one proviso: I was not to be over-critical in my judgments lest BFN's free supply of records from the British companies should be imperilled. We agreed that a good approach would be to include important recordings from the war years which classical enthusiasts might not yet have encountered and I was able to sing the praises unreservedly of Sir William Walton conducting his own *Belshazzar's Feast* and of Sir Adrian Boult's superlative performances of Gustav Holst's *The Planets* and Elgar's Second Symphony.

Outsize butterflies were fluttering wildly in my stomach when I entered the studio to make my first live broadcast and it was reassuring to see that the experienced programme engineer on the other side of the glass panel was a good friend of mine. Thankfully, once we were on the air the butterflies settled down, I read my script without stumbling and in the control studio I could see the discs containing the musical illustrations I had chosen spinning on the turntables ready to be faded in and out at the appointed moments.

It was a truly exhilarating experience and I was lucky enough to present another review a month or two later. Greatly daring, I compiled a comparative review of two recent recordings of Saint-Saëns's Second Piano Concerto, the soloists being Moura Lympany for Decca and Benno Moiseiwitsch for HMV. This involved much time at the Library's turntables playing through the two sets and then, stopwatch in one hand, marking with a yellow Chinagraph pencil held in line with the tone arm's needle, the beginning and end of the passages to be broadcast. Script and music then had to be knitted together and I seem to remember at one point there was even a midstream switch from one recording to the other. I cannot now recall which pianist was my personal first choice but, bearing in mind the warning not to be too judgmental, I discreetly declared the result a dead heat.

At regular intervals I went over to the American Forces Network station at Bremen where we had a long-standing exchange arrangement under which each had access to the other's recent non-commercial recordings. If BFN seemed free and easy, AFN on my brief visits appeared positively laid back and the same might be said of the sixteen-inch vinylite LPs I borrowed. With these BFN could treat its listeners to the leading American singers, bands, comedians and symphony orchestras. Recordings made specifically for broadcasting to the American armed forces were not subject to the high-minded constraints imposed on the radio networks in the USA by the commercial sponsors of their programmes. Any of these discs which BFN wished to broadcast therefore had to be checked right through to ensure that no material going out over the air from Hamburg overstepped the British mark.

An acetate dubbing made in 1945 of two examples of items deemed unacceptable by BFN was still being enjoyed in the offices at the Musikhalle two years later when I was there. In one, the greatly admired vocalist Helen Forrest sang a torrid number, the explicit title of which, *Make Love to Me*, would not have disappointed anybody who was tempted to sample the song. Even more instructive (if that is the right word) was an out-of-character performance by Herbert Marshall, that suave actor who had featured in many a Hollywood romantic film. Assuming a gravelly American accent he sang a piece about the frustrations of a man married to a dedicated striptease dancer. Predictably, the song was heartily applauded by the service audience present at the recording.

Although it did not have Berlin's unique atmosphere Hamburg, despite the bombing, still had much to offer newcomers to the historic city and merely to watch the busy water traffic on the sunlit Alster was to glimpse the hopeful prospect of more stable times ahead. Perhaps I did not explore thoroughly enough but I failed to find any record shops; however, consolation was plentiful in the form of live music. Furtwängler was back at the Musikhalle in September conducting the Symphony Orchestra of Northwest German Radio in excerpts from Mendelssohn's *Midsummer Night's Dream* music which the Nazis had banned, the Double Concerto for Violin and Cello by Brahms and Beethoven's Seventh Symphony. I seem to remember at the time that the playing was rather lacklustre, possibly because the orchestra was feeling jaded after the lengthy rehearsals on which Furtwängler had insisted. The Musikhalle was also the scene of my first encounter with Mahler's music, the massive Sixth Symphony played, I believe, by the Hamburg Philharmonic under Eugen Jochum. Elsewhere in town there was a profusion of new British and American films, popular plays, variety shows and one night stopovers by such household names as Geraldo and his Orchestra.

The only opera I recall seeing in Berlin was that rarity (in Britain, at least) *Tiefland* by Eugen d'Albert, staged in a theatre in the Russian sector. To my shame, I remember little of that no doubt worthy production; on the other hand, Verdi's *Un Ballo in Maschera* (A Masked Ball) at Hamburg's State Opera was a totally involving experience, musically, dramatically and visually. The scene in which the heroine meets the gipsy fortune teller under the gallows tree at midnight was quite unforgettable with the enormous gibbet towering high above the stage, the singers and the audience.

Out in the real world of post-war Germany one might still be confronted by the darker side of life at any time. At BFN we mounted a nightly guard on the company's quarters in suburban Hamburg and once when I was commander a youngish woman was brought into the guardroom after being found hanging about our vehicle lines. She was carrying her pitifully few possessions and had apparently been looking for somewhere to sleep. She knew very little English and my conventional German was no match for her dialect but we gathered that her home used to be in the east of the country and that she had wandered westwards in search of a better life than that prevailing under the Russian occupation.

We offered her the use of our very basic facilities so that she could have a wash and brush-up, a luxury she had clearly not enjoyed for some days, and shared our duty rations with her for which simple courtesy she was pathetically grateful. For her night's rest we could offer only a wooden chair and a table on which to rest her head and the following morning we handed her over to the British military and German civil authorities who dealt with refugees and displaced persons. I have often wondered what eventually became of her.

At the beginning of November my demob was only a matter of days away; I do not know who took over from me as Record Librarian nor do I recall giving any instruction to a successor so perhaps there was an interregnum. At Hamburg work and pleasure had been virtually synonymous but when farewells had been said all round I was eager to get back to England and pick up the threads of civilian life again. I was issued with my standard demob kit at a York barracks only about twenty miles from the village where I now live and where this book was written. At the end of a dreary overnight rail journey to Bristol I was met on the platform at Temple Meads Station at some impossibly early hour by my father who, though far from well, had braved the wretched weather to be there to welcome me the moment I stepped off the train. It was Sunday, 9th November, 1947, two days before Armistice Day itself; it felt a right and proper time at which to be leaving the Army and starting out afresh.

Notes

Nicole's discs of music catering specifically for dancers showed the gramophone not only taking advantage of a niche market but also acting as an agent of change in British domestic entertainment. At the upper end of the social scale a band would automatically be engaged to provide the music for a private gathering of friends in spacious surroundings. In smaller, middle class homes, however, a gramophone and a suitable supply of records would gradually eliminate the need for live music; where previously a carefully planned party was "held" or "given" the new mechanical music provider opened up the way to a more informal approach which made it a simple matter to "throw" a party at very short notice.

During the First World War all forms of light entertainment were in constant demand and, with dancers in mind, HMV's catalogue of records on sale between 1914 and 1918 was well stocked with fox-trots, two-steps and waltzes.

The use of the gramophone at private functions continued steadily throughout the 1930s in such contexts as university faculty clubs' parties. The special atmosphere generated by a live band would inevitably be lacking but recorded music that could be used many times over cost less than a band's recurrent fees. The performing style on commercial dance music discs was not always totally suited to these social occasions but this problem was solved to a large extent when in 1935 Victor Silvester and his Ballroom Orchestra began to record their strict-tempo versions of popular tunes for Parlophone before switching to Columbia in November, 1940. Interestingly, their Second World War issues included few of the sentimental and hearty hits of those years, perhaps because Silvester's discs rarely featured a vocalist. The British film *Green for Danger* (1946), set in a cottage hospital during the war, authentically depicts the use of the gramophone at the weekly hop for the doctors and nurses.

Even in the twenty-first century the gramophone has continued to supply the younger generation's music for dancing with disc jockeys introducing and spinning their black vinyl LPs at respectable discos as well as at other less decorous venues.

p.35 *n2* Quoted by Jerrold Northrop Moore in his *Edward Elgar: a creative life.* Oxford, 1984.

p.74 *n3* Dr. James Heyworth-Dunne of the School of Oriental and African Studies, University of London.

p.98 *n4* The copy consulted by the author bore the rubber stamp of Feldwebel [Sergeant] Ed. Kirchner of the Music Corps at the Cracow garrison in occupied Poland.

p.152 *n5* Because Parliamentary proceedings were not allowed to be broadcast or recorded at that time the British Council in 1940 made acetate discs of the radio actor Norman Shelley in this speech which Churchill delivered to the House of Commons on 4th June. After Churchill had approved the discs the British Council sent them to President Roosevelt in the hope that they might be broadcast and so act as an incentive for America to join the Allies. (Letter from Gerard Hayling in *Stage, Screen and Radio*, February, 2001)

p.152 *n6* HMV's 78s of Churchill's wartime broadcast speeches had all departed from the catalogue by 1950 but in 1957 and 1958 they were replaced by LP transfers. In 1964 Decca brought out an even more comprehensive collection that included speeches not previously available on record as well as extracts from Churchill's war memoirs.

p.154 *n7* This disc was remarkable for its two links with Sir Thomas Beecham's 1937 Berlin recording of Mozart's *The Magic Flute.*Strienz, who sang the role of Sarastro, had been the obligatory Aryan substitute for the great but Jewish Alexander Kipnis who, in normal circumstances, would have been Beecham's and producer Walter Legge's first choice. By a strange coincidence, the orchestra on the *Tapfere, kleine Soldatenfrau* recording was directed by Bruno Seidler-Winkler who, quite literally, had put the finishing touch to the *Magic Flute* project. Beecham had not been satisfied with certain parts of the November, 1937 sessions and Legge arranged for him to re-record these in late February/early March, 1938 when Sir Thomas was conducting at the Berlin State Opera. By the time he was due to leave, however, the Queen of the Night's first aria had still not been re-made. Seidler-Winkler had worked closely with and for Deutsche Grammophon (and later Electrola) since before the First World War and, together with Erna Berger and the Berlin State Opera Orchestra in lieu of the Berlin Philharmonic, was secretly brought in by Legge to provide the crucial missing section. Listening through earphones to one of Beecham's rejected takes as he conducted, Seidler-Winkler was able to produce a side that measured up to Legge's demanding standards. The author is indebted to Lyndon Jenkins's notes for Dutton Laboratories' CD transfer of Beecham's *Magic Flute* for this information. It was not Seidler-Winkler's only patchwork job in the recording studio as he was also responsible for completing the second act of Wagner's *Die Walküre* of which Bruno Walter had recorded five sides with the Vienna Philharmonic and a dazzling cast before having to flee from Austria. Only two singers had to be changed and with the Berlin State Opera Orchestra replacing the Vienna Philharmonic Seidler-Winkler made the remaining fifteen sides.

p.159 *n*8   Columbia's equivalent of HMV's Boston Promenade Orchestra was America's Columbia Broadcasting Symphony Orchestra under Howard Barlow. It made its British debut in August, 1939 with Haydn's *Surprise* Symphony and wartime issues ranged from Ravel's delicate *Mother Goose* Suite to one of the most rumbustious accounts of Dvořák's *Carnival* overture on disc.

p.164 *n*9   It is often assumed that the ballet with its conflict between the Children of Darkness and the Children of Light was directly inspired by the invasion of Poland but Ashton himself regarded it as an expression of the evils of war in general. Because the music had to be left behind in Holland, performances after the Company's return to Britain were danced to the Columbia recording until Lambert finished reconstructing the score. Technically, the discs were not amongst Columbia's best and were deleted in October, 1951; they were then largely forgotten until in 2000 a remarkably successful CD transfer was issued by Pearl.

p.167 *n*10   Van Beinum and the Concertgebouw Orchestra had a special rapport with the *Symphonie Fantastique* and another wartime recording was made for Polydor in 1943. After the war Decca made two further recordings with the same artists, first on 78s in 1946 and then on LP in 1951.

275

p.187 *n*11   I am indebted to Lyndon Jenkins's informative liner notes to Dutton Laboratories' CD transfer of Lambert's *Romeo and Juliet* for details of the recording team's problems; from my student days at Birmingham University in the late 1940s I have clear memories of the deafening noise made by the starlings as they performed their mass aerobatics around the Town Hall.

p.196 *n*12   V Disc 44 was an odd exception. Here the black folk and blues artist Josh White sang *Blues in Berlin*, a piece of hard-hitting propaganda in which new words had been grafted on to Jimmie Lunceford's *Blues in the Night*. The revised lyric warned the Germans they would regret the day they attacked Russia and could expect the Red Army to take a terrible revenge.

p.200 *n*13   The Hanover pressings for the Indian market bore the Gramophone Company's Monarch label.

p.203 *n*14   This and all other BBC recordings referred to in this chapter are included in the set of two audio cassettes entitled *BBC War Reports: the Second World War*. At the beginning of the war some of the BBC's more conservative members believed that recording, whether in-house or on location, was not an activity with which the Corporation, primarily a live broadcast provider, should become too deeply involved. The playing of commercial gramophone records was a different matter for these had been a regular feature of the programme schedules since the earliest days of British broadcasting. The disruptive effects of the Blitz triggered a detailed scrutiny of the place of recording in the BBC's wartime functions. A powerful argument in the debate was the need to create and maintain a plentiful supply of pre-recorded talks and other material for use in emergencies such as when, because of an air attack on London, artists might be prevented from getting to the studio on time for a live broadcast. One particular type of recording to influence executive opinion in favour of the BBC stepping up its own recorded output would certainly have been the on the spot reports by war correspondents. These had been transmitted since September, 1939 and their immediacy and consistently high standard were both an object lesson to all broadcasters and a unique source of information on the progress of the war for radio listeners. The outcome of the review was an acknowledgment that if it was to keep pace with world events the BBC as the voice of free Europe could not do so satisfactorily without the assistance of its own

276

recordings. Ironically, once policy had been clarified there was no sudden significant growth in recording activities because of shortages of equipment and trained staff, a situation that would persist for some considerable time.

p.205 *n*15 Almost certainly the HMV recording by Reginald Kell and the London Philharmonic Orchestra conducted by Malcolm Sargent.

p.205 *n*16 This song's title is found in a variety of forms with Lilli alternatively spelt Lili and Marlene alternatively spelt Marleen or Marlen. The author follows the usage of Rust and Forbes in their discography *British Dance Bands on Record 1911 to 1945*.

p.220 *n*17 Decca released its first LPs in June, 1950 but EMI cautiously waited until October, 1952 to make sure the new format was not just a flash in the pan.

p.224 *n*18 The most substantial exception was Miaskovsky's Symphony No. 21 on three ten-inch mid-price discs.

p.227 *n*19 For further details of Telefunken's wartime recordings see the 1999 issues of *International Classical Record Collector*.

p.252 *n*20 The line-up of soloists eventually comprised Heddle Nash, tenor (*Gerontius*), Gladys Ripley, contralto (*The Angel*), Dennis Noble, baritone (*The Priest*) and Norman Walker, bass (*The Angel of the Agony*).

Bibliography

General reference works

The *Britannica, Cambridge, Chambers's, Everyman's, Great Soviet* (English language ed.) and *Waverley* encyclopaedias.

Chambers's biographical dictionary, the *Dictionary of national biography, Who's who* and *Who was who*.

The Times and *The Daily Telegraph* newspapers.

Discographies and record catalogues

ADRIAN, Karlo and BADROCK, Arthur. Edison Bell Winner records: [numerical listing]. 2nd rev. ed. Bournemouth, 1989.

ANDREWS, Frank. Columbia 10″ records 1904-1930. London, 1985.

ANDREWS, Frank and BAYLY, Ernie. A numerical listing of the H.M.V. "B" series of 78 rpm records. Wells-next-the-Sea, 2000.

ANDREWS, Frank and SMITH, Michael. The Parlophone twelve inches diameter E. 10000 catalogue series: a product of the Parlophone Company Limited, 1923-1959: a numerical listing of catalogue numbers. Wells-next-the-Sea, 2000.

ARIEL. See GRAVES RECORDS.

BAUER, Robert. The new catalogue of historical records, 1898-1908/09. London, 1947.

BEKA. The catalogue of "Beka" double sided gramophone records. [c1920].

BERLINER. Record catalogue Nov.16th 1898 [to June, 1900].

BRITISH ZONOPHONE CO. Catalogue of Zonophone disc records. July, 1904.

CENTRAL EDUCATION OFFICE. 1951 catalogue of educational recordings: "His Master's Voice", Columbia, Parlophone. London, 1951.

CLOUGH, Francis and CUMING, G.J. The world's encyclopaedia of recorded music; with Supplements 1-3. 3 vols. London, 1952-57.

COLUMBIA. Alphabetical catalogue of Columbia records ... 1947 [and] 1949.

DECCA. A complete catalogue of Decca records ... September, 1941, April, 1947 [and] March, 1949.

DECCA. Supplementary catalogue of 78 r.p.m. and 33⅓ r.p.m. long playing records, April, 1949 to September, 1950.

"GRAMMAVOX" RECORDS. [Catalogue, pre-1914].

GRAMOPHONE AND TYPEWRITER, LTD. Catalogue of Gramophone 7-inch records. April, [1903].

GRAVES RECORDS. 'Ariel' Grand double-sided [10 in. records and 'Ariel' Concert double-sided 12 in. records]. (First World War period mail order catalogue issued by J.G. Graves, Ltd. of Sheffield. Many of the discs came from the Beka and Grammavox catalogues and were presumably re-labelled for Graves).

GRAY, Michael. Beecham: a centenary discography. London, 1979.

HIS MASTER'S VOICE. Catalogue. 1939-40, 1942-43, 1948-49, 1949-50, 1950-51, 1951-52, 1952-53, 1955-56.

HIS MASTER'S VOICE. Gramophone records of the First World War: an HMV catalogue 1914-1918; introduced by Brian Rust. Newton Abbot, 1975.

HIS MASTER'S VOICE. International special catalogue. March, 1952.

HIS MASTER'S VOICE. Numerical list of recordings. 1911.

HIS MASTER'S VOICE. Special list. 1948.

HIS MASTER'S VOICE. Verzeichnis der deutschen "His Master's Voice" Musikplatten. (German catalogue). 1949.

HUNT, John. Back from the shadows: Mengelberg ... van Beinum: discographies. London, 1997.

HUNT, John. The Furtwängler sound: discography with concert register. 6th ed. London, 1999.

HUNT, John. Giants of the keyboard: Kempff; Gieseking; Fischer; Haskil; Backhaus; Schnabel: [discographies]. London, 1994.

HUNT, John. Gramophone stalwarts ... Bruno Walter: [discography]. London, 2001.

HUNT, John. Mid-century conductors: Böhm; De Sabata; Knappertsbusch; Serafin; Krauss: discographies. London, 1992.

HUNT, John. Musical knights: Wood, Beecham, Boult, Barbirolli, Goodall, Sargent: discographies. London, 1995.

HUNT, John. Philharmonic autocrat: the sound and video recordings of Herbert von Karaian: [discography] with concert and opera register. London, 1993.

HUNT, John. Sächsische Staatskapelle Dresden: complete discography. London, 2002.

HUNT, John. Singers of the Third Reich: Helge Rosvaenge, Tiana Lemnitz, Franz Völker, Maria Müller, Max Lorenz: 5 separate discographies. London, 2001.

HUNT, John. Vienna Philharmonic and Vienna State Opera Orchestras: discography 1905-1989. 2 vols. London, 2000.

KNOWLES, John. Elgar's interpreters on record: an Elgar discography. 2nd ed. London, 1985.

METHUEN-CAMPBELL, James. Catalogue of recordings of classical pianists. Vol. 1. (Pianists born to 1872). Chipping Norton, 1984.

MOORE, Jerrold Northrop. An Elgar discography. London, 1963. (Reprinted from *Recorded Sound*, vol. 2, no. 9, January, 1963).

NICOLE. Record catalogue. 1905/6.

PARLOPHONE. Complete catalogue ... 1934-1935, 1949-50.

RUST, Brian. British music hall on record. Harrow, 1979.

RUST, Brian. Discography of historical records on cylinders and 78s. London, 1979.

RUST, Brian and FORBES, Sandy. British dance bands on record 1911 to 1945. Harrow, 1987.

SEELEY, Robert and BUNNETT, Rex. London musical shows on record 1889-1989: a hundred years of London's musical theatre. Harrow, 1989.

SHAW, Eddie. Date about all those English 78s. Part 1. Commercial. 2nd rev. ed. and Supplement A. London, 1995. Part 2. Private, publishers, etc. London, 1997.

SMITH, Michael. Columbia Graphophone Company Limited: English Celebrity series and 10 and 12 inch D, LB, L, LX series, YB, RO and ROX series, D-40,000 series. Gillingham [Kent], 2002.

SMITH, Michael. The Decca Record Company Limited: Decca 78 rpm records 1929-1954: 12-inch diameter discs - "K", "T", "X", "S"; 10-inch diameter discs - "M", "A", "Z". [Gillingham, Kent?], 1999.

SMITH, Michael. The Gramophone Company Ltd. His Master's Voice black label 12 and 10-inch "D" & "E" 78 rpm series. [Gillingham, Kent?], 2001.

SMITH, Michael. "His Master's Voice" recordings: "BD" series: Magenta label: a discography. Hastings, 1992.

SMITH, Michael and ANDREWS, Frank. The Gramophone Company Limited: "His Master's Voice" recordings: plum label records, "C" series. [Gillingham, Kent?], 2000.

SMITH, Michael and others. Columbia Graphophone Company Limited: Columbia "DX" and "YBX" 12 inch series of 78 rpm discs 1930-1959. (Gillingham, Kent?], 1997.

TAYLOR, Ronald. Columbia twelve-inch records in the United Kingdom 1906-1930: a discography. [London?], 1994.

Gramophone industry

ANDREWS, Frank. Edison Phonograph: the British connection. Rugby, 1986.

ANGELO, Mario d'. La renaissance du disque. (*Notes et Etudes Documentaires*. No. 4890). Paris, 1989.

BATTEN, Joe. Joe Batten's book. London, 1956.

BLOCH, Francine. Le disque en France: sa primauté dans l'enregistrement sonore. (*Notes et Etudes Documentaires*. No. 4418). Paris, 1977.

BULTMANN, Stephan. The record of Grammophon. (*International Classical Record Collector*. No. 13. Summer, 1998).

BULTMANN, Stephan. Telefunken's rise and rise. (*International Classical Record Collector*. No. 19. Winter, 1999).

CHEW, V.K. Talking machines. 2nd ed. London, 1981.

CLASSIC RECORD COLLECTOR (formerly International Classical Record Collector). Quarterly, 1995-.

CULSHAW, John. Putting the record straight: the autobiography. London, 1981.

DE, Santosh Kumar. Gramophone in India: a brief history. Calcutta, 1990.

DEARLING, Robert and others. The Guinness book of recorded sound. See The GUINNESS book of recorded sound.

DICTIONARY of business biography ... 1860-1980. See JEREMY, David J.

GAISBERG, F.W. Music on record. London, 1946.

GELATT, Roland. The fabulous phonograph. 2nd rev. ed. London, 1977.

THE GRAMOPHONE. Monthly, 1923-.

THE GRAMOPHONE jubilee book; [compiled by Roger Wimbush]. Harrow, 1973.

The GUINNESS book of recorded sound; by Robert and Celia Dearling with Brian Rust. Enfield, 1984.

INTERNATIONAL CLASSICAL RECORD COLLECTOR. See CLASSIC RECORD COLLECTOR.

INTERNATIONAL FEDERATION OF THE PHONO-GRAPHIC INDUSTRY. The industry of human happiness; (editor P. Beishuizen). London, 1959.

JEREMY, David J. Dictionary of business biography ... 1860-1980. 5 vols. London, 1984-86.

JONES, Geoffrey. The Gramophone Company: an Anglo-American multinational, 1898-1931. (*Business History Review*. 59. Spring, 1985).

LEWIS, Sir Edward. No C.I.C. [A history of the Decca Record Company]. London, 1956.

MARTLAND, Peter. Since records began: EMI: the first hundred years. London, 1997.

MILLER, Russell and BOAR, Roger. The incredible music machine. London, 1982.

MOOGK, E.B. Roll back the years: history of Canadian recorded sound and its legacy; genesis to 1930. Ottawa, 1975.

MOORE, Jerrold Northrop. A voice in time: the gramophone of Fred Gaisberg 1873-1951. London, 1976.

MOORE, Jerrold Northrop. A voice to remember: the sounds of 75 years on EMI records 1898-1973; edited by Roland Gelatt. London, 1973.

O'CONNELL, Charles. The other side of the record. New York, 1947.

PHILIPS, Frederik. 45 years with Philips. Poole, 1978.

POLLARD, Anthony. *Gramophone*: 75th anniversary. Harrow, 1998.

READ, Oliver and WELCH, Walter L. From tinfoil to stereo: evolution of the phonograph. 2nd ed. Indianapolis, 1976.

RIESS, Curt. Knaurs Weltgeschichte der Schallplatte. Zürich, 1966.

RUSSIA. [Decree of the Soviet Peoples Commissariat on the nationalisation of shops, warehouses and workshops manufacturing and selling keyboard and other musical instruments. Moscow, the Kremlin, 20th August, 1919].

SCHULZ-Köhn, Dietrich. Die Schallplatte auf dem Weltmarkt. Berlin, 1940.

SCHWARZKOPF, Elisabeth. On and off the record: a memoir of Walter Legge. London, 1982.

SMART, James R. and NEWSOM, Jon W. "A wonderful invention": a brief history of the phonograph from tinfoil to the LP. Washington, 1977.

STONE, Christopher. Christopher Stone speaking. London, 1933.

Historical and military sources

ADAM, Peter. The arts of the Third Reich. London, 1992.

The ALMANAC of World War II. See YOUNG, Peter.

ATKINS, David. The reluctant major. Pulborough, 1986.

283

BLUNDEN, Edmund. Undertones of war. Harmondsworth, 1937.

BRIGGS, Asa (Lord Briggs). The history of broadcasting in the United Kingdom. Vol. 2. The golden age of wireless. London, 1965. Vol. 3. The war of words. London, 1970.

BRYANT, Louise. Six red months in Russia: an observer's account of Russia before and during the proletarian dictatorship. London, 1918.

BULLOCK, Alan (Lord Bullock). Hitler: a study in tyranny. rev. ed. London, 1964.

BUTLER, Audrey. Everyman's dictionary of dates. 5th ed. London, 1967.

CALDER, Angus. The people's war: Britain 1939-1945. London, 1969.

CASTLEDEN, Roy. Harrap's book of British dates. London, 1991.

The CENTURY world history fact finder. See McEVEDY, Colin.

CORTADA, James W. Historical dictionary of the Spanish Civil War 1936-1939. London, 1982.

CROZIER, F.P. A brass hat in No Man's Land. London, 1930.

CRUTTWELL, C.R.M.F. A history of the Great War 1914-1918. 2nd ed. Oxford, 1936.

DAILY TELEGRAPH. Record of the Second World War month by month from 1939-1945. London, 1989.

DAVIDSON, Edward and MANNING, Dale. Chronology of World War Two. London, 2000.

DE JONGE, Alex. The Weimar chronicle: prelude to Hitler. London, 1978.

DAS DRITTE REICH. Annual, 1933-194? (Vol. 4, 1936 deals with broadcasting of commercial recordings).

EVERYMAN'S dictionary of dates. See BUTLER, Audrey.

FONTEYN, Margot. Margot Fonteyn: autobiography. London, 1975.

GEORGE, W.R.P. Lloyd George, backbencher. Llandysul, 1983.

GRACE, Alan. This is the British Forces Network: the story of Forces Broadcasting in Germany. Stroud, 1996.

GREENWELL, Graham H. An infant in arms: war letters of a company officer 1914-1918. London, 1972.

GRIGG, John. The young Lloyd George. London, 1973.

Das GROSSE Lexikon des Dritten Reiches. See ZENTNER, Christian and BEDÜRFTIG, Friedemann.

HANFSTÄNGL, Ernst (Putzi). Hitler: the missing years. London, 1957.

HARRAP'S book of British dates. See CASTLEDEN, Roy.

HIBBERT, Christopher. Benito Mussolini: the rise and fall of Il Duce. Harmondsworth, 1965, (reprinted with minor revisions, 1986).

HINDLEY, Diana and Geoffrey. Advertising in Victorian England 1837-1901. London. 1972.

HISTORY of the Great War based on official documents: military operations, France and Belgium, 1916 ... vol. 2. London, 1938.

HOWAT, G.M.D. Dictionary of world history. London, 1973.

JACKSON, Gabriel. A concise history of the Spanish Civil War. London, 1974.

KIPLING, Rudyard. Rudyard Kipling's verse: definitive edition. London, 1940.

KOLLONTAI, Alexandra. The autobiography of a sexually emancipated woman. London, 1972.

LANGER, William L. An encyclopedia of world history. rev. ed. London, 1948.

LASCELLES, George (Lord Harewood). The tongs and the bones: the memoirs of Lord Harewood. London, 1981.

LLOYD GEORGE, David. War memoirs of David Lloyd George. vol. 2. London, 1933.

MACKENZIE, Sir Compton. Gallipoli memories. London, 1929.

MAGNUS, Sir Philip. Kitchener: portrait of an imperialist. London, 1958.

MASON, David. Blackshirts or No-Shirts: Oswald Mosley and his movement on record. (*The Historic Record*, 1997)

McEVEDY, Colin. The Century world history fact finder. London, 1984.

MOOREHEAD, Alan. Gallipoli. London, 1956.

MELODIYA. V.I. Lenin: speeches on gramophone records 1919-21, the Third Communist International: [Russian texts and English translations accompanying Melodiya's CD transfers on Melodiya MCD 003].

ORKNEY'S Italian chapel; [by the] Chapel Preservation Committee. [cl992].

OUSBY, Ian. Occupation: the ordeal of France 1940-1944. London, 1997.

The PAGEANT of the century. London, [1933].

PRYCE-JONES, David. Paris in the Third Reich; a history of the German occupation 1940-1944. London, 1981.

ROOSEVELT, Theodore. The letters of Theodore Roosevelt. vol. 8. Cambridge (Mass.), 1954.

SHEPPERSON, George. Kipling and the Boer War. (in GROSS, John. Rudyard Kipling: the man, his work and his world. London, 1972).

SHIRER, William L. The rise and fall of the Third Reich. London, 1960.

SNAGGE, John and BARSLEY, Michael. Those vintage years of radio. London, 1972.

SNOWDEN, Ethel. Through Bolshevik Russia. London, 1920.

SPEER, Albert. Inside the Third Reich: memoirs; translated by Richard and Clara Winston. London, 1970.

STONE, Christopher. From Vimy Ridge to the Rhine: the Great War letters of Christopher Stone, D.S.O., M.C. Marlborough, 1989.

SUMMERFIELD, Penny. Patriotism and empire: music hall entertainment. (in MACKENZIE, J. Imperialism and popular culture. Manchester, 1986).

TAYLOR, Doreen. A microphone and a frequency: forty years of Forces Broadcasting. London, 1983.

THE TIMES atlas of the Second World War; edited by John Keegan. London, 1989.

TREVOR-ROPER, Hugh (Lord Dacre). The last days of Hitler. 7th ed. London, 1995.

TUNNEY, Christopher. Biographical dictionary of World War II. London, 1972.

UNITED KINGDOM. Foreign Office. [Index to general correspondence and files in the Public Record Office relating to the Gramophone Company's Barcelona branch during the Spanish Civil War and Arabic propaganda recordings attacking Britain, Mussolini and Italy].

VAUGHAN, David. Frederick Ashton and his ballets. London, 1977.

VERNEY, John. Going to the wars: a journey in various directions. London, 1955.

WILLIAMS, John. The other battleground: the home fronts Britain, France and Germany 1914-18. Chicago, 1972.

WILLIAMS, Neville and WALLER, Philip. Chronology of the modern world 1763-1992. 2nd ed. Oxford, 1994.

WILMOT, Chester. The struggle for Europe. Ware, 1997.

WILSON, Angus. The strange ride of Rudyard Kipling. London, 1977.

WILSON, Trevor. The myriad faces of war: Britain and the Great War 1914-1918. Oxford, 1986.

WISTRICH, Robert. Who's who in Nazi Germany. London, 1982.

The YELLOW spot: the outlawing of half a million human beings; a collection of facts and documents relating to three years persecution of German Jews, derived chiefly from National Socialist sources, very carefully assembled by a group of investigators. London, 1936.

YOUNG, Peter. The almanac of World War II. London, 1981.

ZENTNER, Christian and BEDÜRFTIG, Friedemann. Das grosse Lexikon des Dritten Reiches. München, 1985.

Musical sources

BACHARACH, A.L. British music of our time. Harmondsworth, 1946.

BEECHAM, Sir Thomas. A mingled chime. London, 1973.

BLOM, Eric. Everyman's dictionary of music. rev. ed. London, 1964.

BOULT, Sir Adrian. My own trumpet. London, 1973.

CARDUS, Neville. Sir Thomas Beecham: a memoir. London, 1961.

CLARKE, Donald. The rise and fall of popular music. London, 1995.

COPPOLA, Piero. Dix-sept ans de musique à Paris 1922-1939. Paris, 1982.

DAVISON, Peter. A Briton true?: a short account of patriotic songs and verse as popular entertainment. (*Alta: University of Birmingham Review*, Spring, 1970).

DAVISON, Peter. Songs of the British music hall. New York, 1971.

DAWSON, Peter. Fifty years of song. London, 1951.

DÜMLING, Albrecht. Entartete Musik. See ENTARTETE Musik.

EDNEY, Eric. A gramophile in Spain. (*The Gramophone*, December, 1938).

ENGELBRECHT, Henrik. The magic flautist [Marcel Moyse]. (*International Classical Record Collector*, no. 17, Summer, 1999).

ENTARTETE Musik: banned by the Nazis: the exhibition of Düsseldorf 1938/88 in texts and documents; edited by Albrecht Dümling. London, 1995.

EVERYMAN'S dictionary of music. See BLOM, Eric.

EWEN, David. Musicians since 1900. New York, 1978.

FRITH, Simon. Music for pleasure: essays in the sociology of pop. Cambridge, 1988.

GAMMOND, Peter. The Oxford companion to popular music. Oxford, 1991.

GAMMOND, Peter and HORRICKS, Raymond. Big bands. (*Music on record* 2). Cambridge, 1981.

GÄNZL, Kurt. The British musical theatre. 2 vols. London, 1986.

GEISSMAR, Berta. The baton and the jackboot. London, 1988.

GIFFORD, Denis. Bless 'em all!: the World War Two songbook. Exeter, 1989.

GOOSSENS, Sir Eugene. Overture and beginners: a musical auto-biography. London, 1951.

HALL, David. The record book: international edition: a guide to the world of the phonograph. New York, 1948.

HALL, David. Records: 1950 edition. New York, 1950.

HARKER, Dave. One for the money: politics and popular song. London, 1980.

HERZFELD, Friedrich. Wilhelm Furtwängler: Weg und Wesen. Leipzig, 1941 (copyright date). Also dated 2-1942.

HOROWITZ, Joseph. Understanding Toscanini. London, 1987.

JEFFERSON, Alan. Sir Thomas Beecham: a centenary tribute. London, 1979.

KATER, Michael H. Different drummers: jazz in the culture of Nazi Germany. New York, 1992.

KATER, Michael H. The twisted muse: musicians and their music in the Third Reich. New York, 1997.

KENNEDY, Michael. The Oxford dictionary of music. Oxford, 1994.

LÁNG, Paul Henry. Music in western civilization. New York, 1941.

LeMAHIEU, D.L. *The Gramophone*: recorded music and the cul-tivated mind in Britain between the wars. (*Technology and Culture*, vol. 23, no. 3, July, 1982).

LEVI, Erik. Music in the Third Reich. London, 1994.

LEXIKON der Juden in der Musik. See STENGEL, Theo and GERIGK, Herbert.

LUND, Jens. Country music goes to war: songs for the red-blooded American. (*Popular Music and Society*, vol. 1, no. 4, Summer, 1972).

MACKENZIE, Sir Compton. My life and times: octave six, 1923-1930. London. 1967.

MACKENZIE, Sir Compton. My record of music. London, 1955.

MACKENZIE, Sir Compton and MARSHALL, Archibald. Gramophone nights. London, 1923.

MARSH, Robert Charles. Toscanini and the art of orchestral per-formance. London, 1956.

MELBA, Nellie. Melodies and memories. London, 1980.

MEYER, Michael. The politics of music in the Third Reich. New York, 1993.

MILLER, Geoffrey. The Bournemouth Symphony Orchestra. Milborne Port, 1970.

MOORE, Gerald. Am I too loud?: memoirs of an accompanist. London, 1962.

MOORE, Jerrold Northrop. Edward Elgar: a creative life. Oxford, 1984.

MOORE, Jerrold Northrop. Elgar on record: the composer and the gramophone. London, 1974.

The NEW Grove dictionary of music and musicians; edited by Stanley Sadie. 20 vols. London, 1980.

NEWTON, Carl. The nightmare of Gerontius: the story behind a famous recording. (*The Elgar Society Journal*, vol. 10, no. 2, July, 1997).

O'CONNOR, Garry. The pursuit of perfection: a life of Maggie Teyte. London, 1979.

The Oxford companion to popular music. See GAMMOND, Peter.

The Oxford dictionary of music. See KENNEDY, Michael.

PARKER, Derek and Julia. The story and the song: a survey of English musical plays 1916-1978. London, 1979.

PEARSALL, Ronald. Edwardian popular music. Newton Abbot, 1975.

RUSSELL, Dave. Popular music in England 1840-1914: a social history. Manchester, 1987.

SACHS, Harvey. Music in fascist Italy. London, 1987.

SACKVILLE-WEST, Edward and SHAWE-TAYLOR, Desmond. The record guide. Various eds. and supplements. London, 1951-56.

SADIE, Stanley. The new Grove, etc. See The NEW Grove dictionary of music and musicians.

SCHONBERG, Harold C. The great conductors. London, 1968.

STENGEL, Theo and GERIGK, Herbert. Lexikon der Juden in der Musik. Berlin, 1943.

SULLIVAN, Herbert and FLOWER, Newman. Sir Arthur Sullivan: his life, letters and diaries. London, 1927.

TEMPERLEY, Nicholas. The romantic age 1800-1914. (*The Athlone History of Music in Britain*, vol. 5). London, 1981.

TEYTE, Maggie. Star on the door. London, 1958.

TURNER, Michael R. and MIALL, Antony. The Edwardian song book: drawing room ballads 1900-1914. London, 1982.

WALKER, Leo. The wonderful era of the great dance bands. New York, 1989.

WALKER, Malcolm. The early Vienna Philharmonic recordings (1924-1945). (*International Classical Record Collector*, no. 4, Spring, 1996).

WOOD, Sir Henry J. My life of music. London, 1938.

WULF, Joseph. Musik im Dritten Reich: eine Dokumentation. Gütersloh, 1963.

YOUNG, Percy M. Sir Arthur Sullivan. London, 1971.

ZIEGLER, Hans Severus. Entartete Musik: eine Abrechnung. Düsseldorf, 1938.

Index

British Forces Experimental Station (BFES), Algiers, 205-6.
British Forces Network (BFN), Hamburg. 248, 266*ff.*
British Grenadiers, 159, 240, 251.
British (later Royal British) Legion, 143-4.
British Red Cross, 24.
British Union of Fascists, 89, 181.
British Zonophone Company, 10, 14.
Britten, Benjamin, 35, 148.
Brooks, Arthur, 24.
Brown, L. J., 172.
Bruckner, Anton, 113, 122, 246-7.
Brunswick (American), 147.
Brunswick (British), 147.
Brunswick (Canadian), 236.
Brunswick (German), 174.
Brussels Radio Orchestra, 264.
Bryan, William Jennings, 63.
Bryant, Louise, 61.
Bubbly (Revue), 44.
Buchanan, Jack, 139.
Buffalo Philharmonic Orchestra, 223.
Bugle calls (British), 26.
Bukharin, Nikolay, 60.
Burchall, Sidney, 138, 158.
Burning of the Books, 84, 106.
Busch, Fritz, 119, 192.
Busch String Quartet, 239-40.
Business as Usual (Revue), 43-4.
Busoni, Ferruccio, 266.
Butt, Clara, 24, 33.
Byam, Guy, 233, 236.

Cabanel, Paul, 179.
Cadett, Thomas, 250.
Calling all Workers, 159.
Cameron, Basil, 141.
Cammaerts, Emile, 36.
Caniglia, Maria, 256-7.
Capitol (Record company), 197.
Carmirelli, Pina, 72.
Carmirelli String Quartet, 72.
Carol, Stella, 32.
Caruso, Enrico, 17, 43, 51.
Casals, Pablo (Pau), 76-8.
Cassi, Emil, 3-4, 5.
Cavalcade of Martial Songs, 133-4.
Cecilia Choir, Antwerp, 178.
Celebration - for all Occasions, 251.
Cenotaph (London), 54.
Cetra (Record company), 116, 192.
Chabrier, Emmanuel, 219.

Chaliapin, Fyodor, 43, 211.
Chamber music, 18, 222.
Chamberlain, Neville, 126, 127, 128-9, 150.
Charity records, 10, 23, 24, 31, 80, 158, 164, 261.
Charlie and his Orchestra, 182-3, 237.
Cheshire, Leonard, V.C., 254-5.
Chester, Charlie, 210.
Chevalier, Maurice, 171.
Chopin, Frederic, 113, 171, 176.
Chu Chin Chow (Musical comedy), 45.
Churchill, Sir Winston, 6, 49, 150-3, 155, 169, 182, 183, 184, 250, 274n5, 274n6.
Cigna, Gina, 226.
Cinema organs, 185.
City of Birmingham Orchestra, 187, 251.
C.I.V.s (City Imperial Volunteers), 9.
Clare, Helen, 218.
Clark, Alfred, 17, 35-6.
Clarke, Donald, 197.
Classical music, 132, 141-2, 145.
Claudel, Paul, 177.
Clough, Francis, 67, 102, 104.
Coates, Eric, 159, 241.
Cohan, George M., 51.
Colditz Castle, 239-40.
Coldstream Guards Band, 26, 159.
Collins, Anthony, 251.
Colonel Roosevelt's Rough Riders (March), 5.
Colquhoun, Ion, 8, 9, 12.
Columbia (American), 3, 14, 20, 52, 55, 108, 109, 145, 197, 259.
Columbia (British), 22 *et passim*.
Columbia (French), 108, 171, 176, 177, 179.
Columbia (German), 97, 108.
Columbia (Italian), 69, 108, 116.
Columbia (Spanish), 78, 79.
Columbia Band, 14.
Columbia Broadcasting Symphony Orchestra, 275n8.
Comin' in on a Wing and a Pray'r, 197, 217-8.
Compania del Gramofono-Odeon, 78-9.
Concertgebouw Orchestra, 165-7, 247, 266, 275n10.
Condor Legion, 81-2.
Copland, Aaron, 100.
Coppola, Piero, 179.
Corbett, Geoffrey, 241-2.

294

301

303

Schallplattenverordnung, 99-100, 102, 113.
Schiøtz, Aksel, 163.
Schipa, Tito, 160.
Schlageter, Albert Leo, 106.
Schleicher, General Kurt von, 84.
Schmidt, Joseph, 104, 105.
Schmidt-Isserstedt, Hans, 103.
Schmidt-Neuhaus, A. and H., 266.
Schnabel, Artur, 104.
Schoenberg, Arnold, 101, 107, 109.
Schorr, Friedrich, 105.
Schot, Betsy, 8.
Schreker, Franz, 107.
Schubert, Franz, 105, 113, 120, 121, 142, 166, 261.
Schulz-Köhn, Dietrich, 173-6.
Schumann, Elisabeth, 103, 122.
Schumann, Robert, 113, 171, 226, 265.
Schuschnigg, Kurt, 123.
Schwann Long Playing Record Catalog, 91.
Schwedler, Karl (Charlie), 183.
Scott, Bebe, 198.
Scott-Coomber, Billy and his Singing Grenadiers, 138.
Scotto, Renata, 67.
Segovia, Andres, 76.
Seidler-Winkler, Bruno, 188, 274-5n7.
Seligsohn, Richard, 97.
Serafin, Tullio, 256.
Serkin, Rudolf, 104.
Service charity records. *See* Charity records.
Seyss-Inquart, Artur, 125.
Shafran, Danya, 222.
Shakespeare, William, 42, 84, 251.
Shaw, Denis, 261.
Shaw, George Bernard, 42.
Shellac, 25, 131, 143, 153, 197, 259, 264.
Shelley, Norman, 274n5.
Shelton, Anne, 206, 217.
Shields, Ella, 32.
Shostakovich, Dimitry, 188, 223.
Sibelius, Jean, 87, 113, 141, 146, 265.
Siegfried Line (German frontier defences), 130, 139.
Siegfried Line (German parody of British song), 153.
Siemens, Ernst von, 190.
Siemens Spezial (DG label), 190, 266.
Silver Wings in the Moonlight, 218.
Silvester, Victor and his Ballroom Orchestra, 273n1.

Sinatra, Frank, 196.
Skyrockets Dance Band, 210.
Slaughter, Walter, 13.
Sleepy Lagoon, 159.
Slezak, Leo, 80.
Smetana, Bedrich, 162-3.
Smith, Major F.H., 253,
Smith, Michael, 223, 224.
Smoke gets in your Eyes, 202.
Snagge, John, 157, 216.
Snowden, Ethel (Mrs. Philip Snowden), 61.
Society for the Promotion of New Music, 241-2.
Soldatensender Calais (British propaganda radio transmitter), 237.
Soldier Boy (Revue), 44.
Soldiers of the Queen, 9, 258.
Soldiers' Wives and Families Association (Aldershot branch), 10.
Solomon (Pianist), 98, 220.
Somers, Debroy, 136, 158, 251.
Song Spinners, 197, 217.
Soviet Airmen Song, 223.
Soviet Fatherland Song, 223.
Speer, Albert, 227-8.
St. Peter's, Rome (Choir), 239.
St. Thomas's, Leipzig (Choir), 190.
Stalag Luft III, 228-9.
Stalin, Joseph, 56, 60, 212-3.
Stalingrad, 213, 221.
Stanford, Sir Charles Villiers, 18.
Star Spangled Banner, 4.
State Music Trust (Russia), 224.
Steinberg, William, 223.
Stengel, Theo, 98, 102, 113.
Stenka Razin, 221.
Sterling, Sir Louis, 17.
Stignani, Ebe, 192, 256.
Stokowski, Leopold, 109, 159.
Stone, Christopher, 34.
Storm, Erica, 109.
Strasser, Gregor, 84.
Straus, Max, 97-8.
Strauss, Johann, 86, 114, 120, 125, 219.
Strauss, Richard, 41, 69, 86, 115, 117, 166, 191, 226, 264, 266.
Stravinsky, Igor, 107-8, 110, 173.
Strienz, Wilhelm, 119, 154, 274n7.
Stuart, Francis, 181.
Stuart, Leslie, 9.
Submarine warfare, 38-9, 49.
Sugar, 32.

304